opportunities implicit in the present period of religious uncertainty.

Robert Wuthnow is Assistant Professor of Sociology, Princeton University. He is the author of **The Consciousness Reformation**, published in 1976 by the University of California Press.

EXPERIMENTATION
IN AMERICAN RELIGION

EXPERIMENTATION IN AMERICAN RELIGION

THE NEW MYSTICISMS AND THEIR IMPLICATIONS FOR THE CHURCHES

Robert Wuthnow

UNIVERSITY OF CALIFORNIA PRESS
Berkeley   Los Angeles   London

University of California Press
Berkeley and Los Angeles, California

University of California Press, Ltd.
London, England

Copyright © 1978 by
The Regents of the University of California

ISBN 0-520-03446-5
Library of Congress Catalog Card Number: 77-71068
Printed in the United States of America

1 2 3 4 5 6 7 8 9

CONTENTS

To Sally

PREFACE

This book is about one of the more familiar, but still little understood, developments that has taken place in American religion in recent years—experimentation with movements largely outside the Judeo-Christian faith. These movements, and the less organized values and beliefs associated with them, have aroused curiosity because they emerged at a time when many observers were predicting the death of God and a gradual dispersal of his followers. Attention has focused on the new religions also because they seem to appeal to some of the groups that traditional religion has had difficulty attracting—for example, college students, young people, and the educated. Perhaps the most important reason why these movements have drawn attention, however, is because they seem to harken to the ancient religions of the East, to the occult and the psychic, and to humanistic creeds more often than to the religious traditions of the American past.

The aim of the present book is to make a modest contribution to the understanding of these movements by presenting some empirical data bearing upon them. These data will shed additional light on some of the questions that have remained largely unanswered about the new religions. Why are some people attracted to them and others not? What sorts of values and experiences tend to be associated with religious experimentation? Why have some people defected from conventional religion and remained nonreligious or only nominally religious?

A sociological approach is taken in attempting to answer these questions. The data examined are from random-sample surveys conducted by professional interviewers. Admittedly, such data are poorly adapted to understanding many aspects of religious commitment, a fact that becomes increasingly apparent to anyone who works with them for very long. But for all its limitations, a sociological survey still remains a useful way to determine how many people in a population express particular kinds of religious commitments; it remains an efficient way to collect relatively uniform information from a large enough number of people that systematic comparisons of differences can by made; and it remains perhaps the only way to pin down relations among various sorts of commitments and other factors with some degree of statistical precision. A sociological perspective also informs the manner in which questions are framed here, as it does the kinds of answers sought. The concern underlying much of the discussion is to find out what it is about American society that has stimulated the growth of new religions.

In the end, it may seem that we are as far from having an answer as when we began, or it may seem that more questions have been raised than have been answered. That, of course, is how it should be in exploring something about which little is known. It should be kept in mind, however, that the exploration is largely limited to certain kinds of social factors, such as education or age or background, and to certain kinds of social implications. This is *not* a study of the inner composition of religious movements, of the psychology of people who join religious movements, or of the theological or philosophical teachings of these movements. Such studies are highly valuable and more of them need to be done. My own impression, however, is that the internal aspects of religious movements are often written about, if for no other reason than that members and former members write about their experiences, while the larger social contexts of religious movements are often neglected. Hence the focus of the present study.

While affirming the utility of a sociological perspective and attempting to maintain this perspective in the present volume, I have made no effort to adhere faithfully to any single sociological theory. In part this has been necessitated by the kinds of data I have had available. But, more to the point, it has been necessitated by the new religions themselves and by our present state of knowledge about them. A theory that proves helpful for understanding why people become involved with yoga, for example, doesn't seem very helpful for explaining attraction to astrology (as we shall see), nor does the theory that explains astrology shed much light on the reasons why some folks have psychic experiences and others don't. For this reason, the chapters forming the present study should probably be regarded, not as elements of a single argument, but as essays bearing only a loose relation with one another, each attempting to illuminate some rather specific aspect of religious experimentation and defection. It should also go without saying that no attempt has been made to be comprehensive in the problems treated.

My interest in new religions dates from my earliest days in graduate school at the University of California, Berkeley, where I was first able to combine a long-standing personal interest in religion with sociological concepts and tools of inquiry under the tutelage of Charles Glock, Guy Swanson, and Robert Bellah, each of whom served as a provocative mentor and, in combination, provided one of the most creative atmospheres for learning and reflection that one can imagine. At their inspiration, my still amorphous interests in religion quickly became directed toward exploring the new religious currents that were becoming increasingly visible in the Berkeley area at that time. Many of the ideas and quasi-theories in the present study were initially formed in those early explorations.

The chance to devote my full energies to the study of new religions came in 1971, when Professors Glock and Bellah received a sizable grant to support graduate students interested in doing research on new religious consciousness. Between 1971 and 1974, an intensive program of research was carried out at the Survey Research Center on various forms of new religious consciousness, and, since 1974, many of us who participated in that project have continued to pursue these interests. It was also from that project that the idea was born for a series of monographs on new religious consciousness under the general editorship of Professors Glock and Bellah. The present volume is a part of that ongoing series.

The greatest debt I have incurred in preparing this study, as the foregoing bears witness, is to Charlie Glock and Bob Bellah, both for their ideas, which have deeply influenced my own thinking about religion, and for their continued support and encouragement. I also wish to express my appreciation to the staff of the Survey Research Center and to the other members of the religious consciousness project for their assistance in designing and conducting the research and for many constructive suggestions in the course of the analysis.

Three of the chapters are based on papers that have been published previously. Parts of Chapter 2 initially appeared as "Astrology and Marginality," *Journal for the Scientific Study of Religion,* 15 (June 1976), 157–168. Parts of Chapter 5 are taken from "Peak Experiences: Some Empirical Tests," *Journal of Humanistic Psychology* (1977). And parts of Chapter 6 were published in "Recent Patterns of Secularization: A Problem of Generations?," *American Sociological Review,* 41 (October 1976), 850–867. I wish to thank the editors of these journals for permission to reprint this material. Each of these papers has been extensively revised.

Glen Mellinger, who is the co-author of Chapter 7, made available the data on which that chapter is based. He and his staff at the Institute for Research in Social Behavior have been most helpful over the years, not only in sharing the results of their research, but in their continued enthusiasm for investigating the peculiarities of new consciousness and alternative life styles.

Financial support for the research contained in this book came from the Institute for Religion and Social Change (Honolulu), the Ford Foundation, the National Institute of Mental Health, the Institute for Research in Social

Behavior (Berkeley), and the William Paterson Foundation (Princeton University).

Larry Blackwood assisted with much of the computer processing and read most of the chapters for methodological accuracy. My many conversations with him contributed greatly to the enjoyment of pursuing the research as well as to the product itself.

Finally, I wish to express my deepest gratitude to my wife, Sally, to whom the book is fittingly dedicated, and to my daughters, Robyn and Brooke, for their patience and love. People who write books search in vain for ways of acknowledging these forms of personal sentiment without seeming trite. For it is only in personal relationships, not in the printed word, that such feelings can truly be expressed.

Princeton University   Robert Wuthnow
March 1977

INTRODUCTION

In 1971, through a generous grant from the Institute for Religion and Social Change, a research project was initiated at the University of California, Berkeley, to examine the new religious consciousness that was already becoming a social phenomenon of some importance at that time. While much of the project was devoted to in-depth case studies of selected religious and quasi-religious movements present in the San Francisco area, the research design also called for a survey to be conducted among randomly selected representatives of the community to determine what broader shifts in consciousness might be taking place.[1] In addition, the survey was intended to provide an estimate of the relative popularity of some of the more specific movements and associated commitments that were being examined ethnographically. As it turned out, substantially larger proportions of the community were knowledgeable of, attracted to, or involved in some of these movements and experiments than had been expected. Hence, a fortuitous opportunity became available to investigate some of the causes and effects of this religious experimentation using quantitative methods.

When we began our investigation, some systematic research, in addition to numerous journalistic inquiries, had been conducted on the new religions. But even now only the preliminary results from much of this research have been reported.[2] These reports, moreover, have for the most part been ethnographic in method and descriptive in purpose. Some of them have provided rich phenomenological accounts of the inner lives of these move-

1. A collection of ethnographic studies from the Berkeley project has been published in Charles Y. Glock and Robert N. Bellah (eds.), *The New Religious Consciousness* (Berkeley and Los Angeles: University of California Press, 1976). An examination of broader cultural patterns documented by the survey part of the project is found in Robert Wuthnow, *The Consciousness Reformation* (Berkeley and Los Angeles: University of California Press, 1976).
2. A large number of studies on various aspects of the new religions, mostly from an anthropological point of view, have been published in Irving I. Zaretsky and Mark P. Leone (eds.), *Religious Movements in Contemporary America* (Princeton: Princeton University Press, 1974). Brief journalistic descriptions of many of the new religious movements can be found in Peter Rowley, *New Gods in America* (New York: David McKay, 1970); and Jacob Needleman, *The New Religions* (Garden City, N.Y.: Doubleday, 1969). Some of the literature from the new religions themselves has been collected in Robert S. Ellwood, Jr., *Religious and Spiritual Groups in Modern America* (Englewood Cliffs, N.J.: Prentice-Hall, 1973); Jacob Needleman, A. K. Bierman, and James A. Gould (eds.), *Religion for a New Generation* (New

ments and their adherents. What has been missing above all, it has seemed, is evidence on the relations between the current religious experimentation and the larger society.

In the absence of much previous evidence, together with the fact that we had not foreseen being able to make as much use of the survey data as the results indicated we could, the clues for conducting our investigation had to be taken largely from prevailing imagery about the new religions. This imagery tended to suggest that a number of new religious movements and less organized religious experiments had been born on the periphery of established religion and that many of them were advocating beliefs and practices that might be characterized as non-Christian, a-Christian, or post-Christian. Beyond this, the imagery was either vague or in disagreement.

A question on which there seemed to be considerable disagreement concerned the causes of the new religious experimentation. One notion was that it had occurred because of some failure within the churches. Another explanation was that it was the result of social unrest surrounding the Vietnam war. Some linked it more to shifting attitudes toward sex and marriage. Others attributed it in varying degrees to high standards of living, rising levels of education, and more general feelings of alienation from science, technology, and bureaucracy. These were only some of the explanations that had been proposed.

Which of these explanations, or which combination, was correct seemed obviously to depend on the kind of experimentation that was being explained. The conditions leading people to engage in Transcendental Meditation, for example, might well be different from those leading people to join a Jesus movement. These, in turn, might be quite different from those causing interest in the occult. And so on. Part of the imagery was also that some people experimented habitually with one movement and then another, giving some of these movements overlapping or rotating memberships. Nevertheless, it seemed clear that the search for explanations had to begin by looking at specific forms of experimentation.

Since movements rooted in Asian traditions had attracted much publicity, we asked questions about involvement in several of these movements. Three of them—Transcendental Meditation (TM), Zen, and yoga groups—turned out to have elicited sizable enough followings and participation to allow some investigation of the kinds of people who were

York: Macmillan, 1973); and Lowell D. Streiker (ed.), *Who Am I? Second Thoughts on Man, His Loves, His Gods* (New York: Sheed and Ward, 1970). See also Edward F. Heenan (ed.), *Mystery, Magic, and Miracle: Religion in a Post-Aquarian Age* (Englewood Cliffs, N.J.: Prentice-Hall, 1973); and Edwin Scott Gaustad, *Dissent in American Religion* (Chicago: University of Chicago Press, 1973).

interested in them. Preliminary investigation also indicated that experimenters in these groups were similar enough to one another that they might reasonably be combined for certain purposes, making it possible to do some multivariate analysis. The fact that this investigation could be based on data from a pre-defined sample of the community made it possible to compare experimenters with nonexperimenters from the same population, thereby providing a chance to learn something of the social conditions leading to this particular kind of religious experimentation. Unfortunately, too few in the sample had participated in other movements of a different nature, such as Hare Krishna, Satanism, or any of the so-called Jesus People groups that remained more within the bounds of Christianity, to warrant a systematic examination of these kinds of experimentation.

In addition to these questions on Asian religions, we had also asked some questions about the occult, specifically about astrology and extrasensory perception (ESP). Both of these had been discussed in connection with other forms of religious experimentation during the late 1960s and early 1970s. Yet it didn't seem self-evident that these were "new" to American culture in substance, scope, or constituencies in quite the same way that some of the other religious experiments seemed to be. Again the problem was simply that very little research had been done to determine what kinds of people were interested in astrology and ESP. Having found considerable interest in these two phenomena in our own sample, we decided, therefore, to see what we could learn about the conditions leading to these interests. One of the specific things we wanted to find out (and the reason for including these examinations in the present study) was whether the same kinds of conditions that promoted other forms of religious experimentation, or more particularly, Eastern experimentation, also led to experimentation with the occult.

A second general type of question over which there seemed to be much disagreement concerned the consequences of the new religious experiments. What effects were they having on people's life styles, values, political attitudes, and other interests? The answer to this question also clearly depended on what kind of experimentation was being discussed. But here some of the prevailing debates seemed to be somewhat more specific. They were still numerous and largely unresolved, but two of them in particular seemed to be ones on which our own data might be able to shed some light.

One notion that had been expressed recurrently in discussions of the new religions and that gained credence as one radical leader from the campus turmoil of the 1960s after another turned to religious experimentation, was that the new religions were draining off the political energies of the sixties, turning them into perhaps more quietistic directions. We hadn't the data to test out this notion directly (except for some very limited evidence from some longitudinal studies of Berkeley students, about which more will be said later). Part of this notion, however, seemed reminiscent of theories which Max Weber and other students of religion had advanced about the relations between particular kinds of religious orientations and political involvement. Specifically, Weber and others had suggested that mystical religious orientations are likely to cause withdrawal from political involvement. By the early 1970s, there indeed seemed to be signs both of mysticism and of political withdrawal. For our part, we had asked some questions about mysticism, and a substantial number of people had indicated some interest or involvement in it. Thus, by examining the relations between mysticism and indicators of political involvement, we were afforded an opportunity to possibly add some empirical evidence to this particular discussion.

Another debate concerning the consequences of the new religions had centered on the effects of what seemed to be a renewed sensitivity to religious experiences. Many of the new movements seemed to stress the experiential dimension of religion much more than the churches had done, at least in the recent past. As time progressed, it also seemed that this new interest might be spreading beyond the new movements themselves into the cultural mainstream and into the churches. The debate seemed to concern mostly whether this interest was somehow "unhealthy" or "healthy" for the individual. Some had argued that religious experientialism has often resulted in some form of antinomianism or social irresponsibility. Others, of whom the psychologist Abraham Maslow had been a chief spokesman, had argued instead that religious experiences (or what Maslow called "peak" experiences) promoted psychological well-being, which in turn fostered better, more self-sacrificing relations with others. Since we had asked some questions about religious experiences, we decided to see what our data might have to say on this debate.

There were many other unanswered questions about the effects of the new religious movements and about the values and life styles which the popular press had associated with them—questions about which we had no information. Lacking the data to conduct a complete examination of all these effects, it nevertheless seemed useful to pursue those questions that we could.

A third general type of question which had aroused considerable discussion concerned the status of established religion. For some, the religious experimentation and, more generally, the social unrest that had become so evident by the early 1970s had raised questions about the institutional strength of the churches. Were the new religions gaining at the expense of the churches? Were important changes happening within the churches? Clearly the churches remained a major social institution. This was very much evidenced by data on religious commitment from national polls in the United States and in other modern countries. For example, a series of polls done in 1969 had shown that 98 percent of the people in the United States claimed to believe in God, whereas the figure for Switzerland was 84 percent, the figure for Great Britain was 77 percent, the figure for France was 73 percent, and that for Sweden was 60 percent. The United States also ranked highest of these countries on other Christian beliefs, such as belief regarding the devil, life after death, heaven, and hell (see Table 1). On church attendance, polls in 1974 still showed that 40 percent of the population attended weekly in the U.S., in comparison with 30 percent in Switzerland, 25 percent in France, and only 9 percent in Sweden. And among young people, who presumably had been most affected by the recent religious experimentation, a poll in 1973 showed that 35 percent in the U.S. included going to church as a typical weekend activity, in comparison with 18 percent in Switzerland, 11 percent in Great Britain, 8 percent in France, and 6 percent in Sweden.

Interestingly, there was also contrary evidence throughout the late 1960s and early 1970s that commitment to the churches was declining and that considerable numbers in some parts of the society claimed to be without any religion. This evidence elicited a host of would-be explanations—again, without benefit of very much systematic research. It was not clear, for example, whether these declines were related to the specific social unrest of the period or whether they might be rooted in long-term social forces. Nor was it clear whether these trends in the churches bore any direct relation to the new religious experiments. The possibility that there might be some relation, however, seemed sufficient to warrant some effort to find out what was causing them.

Some of the data we collected in the Bay Area had to do with conventional religious commitments. These data were all collected at one time, so we could not explore the causes of *trends* in these commitments. But, using other data to establish the trends, it seemed that the Bay Area data could still reveal something about who was defecting from the churches and who was remaining loyal. We were also able to supplement this evidence with some data from Berkeley students concerning actual changes in their religious preferences.

The other question about the strength of established religion that seemed to appear frequently in discussions of contemporary religion was one which social scientists had been discussing well before the new religions appeared—namely, whether the churches, apart from their size, were remaining "strong" in terms of influence on their members' behavior in other areas of their lives, or whether the churches were also losing this form of influence. The discussion of this question was kindled anew by the argu-

Table 1. **RELIGIOUS COMMITMENT IN FIVE MODERN COUNTRIES**

	United States	Switzerland	Great Britain	France	Sweden
Percent in each country who:					
Believe in God	98%	84%	77%	73%	60%
Believe in the devil	60%	25%	21%	17%	21%
Believe in life after death	73%	50%	38%	35%	38%
Believe in heaven	85%	50%	54%	39%	43%
Believe in hell	65%	25%	23%	22%	17%
Attend church weekly*	40%	30%	NA	25%	9%
Include church in weekend activities (age 18–24 only)	35%	18%	11%	8%	6%
Not interested in religion (age 18–24 only)	12%	15%	32%	19%	41%

*Figure for 1974; youth figures for 1973; all others for 1969.
NA = not available.
Source: Gallup Opinion Index, No. 44, No. 114.

ments of critics who suggested that the new religious experiments had appeared precisely because the churches had become irrelevant to the everyday lives of many of their members (or of their children).

The strength and nature of the relations between conventional religious commitment and other attitudes and activities had been the subject of considerable research in the past, although the pattern of many specific relations still seemed unclear. We realized that the items in our survey, designed largely for other purposes, could scarcely hope to go beyond much of the research that had already been done on these relations. One unusual characteristic of the Bay Area sample, however, was that it contained persons committed not only to conventional religions, but also to new religions, as well as a disproportionate number of persons not committed to any religion. Thus, the values of all these religious types could be compared directly as a way of assessing how different or how similar the conventionally religious might be from other religious or nonreligious persuasions.

In sum, this study concerns only a few of the many questions that have been raised in recent years about the new religions. It does not claim to provide definitive answers to the questions it addresses—it is clearly exploratory. What we have sought to do is to present evidence of a preliminary sort that may be useful in shaping further discussion and investigation of the new religious experiments.

THE SAN FRANCISCO BAY AREA SURVEY

The survey from which our data are taken was conducted in the San Francisco Bay Area in 1973. The sample, drawn to be representative of the nearly three million people living in the four counties (Alameda, Contra Costa, San Francisco, and San Mateo) comprising the San Francisco-Oakland Standard Metropolitan Statistical Area (excluding Marin County), was chosen by randomly selecting, first, census tracts; then, blocks within census tracts; and finally, individuals age 16 and over within randomly selected households. In order to ensure a sufficient number of young people for examining age differences, which we expected to be an important factor in religious experimentation, persons age 16 through 30 were sampled at a ratio of approximately two to one relative to their actual number in the total population as indicated by the 1970 census. In parts of the inquiry not concerned with age differences, this disproportionate sampling is compensated for by assigning a weight of .5805 to each person between 16 and 30 and a weight of 1.5448 to each person over age 30. This weight adjusts the sample to make it representative of the Bay Area population.

A total of 1,000 persons participated in the survey, representing 78 percent of those initially included in the sample. As the comparisons shown in Table 2 indicate, the characteristics of these respondents match closely those of the Bay Area population, with the exception that poorly educated respondents and males tend to be underrepresented.

The data were collected by interviewing respondents in their homes. Each interview lasted approximately one hour and fifteen minutes, covering topics such as the respondent's religious beliefs and practices, attitudes toward new religions and religious surrogates, political opinions, personal values and life styles, and background characteristics. The interviews were

Table 2. REPRESENTATIVENESS OF THE BAY AREA SAMPLE

	Bay Area Census Figures, 1970	Bay Area Survey, 1973
Age:		
16–24	21.6%	19.7%
25–34	19.4	22.9
35–44	16.2	17.2
45–54	17.0	14.5
55–64	12.8	11.9
65 and over	12.9	13.3
Education:		
Grade school	18.0%	10.3%
High school	48.6	40.3
Some college	16.6	22.1
College graduate	16.8	27.3
Occupation:		
Professional	18.2%	23.5%
Other white collar	40.6	36.6
Total white collar	58.8%	60.1%
Blue collar	27.8	25.3
Service and domestics	12.8	13.3
Sex:		
Male	48.2%	43.2%
Female	51.8	56.8
Race:		
White	82.8%	85.2%
Nonwhite	17.2	14.8

conducted by a staff of forty professional interviewers from the Survey Research Center at the University of California, Berkeley.[3]

The fact that the survey was conducted in the Bay Area rather than, say, on a national sample obviously raises difficult questions about how similar or dissimilar the present findings may be to those that might have been found in other parts of the country. Regrettably, comparable studies in other regions of the country have yet to be conducted, so no precise answers can be given to such questions. Lacking precise answers, some comments about the nature of the Bay Area and the reasons for conducting the survey there seem in order.

The Bay Area was selected as the location for the survey in large measure because we wanted information from the same population in which the ethnographic studies of the larger project were being conducted. Most of these were being done in the vicinity of the University of California, Berkeley. Therefore, it made sense that the survey should be done locally as well. This decision had the further advantage, of course, that the survey could be administered more efficiently than if it were done elsewhere.

In addition to these reasons for choosing the Bay Area, we were also convinced that religious experimentation was probably more widely in evidence in the Bay Area than in almost any other part of the country we could think of, meaning that we could study it more readily. This conviction was based mostly on our own impressions that the new religions seemed to be more prominent on the West Coast than in other regions of the country and that many of the new movements had first appeared in the Bay Area. Even at this writing there appears to be no solid evidence with which to support these impressions. One piece of evidence that does seem to fit, however, came from looking at the location of groups listed in the *Spiritual Community Guide for North America,* one of the most comprehensive directories of new religious and spiritual movements available.[4] Included in this guide and its supplements are over 3,000 "spiritual communities," the common denominator of which is some concern for alternative forms of consciousness and alternative life styles. This means that groups other than strictly religious groups, such as alternative bookstores and food shops or communes, are also included, but most of the groups seem to be oriented to some form of new consciousness. As one would probably expect, these communities tend to be congregated in areas having large populations— over 800 in California, for example, and over 300 in New York. But when

3. Further details of the sample and a copy of the interview schedule are found in Wuthnow, *The Consciousness Reformation.*
4. *Spiritual Community Guide for North America* (San Rafael, California: The Spiritual Community, 1972–1975).

the number of communities per 100,000 population is examined, the greatest concentrations tend to be in the West (see Table 3). For instance, nine of the top ten states are in the West, Colorado being the farthest east of these. The highest rates are in states like California, Oregon, Arizona, and New Mexico, and the lowest tend to be in the South: Mississippi, South Carolina, Kentucky, Alabama, and Tennessee. As far as the Bay Area specifically is concerned, the guide listed over 300 groups in that area alone,

Table 3. "SPIRITUAL COMMUNITIES" PER 100,000 POPULATION BY STATE

State	Rate	State	Rate
Arizona	5.3	Illinois	0.8
New Mexico	4.9	Iowa	0.8
Alaska	4.7	Louisiana	0.8
Oregon	4.6	Michigan	0.8
California	4.0	Virginia	0.8
Colorado	3.6	Wisconsin	0.8
Hawaii	3.5	New Jersey	0.7
New Hampshire	3.3	Ohio	0.7
Wyoming	2.8	Oklahoma	0.7
Washington	2.4	Kansas	0.6
Massachusetts	2.4	Pennsylvania	0.6
Montana	2.0	Indiana	0.5
Idaho	1.9	North Carolina	0.4
New York	1.9	Tennessee	0.4
Connecticut	1.8	West Virginia	0.4
Florida	1.5	Alabama	0.3
Maine	1.5	Kentucky	0.3
Maryland	1.3	Nebraska	0.3
South Dakota	1.3	South Carolina	0.3
Missouri	1.2	Mississippi	0.1
Texas	1.1	Delaware	NA
Minnesota	1.0	Nevada	NA
Arkansas	1.0	North Dakota	NA
Georgia	0.9	Rhode Island	NA
Utah	0.8	Vermont	NA

NA = data not available.

Source: *Spiritual Community Guide for North America,* 1973, 1975.

giving it a ratio of approximately 10 per 100,000 population, a ratio substantially larger than that for California as a whole or for any other state in the West.

If religious experimentation seemed likely to be more readily observable in the Bay Area than in many other places, there also seemed to be some evidence that *nonreligion* might also be especially prominent. The West in general, judging from national polls, has shown somewhat less commitment to conventional religion than other regions. For example, a poll in 1974 found that people in the West were 10 percent less likely than the nation at large to attend church in any given week, they were 13 percent less likely to express a "great deal of confidence" in organized religion, and they were 6 percent less likely to say they were "very religious." Other polls had found that people in the West were less likely to espouse orthodox beliefs about heaven, hell, the devil, and life after death (see Table 4). Clergymen in the West were more likely than their counterparts nationwide to say they'd considered leaving the ministry. And, although the West made up only 17 percent of the nation's population, polls showed that 36 percent of the population who described themselves as nonreligious lived in the West. As for the Bay Area itself, one poll conducted in 1972 found 18 percent there identified as "nonreligious." The comparable figure for the nation at this time was only 4 percent.

The overall religious profile of the Bay Area, therefore, appears to be

Table 4. **MAINSTREAM RELIGION IN THE WEST**

	West	U.S.
Weekly church attendance, 1974	30%	40%
Very religious, 1974	20%	26%
Great deal of confidence in organized religion, 1974	31%	44%
Believe religion can answer most of today's problems, 1974	57%	62%
Believe in heaven, 1969	77%	85%
Believe in hell, 1969	52%	65%
Believe in the devil, 1969	50%	60%
Believe in life after death, 1969	70%	73%
Ever considered leaving the religious life, clergymen 1971	39%	32%

Sources: Gallup Opinion Index, No. 114, No. 44, No. 70; "West" includes California, Oregon, Washington, Hawaii, Alaska, Montana, Arizona, Colorado, Idaho, Wyoming, Utah, Nevada, and New Mexico.

substantially different from the rest of the nation.[5] For this reason we shall not be able to make any generalizations about the *incidence* of religious experimentation beyond the Bay Area itself, except perhaps to say that the incidence outside the Bay Area is likely to be lower than it is in the Bay Area. Instead, most of our conclusions will concern the *relations* between religious experimentation and other social or psychological variables. These conclusions should also be considered tentative as far as the society outside the Bay Area is concerned. What we have attempted to do, however, is to consider relations that reasonably could exist anywhere, rather than limiting ourselves to relations that clearly could apply only in the Bay Area.

THE BERKELEY STUDENT SURVEYS

In addition to the general population survey of the Bay Area, some evidence from students at the University of California, Berkeley, also became available. These data were collected by the Institute for Research in Social Behavior, Berkeley, under the direction of Dean Manheimer, Glen Mellinger, and Robert Somers, as part of a larger study of changing values and life styles among university males, funded by the National Institute of Mental Health.[6] As part of the study, some information was obtained on religious orientations. This information revealed sizable amounts of religious defection and experimentation among these students, again making it possible to learn something of the causes of this defection and experimentation. But more importantly, the data are longitudinal. They are from two panel studies conducted at three-year intervals among two samples of students. Thus, they afford a chance to explore some of the actual *changes* in religious orientation among these students. These data are analyzed in Chapter 7, where the details of the samples are described more fully.

5. For a sketch of social, economic, demographic, and historical differences between the San Francisco Bay Area and other large metropolitan areas, see Wuthnow, *The Consciousness Reformation,* Appendix A.
6. Identified as National Institute of Mental Health Grant MH-21425 to study "Changing Life Styles and Values among University Males."

I. THE NEW EXPERIMENTATION

CHAPTER 1

Experimentation
with Eastern Religions

Eastern religious movements became widely evident in the San Francisco Bay Area during the late 1960s and early 1970s, both in reputation and participation. Virtually every known group was locally represented, some of the larger of these being Zen, Transcendental Meditation (TM), various yoga groups, the Happy-Healthy-Holy Organization (3HO), Meher Baba, and Divine Light. This chapter examines some of the social and cultural conditions that seem to facilitate attraction to and participation in three of these movements: TM, yoga groups, and Zen.

TM, founded by the Maharishi Mahesh Yogi, became popular in the late 1960s in the United States and, at this writing, claims to have taught over 300,000 people its meditation techniques. Yoga, of course, is not a specific group, but encompasses a variety of different yoga techniques. Hatha yoga seems to have been the most common type in the Bay Area at the time of the survey. Zen Buddhism has been practiced in the United States for many years, but gained considerable popularity in the 1960s, perhaps in large measure because of the writings of Alan Watts and D. T. Suzuki. At the time of the survey, there were large Zen Centers in San Francisco and in the Carmel area.

These particular movements are analyzed because enough people had been attracted by them or had participated in them to make analysis possible. It should be kept in mind, of course, that the results obtained here may well not apply to all kinds of Eastern religious movements. It should also be noted that experimentation with these movements doesn't necessarily imply "religious" experimentation (some yoga groups, for example, are strictly exercise programs). Our reason for characterizing them as Eastern religions is only because each of them draws on religious traditions from the East.

15

The data show that familiarity—at least casual familiarity—with these groups is fairly widespread in the Bay Area. One of every two residents (49 percent) claims to know at least a little about yoga groups, and one of every three claims to know something about TM (32 percent) and Zen (30 percent). Knowing a lot about each group is, of course, less common: only 4 percent claim to know a lot about yoga and about TM, and only 3 percent claim to know a lot about Zen. But at least a sizable segment of the population is aware of the presence of these religions.

Among those who have heard of each movement, the response is also generally favorable. Forty-three percent of those familiar with yoga say they are at least mildly attracted to it, 40 percent say this about Zen, and 39 percent are attracted to TM. This is in comparison with only 10 percent who answer that they are "turned off" by yoga, 11 percent who are "turned off" by Zen, and 12 percent who are "turned off" by TM (the remainder say they have no reactions either way). Thus, these groups have elicited positive feelings at a ratio of about three to one over negative feelings.

Actual participation is difficult to assess accurately with a survey. Nevertheless, we thought it important to at least ask people whether or not they had ever participated in these groups. The data show that participation is much less prevalent than attraction, but they also suggest that the absolute numbers of at least one-time participants may not be small. Among those who have heard of yoga, 16 percent claim to have taken part in it. TM registers the same percentage among those familiar with it. Among those familiar with Zen, 8 percent have participated. Translating these figures into percentages for the entire sample suggests that approximately 8 percent have participated in yoga groups, 5 percent have participated in TM, and 3 percent have participated in Zen.

Yoga, TM, and Zen are perhaps the best known of all the Eastern religions in the Bay Area, and even they, the above figures suggest, have attracted relatively small fractions of the total community. Yet the fractions that have been attracted are sizable enough to warrant examination. Who are the religious experimenters? What are the social conditions leading them to experiment?

EXPLANATIONS OF RELIGIOUS EXPERIMENTATION

A variety of arguments has been put forth to explain why some people have defected from conventional religion and experimented with religions rooted in other traditions, such as yoga, TM, and Zen. Some observers have stressed the tensions seemingly endemic in modern society—pressures to compete and succeed academically and vocationally, the anonymity and associated alienation of urban life, instability within the family and transience in the community, structured inequality and bureaucratic intransigence—tensions that supposedly cause dissatisfaction with the conventional and fascination with alternatives. Some have pointed instead to subtle but profound changes in the cultural sphere: the declining work ethic, the quest for self-expression, disillusionment with scientific rationality, or the collapse of a three-tiered universe in religion. Cultural shifts such as these, they have suggested, have tended to undermine the credibility of established religion, but have not offered something concrete in its place; hence, the search for new sources of meaning and transcendence. Others have focused more on the opportunities to experiment made possible by sustained affluence, labor-saving technology, the mass media, and advanced education. This perspective suggests that religious movements are always likely to be available; the main thing determining their attractiveness is whether or not people have the opportunity to experiment. Still others have found simpler explanations, such as the Vietnam war, the civil rights movement, the Pill, television, campus clergymen, college professors, the Beatles, the devil, and even the stars.[1]

Most of these explanations are plausible; the problem has been knowing which to believe—a matter of some importance, since different explanations imply different conclusions about the significance and future of the new religions. Some accounts have been argued more persuasively than others, but little has been done to test them against solid empirical evidence.

THE NEW RELIGIONS AS CULTURAL INNOVATION

It seems useful, in attempting to account for something presumably new, to bear in mind that cultural innovations have been rather commonplace in human history and, as such, have been the objects of much thought. New religions are not dissimilar in many respects from medical discoveries, inventions, scientific breakthroughs, oil booms, gold strikes, and other cultural innovations. They all add something qualitatively different from that which has gone on before. Some insights into the sources of the new

1. For some of the more persuasive of these arguments, see John Charles Cooper, *Religion in the Age of Aquarius* (Philadelphia: Westminster Press, 1971); Edward F. Heenan, "Introduction: The Second Reformation," in Edward F. Heenan (ed.), *Mystery, Magic, and Miracle: Religion in a Post-Aquarian Age* (Englewood Cliffs, N.J.: Prentice-Hall, 1973), pp. 1–12; Kenneth Keniston, *Youth and Dissent: The Rise of a New Opposition* (New York: Harcourt, Brace, Jovanovich, 1971), especially pp. 27–172; Henry Malcolm, *Generation of Narcissus* (Boston: Little Brown, 1971); and Theodore Roszak, *The Making of a Counter-Culture* (Garden City, N.Y.: Doubleday, 1969).

religions can perhaps be obtained, therefore, by drawing on what has been learned from investigations of other cultural innovations.[2]

Why such innovations happen in the first place seems to depend on a number of things, many of which are unpredictable—chance, genius, serendipity, leadership, creativity. But innovation by itself means little. The important factor is whether or not it catches on. To be of lasting cultural significance, it must be adopted. And adoption depends on the conditions present in its environment.

Specifically, four conditions seem necessary for any cultural innovation to take root and to grow. First, people have to be *exposed* to it. One is scarcely likely to adopt something he doesn't know at least a little about. New products have to be advertised, word of a gold strike has to spread before a gold rush can take place, and new religious movements have to make themselves known if they are to survive. Second, successful innovations must be accorded *legitimacy*. They will flourish only where they make sense, only where it seems reasonable to adopt them. There must be a climate of openness toward novelty and experimentation. Third, people must have *opportunities* to experiment with innovations. New activities cannot diffuse effectively in populations whose time and energy has already been totally committed. Successful innovations require an audience that can change its loyalties, an audience that has freedom to experiment. And fourth, people have to be *motivated* if they are to adopt an innovation. Some need or problem has to be experienced in their present way of life, a problem for which the innovation offers a potential solution. The greater the extent to which all these conditions are met, the more likely it would seem that cultural innovations will be adopted.

It is important to recognize that any one of these conditions seems capable of facilitating the diffusion of cultural innovation independently of the others. We are not suggesting that there must be some sequence whereby legitimacy, for example, can make a difference only if exposure has already reached a high level. What we are suggesting is that the diffusion of a cultural innovation can be understood more fully by taking into account all of these conditions than by limiting attention to any one of them. Statistically this argument is supported if each of the four conditions we have outlined is associated with religious experimentation *independently* of the others.

2. H. G. Barnett's study, *Innovation: The Basis of Cultural Change* (New York: McGraw-Hill, 1953), remains the most suggestive of this literature. Other useful sources include Everett M. Rogers, *The Diffusion of Innovations*, rev. ed. (New York: Free Press, 1971); and James S. Coleman, Elihu Katz, and Herbert Menzel, "The Diffusion of an Innovation Among Physicians," *Sociometry* 20 (December 1957): 253–269. The conditions of cultural innovation discussed here also parallel in some respects those in Neil Smelser's *Theory of Collective Behavior* (New York: Free Press, 1962).

Seeing the new religions in this light suggests that their recent prosperity can probably be understood best as the result of social and cultural developments which in *combination* have provided the necessary exposure, legitimacy, opportunity, and motivation for them to be widely adopted: the mix has been as important as the ingredients. What we are proposing, therefore, is an additive theory emphasizing the combined importance of exposure, legitimacy, opportunity, and motivation. Had conditions been such that any one of these were missing, the popularity of the new religions would likely have been diminished.

This interpretation can be tested by examining the characteristics of persons in the San Francisco Bay Area who became attracted to and who participated in Zen, TM, and yoga groups.[3] Our interest is in determining both the separate and combined effects of being in a part of the society that encourages exposure to such movements, of having values that give them legitimacy, of having the opportunity to take part in them, and of being in a position that motivates one to experiment with new activities.

EXPOSURE TO NEW IDEAS

Modern society has supplied the means whereby large populations can be exposed, sometimes instantaneously, to newsworthy ideas and events through the mass media, books, magazines, the schools, and institutions of higher learning. In the past generation this potential has mushroomed dramatically. For example, during the quarter century between 1950 and 1974, the number of radios produced annually tripled from 9.8 million to 33.2 million, the number of television sets sold annually doubled from 7.5 million to 15.3 million, and the number of commercial broadcasting stations grew from 2,336 to 7,526. During the same period, annual book sales climbed from $456 million to $2,915 million, consumption of newsprint rose from 5.8 million tons to 10.1 million tons, the total volume of mail increased from 45 billion pieces to 90 billion pieces, telephones multiplied from 43 million to 144 million, and telephone calls per year expanded from 176 million to 613 million. Advanced education, another source of exposure to cultural innovations, underwent an equivalent expansion; for instance, college graduates increased from 0.4 million annually to 1.5 million, currently including about 30 percent of all 23-year-olds, and high school graduates rose from 1.2 million annually to 3.1 million annually, currently including 75 percent of all 17-year-olds. At present, the average

3. These groups all gained considerable popularity during the countercultural unrest of the late 1960s and since that time have adapted well to a more settled environment, suing the mass media and established institutions, including the schools, to effectively broaden their audience. Of the various new Eastern groups, they appear to be among the more flexible and least authoritarian.

American has finished high school and has taken some college training, owns a television set which he or she watches an average of five hours a day, makes at least three phone calls each day, receives at least one piece of mail every day, takes a daily newspaper and otherwise consumes more than a hundred pounds of newsprint each year.[4]

All this has made it easier for religious movements to grow than ever before. Unlike their predecessors, dependent on word-of-mouth communication or mass meetings and often little known outside their immediate vicinity, modern gurus can easily make themselves known to vast audiences through established channels of communication. From the standpoint of the average citizen, never before has it been so easy to hear the message of the new religions.

The benefits of modern communication have their costs, of course. Some segments of the society—the young, the educated, and the prosperous—can be reached easily, while others remain relatively more isolated. The constituency of a religious movement, therefore, will be partly determined by the channels through which the movement is made public. In times past, accordingly, the members of religious movements may have been located chiefly along trade routes or in limited geographic regions. Today, it seems more likely that they will be drawn, other things being equal, from the better educated and otherwise informed sectors of the society, simply because these sectors will be most aware of the presence of the new religions.

This expectation can readily be put to the test with our data from the San Francisco area. In Table 5 we have presented the percentages who scored positively on various measures of cultural exposure among those who said they were attracted to TM, to yoga, and to Zen, or to any one of these groups. We have also presented these percentages for those who had taken part in any of these groups and, for comparison, the entire Bay Area sample.[5] On the assumption that college-educated persons and persons from better educated backgrounds tend to be more exposed to new ideas

4. The figures cited in this paragraph are all from the *Statistical Abstract of the United States, 1975* (U.S. Department of Commerce: Bureau of the Census, 1975).

5. The questions from which these responses are taken were framed as follows: For each religious group, respondents were asked first whether they knew nothing, a little, or a lot about it; those who knew a little or a lot about the group were then asked whether they were strongly attracted by the group, mildly attracted, turned off by the group, or whether they had no feelings either way; finally, these respondents were asked if they had ever taken part in the group. Those who said they were strongly attracted and those who said they were mildly attracted are considered together throughout the chapter. Percentages giving the various responses to these questions have been discussed in Robert Wuthnow, *The Consciousness Reformation* (Berkeley and Los Angeles: University of California Press, 1976), pp. 32–33; and in Robert Wuthnow, "The New Religions in Social Context," in Charles Y. Glock and Robert N. Bellah (eds.), *The New Religious Consciousness* (Berkeley and Los Angeles: University of California Press, 1976), pp. 267–293.

Table 5. **INDICATORS OF EXPOSURE BY RELIGIOUS EXPERIMENTATION***

| | | *Persons attracted to:* | | | | |
Percent having:	TM	Yoga	Zen	Any one	Took part	Total Bay Area Sample
Some college	81%	77%	84%	77%	81%	59%
Mother with some college	31%	31%	34%	31%	31%	21%
Father with some college	33%	38%	45%	39%	46%	27%
Intellectual sophistication rated above average	66%	62%	77%	62%	71%	48%
Number	(126)	(207)	(121)	(283)	(114)	(1000)

*Numbers weighted to compensate for oversampling of youth.

than persons less educationally advantaged, we have presented the percentages of persons having some college themselves and the percentages of persons whose mother or father had some college education.[6] We also use information obtained by the interviewers, who were asked to make a general appraisal of the overall intellectual sophistication of each person they interviewed. If exposure to up-to-date ideas encourages attraction to new religious movements, we would expect the percentages to be greater on these items among the religious experimenters than in the sample at large, or more accurately, we would expect religious experimenters to be recruited disproportionately from the better informed segments of the population. These are rather limited indicators of cultural exposure, to be sure, but they afford some evidence as to the importance or unimportance of exposure as a source of the new religions.

The data consistently support our expectation that religious experimenters should rank above average on indicators of cultural exposure. For example, 81 percent of the persons attracted to TM have had some college education, compared with 59 percent of the total sample. The proportion among those attracted to Zen is even higher (84 percent), and among those attracted to yoga it is nearly as high (77 percent). Of those who have taken part in one of these groups, 81 percent have had some college. Similar differences are evident concerning mother's education and father's education and interviewers' ratings of intellectual sophistication. For instance, 48 percent of the total sample were judged to be above average on intellectual sophistication, but among those attracted to TM this proportion was 66 percent; it was 62 percent among those attracted to yoga, and 77 percent among those attracted to Zen.

The effects of different kinds of cultural exposure also seem to be cumulative. This is demonstrated by combining the foregoing measures to form an index affording comparisons between persons highly exposed to sources of new ideas and persons less exposed: giving persons a score of one for each of the items on which they scored positively—having had some college education, having a college-educated mother, having a college-educated father, and having been rated above average on intellectual sophistication—yields an index ranging from 0 (low) to 4 (high). As a look at Table 6 reveals, only 11 percent of those scoring 0 on the index say they are attracted to any of the new groups, and only 3 percent claim to have taken part in any of them. But these proportions increase with each increase on the index, such that 24 percent of the persons scoring 1 are attracted and 7 percent have participated, 36 percent of those scoring 2 are attracted and 15 percent have

6. For young people (age 16 through 30) not yet having finished their education, expected level of educational attainment was substituted for actual education.

requires considered choice, are different. Their legitimacy depends on the presence of supportive values and beliefs that make them seem proper and good (for example, conversion to the metric system requires deliberation over its costs and benefits).

An innovation may be considered legitimate because it is recognized as the only solution to a pressing social problem (for example, gasoline rationing), or because it can be justified in relation to a society's highest values (for example, congressional redistricting), or because it has earned a stamp of approval from authorities in the know (for example, a new drug). But innovations may be experimented with simply because the idea of experimentation has become a value in itself.

A mood of this nature, which tolerates nonconventionality because tolerance itself is of value, has become widely apparent in American culture since the close of World War II. In matters of sexual conduct, for example, the numbers who approve of homosexuality, prostitution, pornography, and premarital sex have risen substantially since the 1950s.[8] In religion, tolerance of atheists has increased in the polls, even though virtually everyone himself still claims belief in God.[9] In politics, both the numbers who call themselves "independents" and those who approve of splinter groups and nonconventional political methods have grown.[10] Especially among young people and on campuses, where anti-war sentiment added alienation from established institutions and life styles, an ethos favoring experimentation in all realms of life became increasingly prominent during the 1960s. Why this ethos and its accompanying unrest occurred when it did has been the

8. Between 1965 and 1973, acceptance of the statement "homosexuals do more harm than good for the country" on Harris polls dropped from 70 percent to 50 percent (*Current Opinion*, November 1973, p. 116), and the idea that relations between consenting homosexuals are morally wrong dropped among college students nationally from 42 percent in 1969 to 25 percent in 1973 and among noncollege youth from 72 percent to 47 percent (Daniel Yankelovich, *The New Morality*, New York: McGraw-Hill, 1974, p. 93). Gallup polls have shown a decrease in the numbers who think premarital sex is wrong, from 68 percent in 1969 to 48 percent in 1973 (*Current Opinion*, September 1973, p. 93). Harris polls have documented a decline from 70 percent in 1965 to 46 percent in 1973 in the proportion who think prostitutes do more harm than good for the country (*Current Opinion*, November 1973, p. 116). Questions about nude actors and actresses, nude pictures in magazines, and topless waitresses have shown decreases of about 16 percent between 1969 and 1973 in the proportions on Gallup polls finding these things objectionable (*Gallup Opinion Index*, August 1973, No. 98).

9. Between 1965 and 1973, the proportion who felt that people who don't believe in God do more harm than good for the country declined in Harris polls from 72 percent to 46 percent (*Current Opinion*, November 1973, p. 116), yet 98 percent of the public still claims to believe in God (See Table 3).

10. In 1974, independents comprised 41 percent of the electorate, up from 28 percent in 1966, according to national surveys conducted at the University of Michigan (*San Francisco Chronicle*, May 5, 1974). Trends in other political attitudes are discussed in Wuthnow, *The Consciousness Reformation*, pp. 12–23.

Table 6. **RELIGIOUS EXPERIMENTATION BY EXF**

| | *Exposure Index* | | | |
| | *Low* | | | |
	0	*1*	*2*	
Percent attracted to any one Eastern religious movement	11%	24%	36%	44%
Percent having participated in any one movement	3%	7%	15%	20%
Number	(270)	(249)	(247)	(149)

*Numbers weighted to compensate for oversampling of youth.

participated, 44 percent of those scoring 3 are attracted and 20 percei participated, and 45 percent of those scoring 4 (highest on exposu. attracted and 23 percent have participated.[7]

These results indicate that the Eastern religious experimenter tends better educated, from a better educated background, and more tellectually sophisticated than the average person in the Bay Area, and the more one has of these characteristics, the more likely he is to be attra to Eastern religions and to have participated in them. By inference, the suggest that the present popularity of these religions has probably b facilitated by the growth in recent decades of higher education, the m media, and other sources of cultural exposure. Education and intellectu sophistication function in other ways, of course, than merely exposin persons to new ideas. These conclusions will have to remain tentative therefore, till we have examined the effects of the other conditions out lined at the beginning of this chapter.

LEGITIMATION

The second condition essential for the birth of successful cultural innovation, we suggested, is a cultural milieu that accords it legitimacy. The process by which things become legitimated is a curious one. Once they become familiar and widely practiced, social patterns retain legitimacy simply by being taken for granted (it never occurs to us, for example, to drive on the left side of the road). But innovations, the adoption of which

7. The chi-square value for the relation between exposure and attraction is 81.2 for 4 degrees of freedom, significant at or beyond the .001 level; for participation, chi-square equals 47.5 for 4 degrees of freedom, significant at or beyond the .001 level.

subject of considerable study itself, but in part it appears to have been rooted in an even broader cultural change, a change in cultural meaning systems, which eroded traditional sanctions against experimentation with the nonconventional.[11] In this climate of experimentation, the new religions have found legitimacy.

Evidence to this effect is shown in Table 7. There we have presented the percentages of persons involved with TM, yoga, or Zen, who express a general tolerance, for example, toward homosexuality, cohabitation, and legalizing marijuana, and who mostly identify themselves as political liberals. On each of these issues the religious experimenters are substantially more likely than the average Bay Area resident to express tolerance. For example, 82 percent of those in the sample who are attracted to TM favor granting more freedom to homosexuals, as do 77 percent of those attracted to yoga, and 79 percent of those attracted to Zen. This is in comparison with only 45 percent of the total sample. One kind of experimentation, in other words, seems to reinforce another.

The importance of having a mindset which legitimates nonconventionality in general, as a factor encouraging religious experimentation, is demonstrated further by comparing persons who consistently register approval on all the issues just considered with persons who answer with less consistent approval. Giving persons a point for each of the four items they answer affirmatively, we see (in Table 8) that only 10 percent of those receiving scores of 0 say they are attracted to any one of the Eastern groups, compared with 18 percent of those with a score of 1, 25 percent of those scoring 2, 36 percent of those scoring 3, and 64 percent of those scoring 4. Similarly, the percentages having participated in any of the groups range from 3 percent among those with scores of 0 to 29 percent among those with scores of 4.[12] Thus, it appears that the *more* legitimacy one gives to nonconventionality, no matter what the specific issue, the more likely he is to be attracted to the new religions.

Our theory, it will be recalled, also suggested that the various conditions of cultural innovation—exposure, legitimacy, opportunity, and motivation—should have a cumulative impact on religious experimentation. With regard to the two conditions considered thus far, persons should be most likely to engage in religious experimentation if they hold values that legitimate novelty *and* if they belong to more sophisticated segments of the

11. This argument has been developed in *The Consciousness Reformation*; see also Charles Y. Glock, "Images of 'God,' Images of Man, and the Organization of Social Life," in Charles Y. Glock (ed.), *Religion in Sociological Perspective* (Belmont, Calif.: Wadsworth, 1973), pp. 297–311.
12. The chi-square for attraction is 195.1 for 4 degrees of freedom, significant at or beyond the .001. level; for participation, 91.5 for 4 degrees of freedom, significant at or beyond the .001 level.

Table 7. **LEGITIMATING VALUES BY RELIGIOUS EXPERIMENTATION***

	Persons attracted to:				Took part	Total Bay Area Sample
	TM	Yoga	Zen	Any one		
Percent who are:						
Politically liberal	70%	61%	62%	58%	62%	34%
Approving of cohabitation	83%	80%	80%	77%	81%	55%
Favoring more freedom for homosexuals	82%	77%	79%	75%	79%	45%
In favor of legalizing marijuana	76%	68%	70%	67%	73%	41%
Number	(126)	(207)	(121)	(283)	(114)	(1000)

*Numbers weighted to compensate for oversampling of youth.

Table 8. RELIGIOUS EXPERIMENTATION BY LEGITIMACY INDEX*

| | Legitimacy Index | | | | |
	Low 0	1	2	3	High 4
Percent attracted to any one Eastern religious movement	10%	18%	25%	36%	64%
Percent having participated in any one movement	3%	5%	11%	13%	29%
Number	(308)	(191)	(159)	(138)	(204)

*Numbers weighted to compensate for oversampling of youth.

population. They should be least likely to be religious experimenters if they score high neither on legitimacy nor on exposure. This is tantamount to saying that *both* legitimacy and exposure are important, that neither explains away the effects of the other. This warrants examination, of course, since the more sophisticated usually tend to be more tolerant as well.

The combined effects of exposure and legitimacy on religious experimentation can be assessed by comparing the percentages who are attracted to Eastern religions and who have participated in them among persons with different combinations of scores on the Exposure Index and Legitimacy Index. If our expectations are correct, there should be a relation between experimentation and each index within each level of the other index, and the two indexes in combination should produce greater variation in experimentation than either did separately.

This is what the data show. Looking across the rows in the top half of Table 9, we see that each increment in legitimacy among people having the same scores on exposure is associated with an increasing likelihood of being attracted to Eastern groups. And reading down each column shows that each increase in exposure among persons with the same legitimacy scores tends to be associated (barring several exceptions) with an increase in the proportion who say they are attracted. A look at the bottom half of Table 9 reveals similar results for participation in these groups. In other words, religious experimentation is associated with conditions facilitating exposure to new ideas independently of conditions that legitimate innovation, and it is associated with legitimacy independently of exposure. Furthermore, the effects of legitimacy and exposure are additive. The least amount of experimentation is among persons scoring low on both indexes, and the most experimentation is among persons scoring high on both. Thus, only 7 percent of those with scores of 0 on both the Exposure Index

Table 9. **RELIGIOUS EXPERIMENTATION BY LEGITIMACY AND EXPOSURE****

| | | Legitimacy Index | | | | |
		Low 0	1	2	3	High 4
Percent attracted to new religions:						
Exposure Index						
Low	0	7%	10%	10%	22%	*
		(131)	(64)	(48)	(19)	(8)
	1	9%	11%	20%	30%	67%
		(86)	(46)	(41)	(31)	(44)
	2	11%	23%	39%	38%	57%
		(47)	(43)	(41)	(43)	(72)
	3	19%	36%	45%	50%	66%
		(28)	(27)	(20)	(33)	(42)
High	4	11%	32%	16%	33%	72%
		(15)	(12)	(10)	(12)	(37)
Percent having participated:						
Exposure Index						
Low	0	1%	5%	7%	0%	*
		(131)	(64)	(48)	(19)	(8)
	1	0%	5%	10%	11%	18%
		(86)	(46)	(41)	(31)	(44)
	2	4%	4%	18%	14%	27%
		(47)	(43)	(41)	(43)	(72)
	3	17%	4%	17%	16%	37%
		(28)	(27)	(20)	(33)	(42)
High	4	0%	18%	0%	28%	39%
		(15)	(12)	(10)	(12)	(37)

**Numbers weighted to compensate for oversampling of youth.
*Less than 10 cases, too few for reliable percentaging.

and the Legitimacy Index say they are attracted to an Eastern religion, but 72 percent say they are attracted among those with scores of 4 on both indexes. Similarly, only 1 percent of the former have ever taken part in an Eastern group, compared with 39 percent of the latter.[13]

These results suggest that much of the appeal of the new religions may be understandable as a function of cultural conditions that have facilitated exposure to the novel and accorded it legitimacy. But other factors have also played a role.

OPPORTUNITY TO EXPERIMENT

The third condition we posited as being necessary for the growth of Eastern religions and of any cultural innovation is the opportunity for people to experiment. What we have in mind is more than just free time, although this certainly is important. People also need to be in situations that do not

13. The significance of three-way relations in this chapter will be examined using Leo Goodman's hierarchical model technique (see Leo A. Goodman, "A Modified Multiple Regression Approach to the Analysis of Dichotomous Variables," *American Sociological Review* 37 (February 1972): 28–46; for a nontechnical introduction to Goodman's methods, see James A. Davis, "Hierarchical Models for Significance Tests in Multivariate Contingency Tables: An Exegesis of Goodman's Recent Papers," in Herbert L. Costner (ed.)., *Sociological Methodology, 1973–1974* (San Francisco: Jossey-Bass Publishers, 1974), pp. 189–231. Briefly, the logic of the Goodman method is to generate alternative hypothetical models that include or omit various of the relations among the variables at issue and compare these models with the actual data and with each other to see if one model fits the data significantly better than another model. In the present instance, we let participation = A, legitimacy = B, and exposure = C. Our expectation is for there to be a relation between A and B and between A and C; we also assume there is a relation between B and C. These relations can be summarized as $\{BC\}\{AB\}\{AC\}$. Goodman has devised a computer program that generates hypothetical numbers for a model having such relations and compares these numbers with the actual data (as shown in Table 9). It describes the degree of fit between the two with the likelihood-ratio chi-square statistic. In this case, it is 21.82 for 16 degrees of freedom. To see if relation $\{AB\}$ is significant, taking into account relation $\{AC\}$, we generate another model which leaves out $\{AB\}$ and see how well it fits the actual data. The likelihood-ratio chi-square for this model is 176.30 for 20 degrees of freedom. Subtracting chi-square values (176.30 − 21.8 = 154.48 for 4 degrees of freedom, significant beyond the .001 level) shows us that relation $\{AB\}$ is significant. We compute the significance of relation $\{AC\}$ in the same manner, finding it to also be significant at the .001 level. Thus, we can conclude, as hypothesized, that both exposure and legitimacy independently affect religious participation. A comparable analysis substituting attraction for participation shows that the relation between attraction and legitimacy is significant, taking into account the effects of exposure. The relation between exposure and attraction is *not* significant, taking into account the effects of legitimacy ($\chi^2 = 4.61$, d.f. = 4, p greater than .30). But none of the models taking into account only the two-way relations among the variables fits the data well; thus, we are forced to conclude that an interactive relation is present among the variables such that the relations between any two varies depending on the level of the third (the difference between the interactive model, which in three-variable relations is always the actual data, and the model which includes relations $\{BC\}\{AB\}\{AC\}$, is 40.67 for 16 degrees of freedom, significant at the .001 level).

require them to conform to conventional expectations all the time. Nothing kills innovation as quickly as demanding, established institutions.

Religious movements typically begin and find their largest audiences among persons marginal in one way or another to the mainstream of society.[14] Part of the reason for this seems to be the frustration and alienation that accompanies marginality, to which we shall give attention in the next section. In part, however, the socially marginal also seem to be less constrained by conventional expectations and therefore have more liberty to engage in religious experimentation.

Marginality has traditionally carried the connotation of being poor, uneducated, perhaps elderly, and more than likely a member of a racial or ethnic minority. Such persons have been little in evidence in the new religions of recent years, perhaps because they lack the exposing and legitimating characteristics seen to be important in creating attraction to the new religions. Instead, popular imagery has cast the religious devotee as typically young and fairly well-educated. These persons, it has been recognized, also manifest characteristics of marginality to the larger society, giving them opportunities to try out nonconventional social experiments. Many may still be in school, where they can enjoy flexible schedules and an atmosphere that encourages new ideas, rather than in the labor force, where job responsibilities would likely be more constraining. Many also remain unattached to marital, child-rearing, and civic obligations.

These kinds of marginality have not grown uniformly, like the conditions facilitating exposure and legitimacy have, but some of the demographic trends of recent years suggest that there may be a larger body of persons having the freedom to experiment with social alternatives now than ever before. In 1960, for example, young people between the ages of 14 and 34 made up about one-fourth (27.6 percent) of the population, but in 1974 over a third (34.6 percent) of the population fell into this category. Furthermore, substantially larger proportions of young people stay in school now than in the past. Between 1950 and 1973, for example, the proportion of 18- to 21-year-olds in school rose from 30 percent to 46 percent. This increase, together with the increase in numbers of young people in general, placed eight million more students on college campuses in 1976 than there had been in 1950.[15]

Accompanying these trends in higher education, there is also evidence

14. The importance of marginality, or what has also been called deprivation, for the origin and evolution of religious movements has been discussed in Charles Y. Glock, "On the Origin and Evolution of Religious Groups," in Charles Y. Glock (ed.), *Religion in Sociological Perspective*, pp. 207–220.

15. All of the figures presented in this section are from the *Statistical Abstract of the United States, 1975*.

that young people are postponing the usual obligations of adult life till they are older and out of school. Between 1950 and 1974, for instance, the proportion of 20- to 24-year-olds remaining single edged up from 52 percent to 57 percent among males and from 31 percent to 40 percent among females. More and more young people also have been putting off having children till they are older; for example, the proportion of women aged 20 to 24 remaining childless increased from 24 percent in 1960 to 36 percent in 1971.

In considering social conditions providing opportunities to engage in religious experiments, the affluence of the recent period also deserves mention, of course. After-tax incomes have grown steadily at a rate of about 2.7 percent each year since 1950, taking into account the declining purchasing power of the dollar. Reflecting this propserity, Americans spent over $800 billion on consumer goods in 1973, which, when adjusted for inflation, is still 2.6 times more than they had spent in 1950. Over $50 billion of this was for recreation, three times as much as had been spent in 1950, again taking inflation into account. In addition, some $25 billion was given to religious, civic, educational, and other charitable organizations.[16]

Apart from these trends, though, what evidence is there that such conditions have actually been associated with religious experimentation? It is difficult to find indicators that measure precisely the opportunities people have to experiment, but three pieces of information in our data seem suggestive of the importance of these factors. First, the data show that religious experimenters tend to be younger than the average resident; for example, 57 percent of those who have ever participated in TM, yoga, or Zen fall between the ages of 16 and 30, while only 33 percent of the total sample is composed of this age group (see Table 10). Second, religious experimenters are disproportionately single: half of the participants have never been married, in comparison with only a fourth of the sample at large. Third, there seems to be a tendency for religious experimenters to be more geographically mobile than average—about one in four have moved in the past two years, compared with one in six in the total sample. The last two factors may be partly a function of the differences in age between experimenters and others. What all three suggest, however, is that religious experimenters are probably less tied down by the ordinary obligations of home, job, and community than the average adult.

Again, the effects of these various characteristics seem to reinforce one another. Sixty-two percent of those having all three characteristics claim

16. Sources: U.S. Department of Commerce, Bureau of Economic Analysis, *Survey of Current Business* (July 1974); and Constant H. Jacquet, Jr. (ed.), *Yearbook of American and Canadian Churches, 1975* (New York: Abingdon Press, 1975).

Table 10. OPPORTUNITY ITEMS BY RELIGIOUS EXPERIMENTATION*

| | Persons attracted to: | | | | | |
	TM	Yoga	Zen	Any one	Took part	Total Bay Area Sample
Percent:						
Age 16 to 30	47%	54%	40%	49%	57%	33%
Never married	45%	44%	39%	41%	50%	26%
Moved twice in the past two years	26%	25%	25%	24%	27%	16%
Number	(126)	(207)	(121)	(283)	(114)	(1000)

*Numbers weighted to compensate for oversampling of youth.

Table 11. RELIGIOUS EXPERIMENTATION BY OPPORTUNITY INDEX*

| | Opportunity Index | | | |
	Low 0	1	2	High 3
Percent attracted to any one Eastern religious movement	19%	37%	37%	62%
Percent having participated in any one movement	7%	13%	18%	33%
Number	(565)	(177)	(199)	(59)

*Numbers weighted to compensate for oversampling of youth.

attraction to at least one of the three Eastern religions, in comparison with 19 percent of those having none of these characteristics. By the same token, 33 percent of the former have taken part in at least one of the groups, compared with only 7 percent of the latter (see Table 11).[17]

There is a problem in drawing inferences from the youthfulness, marital status, and mobility of religious experimenters, of course. People with these characteristics probably have the other characteristics we have been considering too—better educations, more liberal, and so on. If we wish to know whether having the opportunity to experiment plays an important role in itself, therefore, we must look at its effects while also taking into account these other characteristics. Since we have already shown that exposure and legitimacy each make a difference, it will simplify matters to construct a single index encompassing both these factors. This is done by adding scores on the Exposure Index and the Legitimacy Index, yielding a scale ranging from 0 (low) to 8 (high) which, for want of a better label, we shall refer to as the Cultural Availability Index.

The three-way relations between religious experimentation (attraction and participation), opportunity, and cultural availability are reported in Table 12. Looking first across the rows, we see that the percentages generally get larger from left to right, assuring us that the effects of exposure and legitimacy remain when opportunity is taken into consideration. Looking down the columns gives more mixed results. For both attraction and participation, opportunity tends to be associated with religious experimentation if cultural availability is low or if it is high, but not if it is intermediate.

17. Chi square for attraction equals 69.9 for 3 degrees of freedom, significant beyond the .001 level; for participation, 49.0, d.f. = 3, significant beyond the .001 level.

Table 12. RELIGIOUS EXPERIMENTATION BY CULTURAL AVAILABILITY AND OPPORTUNITY**

| | Cultural Availability Index | | | | | | | | |
	Low 0	1	2	3	4	5	6	7	High 8
Percent attracted to new religions: Opportunity Index									
Low 0	6% (117)	7% (116)	11% (97)	20% (76)	32% (57)	53% (53)	21% (29)	* (9)	* (8)
1	16% (10)	17% (22)	0% (14)	28% (25)	33% (30)	51% (20)	65% (36)	45% (14)	* (6)
2	* (2)	16% (11)	14% (26)	13% (26)	33% (26)	44% (36)	54% (42)	59% (20)	56% (10)
3 High	* (2)	* (1)	* (3)	* (5)	* (9)	44% (10)	* (8)	77% (10)	87% (13)
Percent having participated in new religions: Opportunity Index									
Low 0	0% (117)	3% (116)	3% (97)	8% (76)	11% (57)	17% (53)	0% (29)	* (9)	* (8)
1	16% (10)	0% (22)	4% (14)	8% (25)	4% (30)	9% (20)	32% (36)	8% (14)	* (6)
2	* (2)	0% (11)	14% (26)	7% (26)	16% (26)	18% (36)	23% (42)	32% (20)	27% (10)
3 High	* (2)	* (1)	* (3)	* (5)	* (9)	22% (10)	* (8)	46% (10)	57% (13)

**Numbers weighted to compensate for oversampling of youth.
*Less than 10 cases, too few cases for reliable percentaging.

For instance, the percentages attracted to Eastern religions increase with increases on the Opportunity Index from 6 percent to 16 percent among those with Cultural Availibility scores of 0, from 7 percent to 16 percent among those with scores of 1, from 21 percent to 54 percent among those with scores of 6, and from 45 percent to 77 percent among those with scores of 7. Among those with scores of 4, however, the difference is only from 32 percent to 33 percent. Those with scores of 2, 3, and 5 also fail to show consistent differences. These are unanticipated findings and consequently are difficult to interpret, but what appears to be happening is that opportunity counts among people who are already highly predisposed to experiment because of exposure and legitimacy. Indeed, among those few with the highest scores on exposure, legitimacy, and opportunity, 7 out of 8 are attracted to a new religion, and over half have actually participated. Opportunity also seems sufficient in itself to encourage some experimentation among persons not at all predisposed because of exposure and legitimacy. For the majority of persons who are somewhere in the middle in terms of exposure and legitimacy, however, it makes no difference whether they have opportunities to experiment or not. The decisive factor for them is how much exposure and legitimacy they have had. Thus, opportunity is a factor to be included in attempting to explain the appeal of the new religions, but its importance is qualified by the other factors that condition people differently to engage in experimentation.[18]

MOTIVATION

The final condition we proposed to examine as a possible source of the new religions' popularity is motivation. Given that someone is in a position to be exposed to new ideas, that he or she has a value system which gives legitimacy to the nonconventional, and that he or she has opportunities to engage in experimentation, it still makes a difference to be motivated. Becoming a religious experimenter presupposes some reason for doing so.

18. Letting A = attraction, B = opportunity, and C = cultural availability, the χ^2 value for model $\{BC\}\{AB\}\{AC\}$ is 52.91 (d.f. = 24); the χ^2 value for model $\{BC\}\{AC\}$ is 69.08 (d.f. = 27); and for model $\{BC\}\{AB\}$, 103.38 (d.f. = 32). Subtracting the appropriate χ^2s and degrees of freedom shows that both the relations between opportunity and attraction and between cultural availability and attraction are significant beyond the .001 level. Again, however, the interactive model fits the data significantly better than any of the other models. Substituting participation for attraction gives the following estimates: for model $\{BC\}\{AB\}\{AC\}$, $\chi^2 = 65.17$ (d.f. = 24); for model $\{BC\}\{AB\}$, $\chi^2 = 135.04$ (d.f. = 32); and for model $\{BC\}\{AC\}$, $\chi^2 = 79.68$ (d.f. = 27). Making the appropriate subtractions shows both the effects of opportunity and cultural availability to be significant. Because of the presence of a zero cell in the hypothetical models, we cannot examine the significance of the interactive model.

The literature on religious conversion uniformly emphasizes the importance of personal problems, stress, or crises causing one to try out a new faith in hopes of finding a better life.[19]

Some observers of the social unrest of recent years have attributed it almost entirely to the stress produced by modern society, arguing that young people especially have been subject to unprecedented tensions from the demands of higher education, the uncertainities of career plans, and the pressures levied by other powerful institutions.[20] It is hard to say. Certainly the divorce rate, suicide rate, crime index, drug use figures, numbers seeking psychological counseling, alcoholism statistics, dollars spent on pills, movies, and other escapes all suggest a high-wired society. But whether things are worse now than during the Depression, the World Wars, or the Twenties seems questionable. Perhaps the most that should be argued is that tensions run sufficiently high most of the time to give some people an incentive to join new religions if other conditions prove favorable. And on occasion (during the Vietnam war, for example), the level of tension easily becomes magnified, so that larger numbers become motivated toward social experimentation.

If participation in a religious movement usually resolved the worries motivating its members to join, we would have to have information at several time periods to say for sure whether stress was a source of experimentation or not. Most of the experimenters in our sample are only casual experimenters, however. It seems doubtful that their religious experimentation would have resolved their problems. Our expectation, therefore, if the argument just outlined is correct, is that experimenters should demonstrate higher frequencies of stress than others.

This tends to be the case (see Table 13). Our measures of stress are admittedly simple: asking respondents themselves to say how much they have been bothered lately about various problems. But each of the problems asked about shows differences between experimenters and others. Forty-four percent of the persons attracted to TM, for example, say they have been bothered wondering about the meaning and purpose of life, as have 41 percent of those attracted to yoga, 34 percent of those attracted to Zen, and 43 percent of those having taken part in at least one of these groups. This is in comparison with 32 percent of the whole sample. Similarly, religious experimenters are about 10 percent more likely than the average respondent

19. See, for example, John Lofland and Rodney Stark, "Becoming a World-Saver: A Theory of Conversion to a Deviant Perspective," in Barry McLaughlin (ed.), *Studies in Social Movements* (New York: Free Press, 1969), pp. 158–180.

20. An argument of this nature pertaining to student unrest more generally has been made by Talcott Parsons, "Youth in the Context of American Society," in Erik H. Erikson (ed.), *The Challenge of Youth* (Garden City, N.Y.: Doubleday, 1965), pp. 110–141.

Table 13. **MOTIVATION ITEMS BY RELIGIOUS EXPERIMENTATION***

| | | Persons attracted to: | | | | |
	TM	Yoga	Zen	Any one	Took part	Total Bay Area Sample
Percent bothered by:						
Meaning and purpose of life	44%	41%	34%	41%	43%	32%
Money problems	65%	66%	57%	62%	64%	52%
Sex life	26%	24%	25%	26%	29%	20%
Work or work plans	58%	56%	55%	56%	59%	44%
Number	(126)	(207)	(121)	(283)	(114)	(1000)

*Numbers weighted to compensate for oversampling of youth.

Table 14. **RELIGIOUS EXPERIMENTATION BY MOTIVATION INDEX***

	Motivation Index				
	Low 0	1	2	3	High 4
Percent attracted to any one Eastern religious movement	19%	22%	34%	43%	38%
Percent having participated in any one movement	6%	10%	13%	15%	21%
Number	(265)	(292)	(213)	(154)	(76)

*Numbers weighted to compensate for oversampling of youth.

to say they are bothered by money problems, about 5 percent more likely than average to say they are bothered by problems with their sex life, and about 15 percent more likely than average to say they are bothered by problems with work or work plans. Perhaps experimenters are merely more open about acknowledging their worries. But then, to acknowledge a problem may be precisely what is needed to motivate one to experiment in hopes of resolving it.

Past research on the effects of stress or deprivation has tended to find that the number of kinds of stress one experiences may be as important as the magnitude with which any single kind is felt.[21] This also seems true with regard to religious experimentation. As evidenced in Table 14, which shows the relations between experimentation and a Motivation Index constructed by giving respondents one point for each of the problems they said had been bothering them, the percentage attracted and the percentage having participated in Eastern religions is smallest among respondents scoring 0 on motivation, and these percentages rise with each increment in motivation, except that more of those with scores of 3 are attracted than of those with scores of 4.

As before, we are also concerned to show that motivation bears a significant relation to experimentation independently of the other factors considered and, therefore, that it adds to the likelihood of persons engaging in

21. For example, in motivating church involvement (see Charles Y. Glock, Benjamin B. Ringer, and Earl R. Babbie, *To Comfort and to Challenge*, Berkeley and Los Angeles: University of California Press, 1967).

experimentation. This is done by examining the three-variable relations among experimentation, motivation, and opportunity and among experimentation, motivation, and cultural availability. Since the greatest differences attributable to motivation seem to appear between those with scores of 1 and 2 on the index, we have collapsed the index for these comparisons so that scores of 0 and 1 are considered "low" and scores of 2, 3, and 4 are considered "high."

The relations among experimentation, motivation, and opportunity are shown in Table 15. The data assure us that opportunity exerts its effects independently of motivation. The percentages on attraction vary from 15 percent to 53 percent and from 27 percent to 67 percent, and on participation from 6 percent to 25 percent and from 9 percent to 38 percent. They also show the effects of motivation to be independent of opportunity. In each column, those scoring high on motivation show larger percentages than those scoring low. This is to say, of course, that the effects of motivation and opportunity are cumulative. Only 15 percent of those scoring low on both motivation and opportunity claim attraction to new religions, and

Table 15. **RELIGIOUS EXPERIMENTATION BY MOTIVATION AND OPPORTUNITY***

	Opportunity Index			
	Low 0	*1*	*2*	*High* 3
Percent attracted to new religions:				
Motivation Index				
Low	15%	29%	29%	53%
Number	(368)	(93)	(76)	(21)
High	27%	46%	42%	67%
Number	(198)	(84)	(123)	(38)
Percent having participated:				
Motivation Index				
Low	6%	9%	16%	25%
Number	(368)	(93)	(76)	(21)
High	9%	16%	18%	38%
Number	(198)	(84)	(123)	(38)

*Numbers weighted to compensate for oversampling of youth.

only 6 percent have taken part; but 67 percent of those scoring high on both are attracted, and 38 percent have been participants.[22]

Table 16 reports the relations among experimentation, motivation, and cultural availability. Reading across each row shows consistent increases in the percentages attracted to Eastern religions, from 5 percent to 74 percent and from 12 percent to 71 percent, and in the percentages of participants, from 2 percent to 20 percent and from 0 to 54 percent. Thus, the effects of exposure and legitimation seem to operate independently of motivation. The effects of motivation also appear to be independent for their part, at least on attraction. In seven of the nine columns, the percentages attracted are greater among those scoring high than among those scoring low. The pattern for participation is different. In columns 0, 1, 3, 4, and 5, high scorers are either about the same or lower on participation than low scorers. In columns 6, 7, and 8, however, high scorers are much more likely to be experimenters than are low scorers.[23] In other words, motivating conditions seem to stimulate participation in new religions only among those who have been sufficiently exposed and who have values that give legitimacy to experimentation. The relations also suggest that the effects of exposure and legitimacy on religious participation are greater among those experiencing some motivating circumstances than among those experiencing no such conditions, as is evident from comparing the percentages in the two rows. This is the first result that has been different for attraction and participation. Attraction seems to increase with stress at any time. It takes more to create participants. Stress results in participation only if the necessary cognitive foundations have been laid.

22. For attraction, letting attraction = A, motivation = B, and opportunity = C, the results of the Goodman analysis are: for model $\{BC\}\{AB\}\{AC\}$, $\chi^2 = 18.99$ (d.f. = 12); for model $\{BC\}\{AB\}$, $\chi^2 = 26.11$ (d.f. = 15); and for model $\{BC\}\{AC\}$, $\chi^2 = 45.56$ (d.f. = 16). Subtracting the appropriate models shows that relation $\{AB\}$ is significant beyond the .001 level and that relation $\{AC\}$ is marginally significant (p is between .10 and .05). For participation, the results are as follows: for model $\{BC\}\{AB\}\{AC\}$, $\chi^2 = 14.81$ (d.f. = 12); for model $\{BC\}\{AB\}$, $\chi^2 = 22.05$ (d.f. = 15); and for model $\{BC\}\{AC\}$, $\chi^2 = 48.80$ (d.f. = 16). Thus, relation $\{AB\}$ is significant beyond the .001 level, and relation $\{AC\}$ is marginally significant (p is between .10 and .05).

23. The Goodman analysis of significance yields the following results for attraction, where attraction = A, motivation = B, and cultural availability = C: for model $\{BC\}\{AB\}\{AC\}$, $\chi^2 = 7.90$ (d.f. = 8); for model $\{BC\}\{AC\}$, $\chi^2 = 18.81$ (d.f. = 9); thus, relation $\{AB\}$ is significant beyond the .001 level, as is relation $\{AC\}$, and there is no significant interactive effect. For participation, the results are: for model $\{BC\}\{AB\}\{AC\}$, $\chi^2 = 8.67$ (d.f. = 8); $\{BC\}\{AB\}$, $\chi^2 = 57.61$ (d.f. = 16); for $\{BC\}\{AC\}$, $\chi^2 = 10.73$ (d.f. = 9); thus, the relation between participation and cultural availability is significant beyond the .001 level; however, the relation between participation and motivation is significant only at the .20 level, probably because it is (as Table 16 shows) a relation that holds only at high levels of cultural availability. This interaction effect, however, does not prove statistically significant.

Table 16. RELIGIOUS EXPERIMENTATION BY MOTIVATION AND CULTURAL AVAILABILITY*

| | Cultural Availability Index | | | | | | | | |
	Low 0	1	2	3	4	5	6	7	High 8
Percent attracted to new religions:									
Motivation Index									
Low	5%	8%	11%	18%	30%	36%	37%	52%	74%
Number	(94)	(101)	(91)	(65)	(72)	(49)	(51)	(17)	(17)
High	12%	12%	9%	23%	38%	53%	64%	62%	71%
Number	(37)	(49)	(50)	(66)	(50)	(70)	(63)	(37)	(20)
Percent having participated:									
Motivation Index									
Low	2%	2%	4%	9%	11%	18%	17%	28%	20%
Number	(94)	(101)	(91)	(65)	(72)	(49)	(51)	(17)	(17)
High	0%	3%	9%	7%	10%	16%	25%	38%	54%
Number	(37)	(49)	(50)	(66)	(50)	(70)	(63)	(37)	(20)

*Numbers weighted tc compensate for oversampling of youth.

CONCLUSION

We have not sought in this chapter to explain why any specific religious movements rooted in Asian traditions initially appeared in the United States or in the Bay Area. (Available histories of these movements suggest that many of them first came into being in the United States because of particular circumstances surrounding the lives of their eventual leaders. As for the three groups on which our own data have focused, yoga and Zen have long been present in America, and TM seems to have been implanted mostly through a highly publicized trip to the United States during the 1960s by the Maharishi.) We have chosen, instead, to examine social and cultural conditions that may have facilitated the wider *adoption* of these movements once they were available to be adopted.

We began this chapter with the suggestion that the appeal of Eastern religious movements in recent years, like that of any cultural innovation, can perhaps be understood best as the result of a combination of social trends facilitating exposure to new ideas, legitimation of nonconventional activities, opportunities to experiment, and motivation to experiment. A profile of the religious experimenter, we suggested, should find him or her to be above average on all these conditions.

Using information concerning attraction toward and participation in TM, yoga, and Zen in the Bay Area, we have generally found support for these expectations. The more chances one has had to be exposed to new ideas, the more values he holds that accord legitimacy to the nonconventional, the more freedom he enjoys from the role constraints of ordinary life, and the more motivated he is by personal forms of stress, the more likely he is to have experimented with at least one of these groups. We have also attempted to demonstrate that each of these conditions is important in itself and that together they produce strong differences in people's propensities to engage in religious experimentation. Examining different combinations of these factors, we have found as few as 5 percent attracted to new religions among persons scoring low on various of these conditions, and as many as 87 percent attracted among those scoring high. On participation, we have been able to isolate groups where no one had participated in one of these new religions and others where over half had participated. In other words, the conditions we have examined go a long way toward identifying parts of the society in which religious experimentation is virtually absent and others in which it is prevalent.

Zen, yoga, and TM seem to attract similar kinds of people, as far as the variables we have examined are concerned. Had we been able to examine Hare Krishna, Divine Light, 3HO, or other Eastern groups, we might have found greater differences. And had we been able to examine Jesus People groups, we might have found even greater differences. It seems reasonable to suggest that exposure, legitimacy, opportunity, and motivation are important preconditions for any kind of religious experimentation. But it seems equally reasonable to suggest that the conditions supplying each of these factors may be different for different movements.

Social conditions that provide exposure, legitimacy, opportunity, and motivation, it should also be observed, are conditions that only make religious experimentation *possible*. Thus, respondents in our sample who happened to manifest any or all of these conditions were more likely than others to express attraction toward, or to have taken part in, a new religious group. But this is not to say that these conditions are the direct "causes" of religious experimentation. The actual process by which a person makes up his mind to join a new religion is something about which our data can say little. Nor have we been able to examine the processes by which a person decides to join one movement rather than another. Many of those processes may in fact be idiosyncratic to the person himself. But whether idiosyncratic or more general, such processes are probably illuminated best by other kinds of data.

What our data have shed light on are some of the broader characteristics of the society that have facilitated religious experimentation. These characteristics, the data have suggested, include high levels of education, liberal values, marginality to traditional family, job, and community responsibilities, and stress about such things as work plans, finding meaning in life, and money problems. We have also cited evidence suggesting that many of these conditions have increased in recent decades.

Movements inspired by Eastern religions, of course, have not been the only form of religious ferment in recent years. Experimentation with the occult, especially with astrology and with psychic phenomena, has also been the subject of much discussion. Chapter 2 examines two of the arguments that have been put forth to account for the popularity of astrology.

CHAPTER 2

The Appeal of Astrology

The practice of astrology, dating as far back as ancient Babylonia, has seemingly experienced in recent years an upsurge of popularity like that of the Eastern religious movements we have just examined. Twenty-five years ago, for example, about 100 newspapers in this country carried daily horoscope columns. Today the number is closer to 2,000. Current estimates of the number of paid astrologers in the United States range between 5,000 and 10,000. And according to some polls, believers in astrology may number in the millions. This chapter examines some of the sources of astrology's contemporary appeal.

The current interest in astrology has generally been explained in one of two ways. On the one hand, it has been portrayed along with Eastern religions as part of the counterculture, a reaction against the impersonality and rationality of modern society. Harvey Cox, for example, has characterized it as a new, playful way of relating to others:

The astrology trip is a form of play, of relating to each other in ways we don't have to take too seriously until we know we want to. In a broader sense, astrology and drugs and Zen are forms of play, of testing new perceptions of reality without being committed to their validity in advance—or ever.[1]

According to Cox, astrology cuts through the mental and social constrictions of life in an otherwise rationalistic society, providing a much-needed element of fantasy and festivity. More generally, astrology has been likened to the other new religious and quasi-religious movements that emerged, especially on and around the nation's campuses, during the late 1960s and early '70s. As another observer has commented:

1. Harvey Cox, "Religion in the Age of Aquarius: A Conversation with Harvey Cox and T. George Harris," in Edward F. Heenan (ed.), *Mystery, Magic, and Miracle: Religion in a Post-Aquarian Age* (Englewood Cliffs, N.J.: Prentice-Hall, 1973), pp. 15–28.

All that is needed is a pair of eyes to see and a radio to hear to learn of the influence of the occult on the young. Many songs clearly call for the Age of Aquarius to come; much of our young people's dress is decorated with the symbols of astrology and magic. At the same time that these young people may be rejecting the church with its symbols of the afterlife, the supernatural is coming back into their lives with a flood of reports of lives lived before this present one.[2]

Astrology has been thought to have found its most receptive audience among young people "turned off" by science and technology. As in the rock musical *Hair*, popularizer of the catchphrase "age of Aquarius," astrology seems to have become a symbol of a realm beyond the rationally ordered world known to science and out of reach of the manipulations of big business and big government.

On the other hand, astrology has been portrayed as an interest, not so much of the young and the better educated, but of those traditionally marginal to the social mainstream. Popular accounts of astrology, though lacking in evidence, have located it more among the old than among the young, among the uneducated rather than among the educated, among housewives rather than students, and among the ill, the lonely, and the bored rather than those reacting against science and rationality. In general, the more popular imagery of astrology has regarded it as a coping mechanism for the deprived instead of a playful new addition to the lives of the privileged. Mild assessments have pictured it as a frivolous fetish, wasteful of time and money. More critical appraisals have looked upon it as exploitative and deceptive. Nathan Adler, for example, has written of its effects:

The individual no longer has to resolve contradictions, but can view them as dichotomies to be treated serially; he no longer has to struggle to overcome obstacles, but can surrender to the preordained and the inevitable.[3]

Which of these popular views is correct? Has astrology, like the Eastern religions, grown because it attracts the young and the better educated who have been highly exposed to "rational" modes of thought and found them wanting? Or is astrology located among the old, the uneducated, and others left behind by the society, people who would like to enjoy the fruits of a modern rational society but who have been deprived of attaining them? Both views are plausible, but neither has been tested empirically.

2. John Charles Cooper, *Religion in the Age of Aquarius* (Philadelphia: Westminster Press, 1971), p. 23. See also Martin Marty, "The Occult Establishment," in William M Newman, *The Social Meanings of Religion: An Integrated Anthology* (Chicago: Rand McNally, 1974), pp. 349–364.
3. Nathan Adler, "Ritual, Release, and Orientation: Maintenance of the Self in the Antinomian Personality," p. 290, in Irving I. Zaretsky and Mark P. Leone (eds.), *Religious Movements in Contemporary America* (Princeton: Princeton University Press, 1974), pp. 283–297.

In this chapter, the data from the Bay Area are used to examine these alternative conceptions of astrology. We also consider a related question: Does astrology function as a surrogate for more conventional forms of religion? Whether its appeal is similar to that of the new Eastern religions or whether it functions as a coping mechanism for the socially marginal, there is reason to suspect that it may.

THE SCOPE OF APPEAL

The data support popular suspicions that casual interest in astrology has become widespread, at least in the Bay Area. Virtually everyone in the sample (96 percent of the youth and 93 percent of those over age 30) knows what a horoscope is. Just about everyone claimed to know his sign (98 percent of the youth and 86 percent of their elders). Less than a fourth of the youth said they weren't interested at all in their horoscopes, as did less than a third of their elders. On another question which asked about belief in astrology:

People who believe in astrology claim that the stars, the planets, and our birthdays have a lot to do with our destiny in life. What do you think about this—are you a firm believer in astrology, are you somewhat doubtful, are you very doubtful, or are you a firm disbeliever?

only 24 percent of the youth and 34 percent of those over 30 said they were firm disbelievers.

Serious commitment to astrology, as might be expected, tends to be much less prevalent than casual interest. Only 10 percent of the youth and 11 percent of the older half of the sample said they were "quite interested" in their horoscopes. Only 8 percent and 10 percent of the two age groups respectively said they were firm believers. And only 4 percent and 2 percent respectively said they knew a lot about astrology. Yet, if only one person in 10 or 15 is firmly devoted to the claims of astrology, its disciples must still be counted in the millions. If the Bay Area is at all representative of the rest of the nation, *Newsweek*'s 1969 estimate of some 10 million fully committed adherents seems reasonable, and Gallup's more recent estimate of 32 million believers also seems accurate.[4]

A more detailed look at the data by age (see Table 17) reveals no clear support for either the counterculture or social marginality explanation for the appeal of astrology. Young people are slightly more knowledgeable about astrology (know what a horoscope is, know their sign, claim to know at least a fair amount about astrology), but the differences, though statistically significant, amount to only several percentage points and may well

4. "Digging the Stars," *Newsweek* (January 19, 1969): 54–55; and George Gallup, "32 Million Believe in Astrology," *Tucson Daily Citizen* (October 20, 1975).

Table 17. **ASTROLOGY BY AGE (Total Unweighted Sample)**

Percent responding as listed among those whose age was:

	16–20	21–30	31–40	41–50	51–60	Over 60
Know what a horoscope is:						
Yes	95%	98%	96%	93%	95%	88%
Know your sign:						
Yes	97%	98%	98%	85%	90%	72%
Knowledge of astrology:						
A lot	3%	4%	2%	1%	4%	2%
A fair amount	29%	33%	26%	14%	22%	14%
Only a little	68%	63%	73%	85%	74%	84%
Interested in horoscopes:						
Quite	10%	10%	9%	14%	14%	9%
Fairly	28%	24%	20%	17%	24%	12%
Slightly	41%	44%	43%	35%	41%	37%
Not at all	21%	22%	28%	34%	21%	42%
Believe in astrology:						
Firm believer	6%	8%	8%	11%	11%	13%
Somewhat doubtful	49%	44%	41%	32%	33%	29%
Very doubtful	23%	23%	22%	22%	24%	17%
Firm disbeliever	21%	25%	29%	35%	31%	41%
Number	(221)	(334)	(135)	(95)	(91)	(114)

Significance (top to bottom):
χ^2 = 17.76, 104.51, 33.35, 30.30, 32.03; df = 5, 5, 10, 15, 15; p = .01, .001, .001, .01, .01

be a function of young people being better educated or more exposed to the mass media than their elders. Interest in horoscopes and belief in astrology, in contrast, tend to be more prevalent among older people, although again the differences are small; and if less serious levels of commitment are included, such as being fairly interested in horoscopes or only somewhat doubtful about astrology, it is the younger people once more who appear slightly more attracted to astrology.

Though inconclusive, these results appear more damaging to the counterculture explanation than to the marginality theory of astrology, for the counterculture has been decidedly a youth phenomenon, while marginality may be characteristic of either the young or the old. We turn, therefore, to other characteristics affording more of a direct test of the marginality theory. As alternative indicators of attraction to astrology, we will be using belief in astrology (firm or only somewhat doubtful belief) and interest in horoscopes (quite interested). Since differences between the younger and older parts of the sample with regard to these items are relatively minor, as we have just seen, we shall combine the younger and older subsamples.

THE SOCIAL LOCATION OF ASTROLOGY

Looking first at the social location of astrology with respect to education, which we take as a sign of relative deprivation or privilege, we see that those with only a grade school education are the most likely to be interested in their horoscopes and to believe in astrology (see Table 18). The least amount

Table 18. ASTROLOGY BY EDUCATION
(Total Unweighted Sample)

		Percent who	
Education (adjusted*)	Are quite interested in their horoscopes		Tend to believe in astrology
Grade school	16%	(45)	64%	(56)
Some high school	16%	(64)	51%	(70)
High school graduate	11%	(186)	53%	(196)
Some college	11%	(205)	55%	(210)
College graduate	11%	(196)	48%	(204)
Graduate school	6%	(251)	41%	(257)

Significance (left to right):
   $\chi^2 = 10.28, 15.90$; df = 5, 5; p = .07, .01
*Expected level of education substituted for actual level for persons under age 30.

Table 19. **ASTROLOGY BY ETHNICITY**
           (Total Unweighted Sample)

	Percent who	
Ethnicity	Are quite interested in their horoscopes	Tend to believe in astrology
Black	18% (79)	58% (88)
Mexican-American	15% (39)	44% (43)
Anglo	10% (742)	48% (768)
Other*	9% (85)	59% (92)

Significance (left to right):
   $\chi^2 = 6.18, 6.74$; df = 3, 3; p = .10, .08
*Includes Spanish-American, Oriental, and other.

of interest and belief is among respondents with (or expecting, in the case of young people) post-graduate training. And with each increase in educational level there is a more or less steady decrease in commitment to astrology, from 16 percent who are quite interested in their horoscopes among the grade school educated to only 6 percent among post-graduates, and from 64 percent to 41 percent on belief.

The location of astrology with respect to ethnic background is also helpful for understanding its appeal: if the marginality perspective is correct, ethnic minorities should demonstrate greater interest than the ethnic majority. Looking at Table 19, we see that blacks are more likely to exhibit commitment to astrology than whites on both interest and belief. Mexican-Americans are more likely than Anglos to be interested in their horoscopes, although they are less likely to be believers. Persons of "other" ethnic descent are similar to Anglos on interest, although they are more likely to believe.

Commitment to astrology also differs between the sexes. Greater proportions of women show interest and belief than men. Specifically, 14 percent of the females in the sample said they were quite interested in their horoscopes, compared with 6 percent of the males, and 55 percent of the women tended to believe in the claims of astrology, in comparison with 43 percent of the men.[5]

All these results tend to support the view that astrology finds its greatest appeal among the traditionally marginal instead of the view that it is part of a new culture among the young and the more privileged. If the latter view were correct, we would have expected to find more commitment

5. Both differences are significant beyond the .001 level.

to astrology among the young, the better educated, and among whites, and to have found no differences between men and women. Instead, we found essentially no differences between the young and the old and found the greatest commitment to astrology among the less well educated, blacks, and women—all of whom tend to find themselves on the fringes of the power, prestige, wealth, and other rewards the society has to offer. This isn't to say that some of the privileged aren't interested in astrology too, perhaps as an alternative to science, rationality, and other dimensions of modern life. The data suggest that some are. But the greatest appeal of astrology, relatively, seems to be to the socially marginal.

To check out this interpretation more rigorously, let us examine other data that bear more directly on whether people are marginal relative to what most people want and expect or whether they are more privileged.

THE ROLE OF MARGINALITY

One expectation that most people share is to marry and lead conventional family lives. A few, of course, never fulfill these expectations, staying single rather than marrying or becoming separated or divorced from their spouses, if once married. If astrology is truly located among the socially marginal, we would expect persons deprived of happy married lives to show greater interest in it than persons leading more normal family lives.

This is what the data show (see Table 20). The separated and the divorced have the highest proportions who are quite interested in their horoscopes and who tend to believe in astrology. The widowed have a relatively high

Table 20. ASTROLOGY BY MARITAL STATUS (Total Unweighted Sample)

	Percent who	
Marital status	Are quite interested in their horoscopes	Tend to believe in astrology
Separated	24% (29)	60% (30)
Divorced	17% (72)	63% (73)
Widowed	16% (55)	46% (63)
Never married	9% (364)	53% (379)
Married	9% (427)	44% (448)

Significance (left to right):
  $\chi^2 = 12.76, 14.93$; df = 4, 4; p = .01, .01

proportion who are interested in their horoscopes, although they do not differ greatly from the married on belief. The never married score above average on belief, but not on interest. It is the married who show the smallest proportions committed to astrology on both belief and interest. The results, therefore, while not entirely consistent, tend generally to suggest that astrology appeals most to persons marginal to conventional family lives.

Most people also expect to have steady jobs during the part of their life when they are members of the labor force. For one reason or another, however, some are either unable to work or unable to find a job to their liking. Work status, therefore, provides another test of our interpretation of astrology.

Focusing attention on persons currently in the labor force—that is, persons either working, looking for work, or presently unable to work, and excluding those in school, retired, or performing household duties—and comparing those unable to work, those looking for work, and those working, we see again that astrology finds its greatest support among the marginal (see Table 21). Sixteen percent of those unable to work and 12 percent of those looking for work, compared with 9 percent of those working are quite interested in their horoscopes. Those looking for work have the highest percentage of believers in astrology (63 percent), and those currently working have the lowest (46 percent).

Another way in which people can be deprived or privileged is physically—for example, by being over- or underweight. Since our data were collected from personal interviews, we asked the interviewers to rate each respondent's weight. We knew these ratings would be biased by the interviewers' predispositions, but with over forty interviewers making

Table 21. **ASTROLOGY BY WORK STATUS (Labor Force Only, Unweighted)**

| | Percent who | |
| | Are quite interested in their horoscopes | Tend to believe in astrology |
Work status		
Unable to work	16% (19)	55% (20)
Looking for work	12% (58)	63% (62)
Working	9% (551)	46% (569)

Significance (left to right):
$\chi^2 = 1.18, 7.25$; df = 2, 2; p = .55, .03

the assessments, we felt confident that many of these biases would cancel one another out.

We would expect the greatest amount of interest in astrology to be found among persons with some kind of weight problem and, as shown in Table 22, this is largely what we find. Being interested in horoscopes is twice as common among persons rated "far above average" on weight as among persons rated closer to the average. The results for belief in astrology are less consistent, but generally indicate the same pattern: both the overweight and the underweight are more likely to believe than those rated average. Thus, our interpretation of astrology as an attribute of the marginal is again sustained.

A somewhat different test of our interpretation is provided by evidence on subjective forms of deprivation. Objective social marginality and subjective feelings of dissatisfaction would seem likely to go together, but the relation is seldom perfect. Some of the marginal are there by choice or at least have learned to be content. At the same time, objective privilege carries no guarantee of satisfaction.

Implicitly, we have assumed thus far that the marginal will be unhappy with their lot in life, resorting to astrology, therefore, as a way of coping with their frustrations or escaping their discontent. We haven't the data to test this assumption directly, and even if we had tried to find out directly why people were interested in astrology, it isn't clear that the marginal would recognize it as a coping mechanism. About the closest we can come to testing this assumption, therefore, is to see if there is a relation between feelings of discontent and commitment to astrology.

Among the questions asked each respondent were items having to do

Table 22. **ASTROLOGY BY WEIGHT (Total Unweighted Sample)**

	Percent who			
Weight	Are quite interested in their horoscopes		Tend to believe in astrology	
Far above average	23%	(30)	52%	(33)
Above average	12%	(194)	52%	(205)
Average	9%	(623)	47%	(651)
Below average	13%	(94)	60%	(99)

Significance (left to right):
$\chi^2 = 7.99, 7.36$; df = 3, 3; p = .05, .06

with such matters as feeling lonely, problems at work, health problems, and problems of grief. Respondents were asked to say whether they were currently bothered a lot, some, had been bothered at some time in the past but not currently, or had never been bothered by each problem. For present purposes, we shall simply compare those who said they were currently bothered a lot with those who gave any of the other responses. Table 23 reports the results.

The results are consistently in the expected direction. For each of the problems listed, persons who said they were bothered a lot are more interested in their horoscopes and more likely to believe in the claims of astrology than their less bothered counterparts. For example, about 10 percent more of those with health worries are interested in horoscopes, and about 10 percent more are believers in astrology than those without health worries. The other differences are of comparable magnitude.

By every measure at our disposal, therefore, the marginal tend to be more committed to astrology than the socially privileged. The greatest amount of interest in horoscopes and the greatest share of belief in the claims of

Table 23. ASTROLOGY BY SUBJECTIVE DEPRIVATION (Total Unweighted Sample)

	Percent who			
Bothered a lot by:	Are quite interested in their horoscopes		Tend to believe in astrology	
Feeling lonely:				
Yes	16%	(104)	58%	(112)
No	10%	(842)	49%	(880)
Problems with your work:				
Yes	16%	(179)	58%	(185)
No	9%	(764)	48%	(804)
Problems with your health:				
Yes	20%	(130)	58%	(137)
No	9%	(814)	48%	(853)
The death of a loved one:				
Yes	17%	(128)	57%	(134)
No	9%	(816)	48%	(856)

Significance (top to bottom), left column:
   χ^2 = 3.81, 6.17, 13.82, 6.55; df = 1 (all); p = .05, .01, .001, .01
right column:
   χ^2 = 3.23, 6.01, 3.87, 2.82; df = 1 (all); p = .07, .01, .05, .09

astrology are found among the uneducated, ethnic minorities, women rather than men, persons with broken marriages or single people more than married people, persons out of work rather than those working, the over-weight, and persons bothered a lot with loneliness, work problems, health problems, and problems of grief.

The reader has probably observed that the differences on many of these items are not great. But marginality is a cumulative phenomenon. Some people experience it in only one part of their lives, while others may be marginal or dissatisfied in many areas of their lives. If astrology appeals most to the marginal, therefore, we would expect it to appeal most to the *most* marginal. Counting the number of ways in which persons are marginal, in other words, should also produce differences, perhaps major differences, in commitment to astrology.

To assess the extent to which respondents are marginal in the different areas of their lives, we constructed a Marginality Index giving respondents one point for each of the following ways in which they may be marginal relative to others in the society: being nonwhite, being female, not having or expecting any education beyond college, being currently unmarried, and being bothered a lot by health problems. This gives an index ranging from 0 (low) to 5 (high).

As shown in Table 24, commitment to astrology varies greatly among persons receiving different scores on this index. Only 5 percent of those scoring 0 are quite interested in their horoscopes, but 46 percent of those scoring 5 are quite interested. With each increase on the index there is a

Table 24. ASTROLOGY BY MARGINALITY INDEX (Total Unweighted Sample)

| | | Percent who | |
| | | Are quite interested in their horoscopes | Tend to believe in astrology |
Marginality Index			
Low	0	5% (38)	25% (40)
	1	4% (190)	38% (199)
	2	8% (362)	48% (371)
	3	15% (268)	58% (288)
	4	24% (76)	66% (83)
High	5	46% (11)	67% (12)

Significance (left to right):
  χ^2 = 46.58, 40.45; df = 5, 5; p = .001, .001

more or less steady increase in the proportions who are quite interested in their horoscopes. Belief in astrology shows a similar pattern: 25 percent of those scoring 0 tend to believe, compared with 67 percent of those scoring 5. Again, each increase on the index is associated with a commensurate increase in the proportions who tend to believe.[6]

Summarizing briefly, our investigation has given clear and consistent support to what has probably been the traditional image of astrology— namely, that it appeals to the down and out much more than to the socially privileged. By inference, we have found no support for the more recent view of astrology; that is, that its popularity has come mostly from the young, the better educated, and the more privileged who are somehow reacting against the rationalism, scientism, and other features of modern society. We turn now to a more direct test of this inference.

ASTROLOGY AND CULTURAL DISENCHANTMENT

On the assumption that astrology may be attracting people disenchanted with modern science, quite apart from what we have observed thus far about marginality, we asked respondents their feelings about the role science has played in the modern world—whether it has done a lot more good than harm for the world, done a lot of good but caused a lot of harm along with it, or done more harm than good. If astrology were appealing to persons react- ing against science, we thought this would be shown by a greater commit- ment to astrology among persons giving the second or third responses than the first. As Table 25 reports, neither interest in horoscopes nor belief in astrology is significantly related to the responses to this question.

We also asked several other questions bearing more directly on involve- ment in the counterculture to see if astrology were related to these. Combin- ing three of these items (been "high" on drugs, participated in a demonstra- tion, and approve of an unmarried couple living together) to form an Index of Countercultural Involvement ranging from 0 (low) to 3 (high), and using the Marginality Index constructed earlier (combining categories 0 and 1

6. These relations between astrology and deprivation also hold when age (over versus under age 30) is controlled. Using the Goodman method for examining the significance of relations in multi-variable contingency tables (see Chapter 1, footnote 13) yields a likelihood-ratio χ^2 of 7.97 (d.f. = 3) for a model which takes into account the effects of both age and deprivation on interest in horoscopes, whereas a model which takes into account only the effects of age yields a χ^2 of 46.03 (d.f. = 3); thus, the first model fits the data significantly better than the second (subtracting gives χ^2 = 38.06, d.f. = 3, p = .001). A comparable analysis for belief in astrology also shows the first model to be a significantly better fit than the second χ^2 = 47.73 minus 9.71 equals 38.02; d.f. = 6 minus 3 equals 3; p = .001). Thus, deprivation is significantly associated with both indicators of commitment to astrology, taking into ac- count the effects of age.

Table 25. **ASTROLOGY BY ATTITUDE TOWARD SCIENCE (Total Unweighted Sample)**

	Percent who			
	Are quite interested in their horoscopes		Tend to believe in astrology	
How do you feel about the role science has played in the world?				
Done a lot more good than harm	9%	(504)	46%	(499)
Done a lot of good and a lot of harm	11%	(456)	54%	(454)
Done more harm than good	11%	(35)	49%	(35)

Significance (left to right):
χ^2 = .812, 5.88; df = 2, 2; p = .67, .06

and categories 4 and 5 to conserve cases), we simultaneously examined the three-variable relation between belief in astrology, marginality, and countercultural involvement (see Table 26; a comparable table for interest in horoscopes is included in the Appendix, Table A-1).

Looking first across each row, we see that belief in astrology increases with each increase on the Marginality Index, except in row 3. In other words, the relation between marginality and commitment to astrology

Table 26. **BELIEF IN ASTROLOGY, MARGINALITY, AND COUNTERCULTURAL INVOLVEMENT**

		Percent who believe in astrology: Marginality Index			
Index of Countercultural Involvement		Low 0	1	2	High 3
Low	0	40%	43%	59%	*
		(175)	(103)	(27)	(4)
	1	45%	47%	62%	*
		(150)	(110)	(37)	(8)
	2	52%	60%	78%	*
		(107)	(74)	(37)	(5)
High	3	59%	61%	44%	*
		(49)	(56)	(32)	(4)

*Too few cases for reliable percentage.

holds controlling for countercultural involvement, except for those heavily involved in the counterculture; for them, marginality makes no difference as far as their belief in astrology is concerned. Looking down the columns, however, we also see that the percentages increase with each increase on the Countercultural Involvement Index. Thus, there appears to be support, after all, for the idea that astrology has been nourished by some of the recent cultural disenchantment associated with the counterculture. This relation, the data show, is independent of marginality. Therefore, the highest proportion believing in astrology tends to be among those *both* relatively marginal *and* fairly involved in countercultural activities.

What is difficult to infer from the table, of course, is whether the greatest share of astrology's appeal remains among the traditionally marginal or whether it has come to be with those involved in countercultural activities. Using other, more sophisticated methods to answer this question, as well as drawing inferences from the evidence on interest in horoscopes, suggests that probably traditional marginality is still the most decisive force behind astrology. For example, the odds of being interested in horoscopes are about ten times greater if one scores 3 on marginality than if one scores 0, taking countercultural involvement into account. But they are only about twice as great if one scores 3 on countercultural involvement as they are if one scores 0.[7]

ASTROLOGY AS SURROGATE RELIGION

Finally, we turn to the question of whether or not astrology serves as a surrogate for more conventional religious practices. Both the finding that it appeals to the socially marginal and the fact that it attracts the culturally disenchanted suggest that it may function similarly to organized religion.

7. A Goodman analysis of the significance of the relations contained in Table 26 shows that a model which takes into account only the relation between belief in astrology and countercultural involvement (letting countercultural involvement and deprivation be related) fits the actual data quite poorly ($\chi^2 = 51.60$, d.f. = 12, p = .000; note that accurate fits are indicated by *high* p-values when comparing models with actual data, i.e., a high probability that discrepancies between the model and the data are simply due to chance). But a model which takes into account the effects of both countercultural involvement and deprivation fits the data significantly better than the first model (comparing the models gives $\chi^2 = 51.60$ minus 8.03 equals 43.57, d.f. = 12 minus 9 equals 3, p = .001). This model also fits the data significantly better than one which takes into account only the relation between astrology and deprivation ($\chi^2 = 29.15$ minus 8.03 equals 21.12, d.f. = 12 minus 9 equals 3, p = .001). In other words, there is a significant relation between astrology and both countercultural involvement and deprivation. Comparing models also shows the effects of deprivation to be considerably stronger than those of countercultural involvement (the model leaving out the former fits the data much less well than the model leaving out the latter). A comparable analysis of the relations with interest in horoscopes yields similar results; see Appendix Table A-2.

Students of religion have observed one of its latent functions to be a source of comfort to those on the social fringe. The church seems to provide a surrogate family for those without spouses, children, or close friends.[8] It sometimes provides an alternative path to social and economic success for those without the necessary education and training to obtain good jobs or for those faced with discrimination. For the ill, religious movements may offer alternative cures, and for the bereaved, comfort and hope.

Astrology may do the same. Those whom society has passed by may find it a comforting alternative reality. One can assume his fate to be governed, not by the rich and the powerful, but by the stars. And if by the stars, then his fortune may change for the better. For the lonely, the daily horoscope column may provide companionship, and for others it may offer clues about making friends, finding lovers, investing money, curing ills, or coping with the blues. One may believe only half-heartedly in its claims and yet find it an intriguing cosmology that somehow stands aloof from the harsher realities of the workaday world.

If interest in astrology has been nourished by countercultural discontent, it may also function as a substitute for conventional religion among those having become disenchanted with the society's basic values, including its traditional religious values. For them, astrology may promise hope for a better day, an age of Aquarius, when different ideals will be realized and, along with Eastern religions, may provide a means of seeking transcendence for one's personal life without commiting oneself to traditional institutions.

One way of examining whether or not astrology performs functions similar to those of conventional religion is to ask whether people who are interested in it show any interest in conventional religion. If astrology performs religious functions, we would expect its adherents to exhibit less commitment to other, more conventional forms of religion than persons uninterested in it.

This possibility is examined in Table 27, which classifies respondents according to their level of marginality, as indicated by their score on the Marginality Index, and according to whether or not they are interested in their horoscopes, and then reports the proportion who attend church weekly in each category. The relevant comparisons are between the top row and the bottom row of the table. Comparing the top and bottom figures in each column, we see that at each level of marginality respondents who are quite interested in their horoscopes are *less* likely to attend church weekly than respondents who are not interested in their horoscopes. In other words,

8. See, for example, Charles Y. Glock, Benjamin B. Ringer, and Earl R. Babbie, *To Comfort and to Challenge* (Berkeley and Los Angeles: University of California Press, 1967), especially Chapter 3.

Table 27. CHURCH ATTENDANCE, HOROSCOPES, AND MARGINALITY

| | Percent who attend church weekly: Marginality Index | | | |
	Low 0	1	2	High 3
And are: "Quite interested" in their horoscopes	11% (9)	11% (28)	13% (39)	4% (23)
Not "quite interested" in their horoscopes	22% (232)	14% (347)	22% (250)	24% (72)

there does seem to be evidence that astrology serves as an alternative for more conventional religious commitment.[9]

This finding also suggests a possible reason for the apparent growth of astrology in recent decades. While much of this growth may have been due to the unrest among young people, to more effective communication in the mass media, or to strains in the society aggravating the experience of marginality, some of it may also have been due to the declining strength of organized religion. As church attendance, belief in God, church construction, seminary enrollments, and other aspects of conventional religion have declined (as we shall see in Chapter 6), astrology appears to have partly filled the gap.

CONCLUSION

In the absence of much previous research of a systematic nature concerning astrology, our discussion in this chapter has been exploratory—and limited at that to exploring some of the more general social correlates of commitment to astrology. We have found some support for both of the explanations for the popularity of astrology that have frequented the literature on the

9. Examining the significance of the relations in Table 27 using Goodman's methods shows that a model which included the effects of both horoscopes and deprivation on church attendance, in comparison with a model which takes into account only the effects of deprivation, provides a significantly better fit of the actual data ($\chi^2 = 8.45$ minus 4.37 equals 4.08, d.f. = 4 minus 3 equals 1, p = .05). In other words, the relation between horoscopes and church attendance is significant at the .05 level, controlling for the effects of deprivation.

subject in recent years. Themes inspired by astrology have been clearly in evidence in the counterculture in recent years, and our data show a positive relation between countercultural involvement and attraction to astrology. But the greatest appeal of astrology appears to remain with the more traditionally marginal members of society. Interest and belief in astrology are about equally present among the young and the old, but whether young or old, it is the poorly educated, the unemployed, nonwhites, females, the unmarried, the overweight, the ill, and the lonely, who are most taken with astrology.

With regard to the claim that astrology has grown as a result of disaffection with the dominant rational, scientific thought-modes of modern culture, we have found no evidence that people with strongly negative views of science differ in their attraction to astrology from people whose views are unreservedly positive.

Astrology does, as church leaders have often suspected, seem to function as a substitute for church involvement. We have not been able, of course, to pinpoint exactly why the astrology buff attends church less than others, but the relation found between marginality and astrology suggests that astrology may provide some of the comforting functions for the ill, the lonely, and the down-and-out that the church has traditionally fulfilled.

The results in this chapter indicate that, at least in the Bay Area, the social location of astrology is somewhat different from the social location of experimentation with Eastern religions such as Zen, yoga, and TM. Both seem to be associated with a more general willingness to experiment with nonconventionality, as evidenced by the relations between both and items having to do with drugs, sexual experimentation, and political liberalism or radicalism. But this is about as far as the similarity goes. Whereas the Eastern movements attracted the young and the educated who, though marginal to the established institutions of the adult society in some ways, still remain part of the relatively privileged strata, astrology attracted the uneducated, those in the labor force but unemployed, the ill and the lonely—in short, those who represent the less privileged social strata.

We turn next to another manifestation of the occult that has aroused considerable interest in recent years: extrasensory perception. As with astrology, our concern is to identify some of the social conditions facilitating experimentation with this phenomenon. It will prove most useful, as the data will demonstrate, to focus directly on the influences of different religious orientations.

CHAPTER 3

Religious Orientations and ESP

Controversies between religious leaders and proponents of psychic phenomena, while scarcely new, seem to have been rekindled by the religious experimentation of the 1960s and '70s. As religious perspectives have come into question, traditional attitudes toward paranormal experiences have also come under scrutiny and revision.

Historically, the churches seem to have generally responded to psychic phenomena largely with skepticism or disapproval. If parishioners could communicate with the gods psychically and, moreover, interpret their experiences as instances of extrasensory perception (ESP), what need, the question has been asked, would there be of the churches? Or if divine revelation could be transmitted through psychic channels, would this not pose a serious threat to the authority of the scriptures? Some positive interest in extrasensory perception has been expressed by churchmen, recognizing potential support from ESP research for biblical claims long pooh-poohed by orthodox science. But for the most part, the risks presented by such ill-codified and little-understood experiences as ESP seem to have caused the churches to lump these phenomena together with magic, fortune-telling, witchcraft, necromancy, astrology, and other manifestations of the occult, all to be viewed with suspicion.[1]

1. Studies giving valuable background information on the relations between the churches and psychic or other occult phenomena include the following: Colin Wilson, *The Occult: A History* (New York: Random House, 1971), a historical survey taking a generally sympathetic view of the occult; Nat Freedland, *The Occult Explosion* (New York: Putnam, 1972), a survey of the major contemporary figures on the psychic scene; Allan Spraggett, *Probing the Unexplained* (New York: World, 1971), a journalistic sketch of some of the major debates and current research on ESP and related topics; H. Richard Neff, *Psychic Phenomena and Religion* (Philadelphia: Westminster, 1971), a relatively sympathetic discussion from a traditional theological perspective; and J. Stafford Wright, *Christianity and the Occult* (New York: Moody, 1972), a generally negative commentary from a traditional theological perspective.

The possibility of extrasensory powers seems to have been entertained somewhat more enthusiastically by many within the new religions. To some of them, ESP represents a higher state of consciousness attainable with increasing facility as one transcends ordinary thought patterns. The ability to communicate telepathically and to perceive clairvoyantly has also been conceived as one of the stages to be passed through on the way to achieving mystical or unitive consciousness. For this reason, the ability to send and receive extrasensory messages has frequently been included as part of the training in meditation and mind control offered by the new religious and quasi-religious movements. To others in the new religions, psychic experiences have been welcomed as further evidence that modern science's formulation of the empirical world is too narrow and needs to be re-examined. Even in the new religions, however, there have been negative responses to the idea of psychic experiences. Some have regarded ESP as an alternative, but overly-scientific, interpretation for what they would rather consider sacred forms of communication with the divine. Others have feared being pegged as frauds by association because of potentially false claims put forth by publicity-seeking psychics.[2]

While there is nothing inherently religious or irreligious about ESP, ample cause seems to exist to suggest that people's religious orientations probably influence their attitudes toward ESP and their involvement with it. What these influences may be has not been established in previous research, however. Some fifty years have passed since the term ESP was coined, and numerous studies have been conducted in the laboratory, resulting in considerable experimental and anecdotal evidence that "something" exists which defies known laws of chance and nature. But hardly any research has been conducted outside of the laboratory to discover what the social and cultural correlates of ESP may be.[3]

2. For a brief but excellent discussion of the links between psychic phenomena and the new religious consciousness, see W. G. Roll, "Postscript: Psychical Research in Relation to Higher States of Consciousness," in John White (ed.), *The Highest State of Consciousness* (Garden City, N.Y.: Doubleday, 1972), pp. 456–471.
3. One recent exception is G. K. Nelson, "Towards a Sociology of the Psychic," *Review of Religious Research* 16 (Spring 1975): 166–173. This paper presents empirical data from England, but on believing in ghosts rather than ESP. Some anthropological research, of course, has considered the relations between religion and psychic phenomena, but usually this research has focused on primitive religions; for example: J. Beattie and J. Middleton, *Spirit Mediumship and Society in Africa* (London: Routledge and Kegan Paul, 1969); Elizabeth Colson, "Ancestral Spirits and Social Structure among the Plateau Tonga," in William A. Lessa and Evon Z. Vogt (eds.), *Reader in Comparative Religion,* 3rd ed. (New York: Harper and Row, 1972), pp. 483–487; A. J. Elliott, *Chinese Spirit Medium Cults in Singapore* (London: London School of Economics, 1955); and I. M. Lewis, *Ecstatic Religions* (London: Penguin, 1971). The importance of the occult for sociological theory has been argued well in Edward A. Tiryakian (ed.), *On the Margin of the Visible* (New York: Wiley, 1974), but little research has been generated thus far.

This chapter examines whether or not ESP experiences and belief in ESP are associated with religious orientations; in particular, whether traditional religious commitments tend to discourage ESP or whether, for some reason, they may encourage it, and whether or not the new religious orientations may be changing people's opinions of ESP. There is little to go on when it comes to formulating specific hypotheses. But it seems that if any part of the culture should be important for understanding ESP, it should be religion, for both concern phenomena that transcend ordinary experience. We shall examine the relations between ESP and three aspects of religious commitment: religious preference, religious belief, and religious experience.

Before turning to these relations, let us consider briefly the frequency with which ESP is familiar to, believed in, and experienced by residents of the Bay Area.

THE INCIDENCE OF ESP

Due to the paucity of research on ESP in the general population, we had little idea whether we would find ESP commonly believed in among our respondents or not. Judging from the frequency with which it has been discussed in the press, we suspected that it might be regarded with fairly widespread interest and credibility. But what we found surpassed our highest estimates. As far as knowledge of ESP was concerned, virtually everyone seemed to have heard of it. Ninety-six percent of the younger subsample (ages 16 through 30) claimed to have heard of ESP when we asked them, as had 87 percent of the older subsample. Among these, opinions about the existence of ESP were overwhelmingly positive. Ninety percent of the youth and 87 percent of their elders thought ESP "probably" exists. Thirty-nine percent and 36 percent respectively were "sure" of its existence, while only 1 percent and 3 percent respectively were confident that ESP doesn't exist.

It will be recalled from Chapter 2 that the proportions registering qualified belief in the claims of astrology were 53 percent among Bay Area young people and 44 percent among older people. By comparison, therefore, ESP elicits considerably more credence than astrology. It also finds more support than spiritualism, the other occult phenomenon on which we obtained data. Respondents were asked:

One of the beliefs of spiritualism is that it is possible to communicate with the dead. Do you think it is definitely possible, probably possible, probably not possible, or definitely not possible to communicate with the dead?

Thirty-four percent of the young people and 23 percent of the older people responded either "definitely" or "probably" possible. In other words, ESP seems to find more believers than other familiar manifestations of the occult.

What is perhaps more noteworthy is that ESP also elicits more belief than many traditional tenets of Christianity—more, for example, than belief in God. Altogether, 54 percent of the young people and 75 percent of the older people said that they definitely believed in God or were uncertain but leaned toward believing, far fewer than the 90 percent and 87 percent respectively who felt ESP probably exists.[4] On another traditional tenet of Christian doctrine—life after death—the proportions who definitely believed or who felt "there must be something beyond death, but I have no idea what it may be like" were 56 percent and 59 percent for the young and the older respectively, and this too was smaller than the percentages on ESP. Or to give another example, 49 percent of the youth and 62 percent of their elders believed that "God created the first man and woman." These are again smaller percentages than those believing in ESP. In terms of belief, therefore, ESP is a phenomenon to be reckoned with on a par with some of the better-established beliefs of conventional religion.

There is also evidence of widespread experience with ESP. Sensational accounts of ESP experiences frequent the newspapers and magazines from time to time. But ESP experiences, our data suggest, are far from uncommon. Of one type or another, they were reported by 54 percent of the younger people and 47 percent of the older people. In other words, one out of every two persons has had some experience he feels may have been ESP.

To find out what kinds of experiences these were, we asked those who said they had experienced ESP to describe their experiences (or if several, their most vivid one). The descriptions ranged from the mundane to the spectacular. As illustrations of the latter, consider the following:

When my husband's ship was shipwrecked, I dreamt that he was only in his underwear and he had a beard and he talked to me and I'd never seen him in a beard before. I woke up from that dream and I started to pray. It was wartime and he really was shipwrecked on an island for three weeks and had nothing to eat. I found out later that he did have a beard and he only had his underwear during the three weeks he was on the island.

My first wife was a medium. We had a lot of conversations with the people from beyond. My father. My mother. My kids. A lot of other people from my country (Puerto Rico). Even the late President Kennedy. While my wife was alive. When she passed away, she came through another medium.

My father's deceased and he came to the house one night. I didn't actually see him, but I had an impression or mental feeling that he was standing in my doorway. I

4. Or if the percentages affirming the existence of ESP are based on the entire sample (including those not having heard of ESP), they are 86 percent and 76 percent respectively, still greater than those for belief in God.

turned to see if he were there and I heard my mother crying in her sleep. I went into her room and asked her if she knew she was crying in her sleep. She said she did and she was dreaming about my father.

I was in North Africa in the Canine Corps. We were about six miles in. A bomb dump and the electricity went out. We had an entire power failure in that area and my dog failed to alert. In the bomb dump site we had sand on the top to see Arabs that might try to steal the stuff. Everything went haywire. The lights failed to come on, the phones didn't work, flashlights wouldn't work, and one dog failed to alert. We saw this one figure on the bomb dump site. After ten minutes it disappeared and the dogs alerted. We went up to look for footprints and there weren't any.

World War II. The Battle of the Bulge. I dreamt about it two days before it happened. Every detail.

The majority of the experiences described tended to be rather ordinary, however, such as having the same thoughts as one's spouse, thinking of a friend and having him or her call on the telephone, feelings of empathy, premonitions, and déjà vu. An effort to categorize these experiences suggested that telepathy and precognition were about equally common, constituting 44 percent and 42 percent of the experiences respectively. Only 2 percent of the experiences were of clairvoyance, 1 percent was psychokinesis, and 3 percent were of apparitions.

Of the telepathic experiences, over half involved merely thinking the same thought at the same time as someone else. About 20 percent were instances of knowing that some friend or relative was in danger, ill, or dying; about 10 percent represented feelings of physical empathy with someone in pain or with someone dying; and about 5 percent involved conscious transfers of information. Virtually all of these experiences were with close friends or with members of immediate families.

The experiences of precognition were divided about equally among premonitions of danger or tragedy, déjà vu experiences, and precognitions of future personal events, such as meeting a new friend, visualizing a future dwelling place, or dreaming about minor experiences before they happened. The mode by which the precognition was received was a dream in about a third of the cases, a feeling or a thought in about a third of the cases, and was unspecified in the remainder.

Many of the respondents who described ESP experiences acknowledged being unsure whether their experiences really had been instances of ESP, and to the critical observer many of the experiences may seem as much a matter of chance as of anything unordinary. But whether real or artifactual, the experiences described indicate a striking *desire* on the part of many respondents to believe in the possibility of ESP and to consider themselves capable of experiencing it.

RELIGIOUS PREFERENCE AND ESP

We suggested earlier that psychic phenomena often have been regarded with suspicion or disapproval by the churches. If so, we would expect church members to believe in ESP less commonly than the nonreligious and probably to say that they've experienced it less often as well. Followers of the new religions would probably be more inclined than church members to believe in ESP, since they seem to be more open toward nonconventionality in general (as seen in Chapter 1). But whether or not they should be more or less inclined toward ESP than the nonreligious is more difficult to say.

The tendency for people of different religious persuasions to believe in ESP (say they are "sure" it exists) and to have experienced ESP is reported in Table 28. Looking first at the conventionally religious, we see that about a third on the average are sure ESP exists and about half think they may have experienced it. Catholics appear slightly more inclined to believe in ESP than Protestants, although the differences are small enough to be due to chance. There are relatively few Jews in the sample, but they appear less inclined toward ESP than either Protestants or Catholics. Among the nonreligious, humanists are most likely to believe in ESP experiences. Agnostics, atheists, and those with no religious beliefs all show about the same propensity to believe in ESP. In general, the nonreligious seem somewhat more inclined toward ESP than the conventionally religious. For example, the percentages believing in ESP range as high as 49 percent among the nonreligious, but among the conventionally religious they range only as high as 34 percent; and among the nonreligious categories as many as 77 percent have experienced ESP, whereas the highest percentage among the conventionally religious is 58 percent. Looking next at Eastern religions, we see that mystics are especially likely to believe in ESP (85 percent) and to have experienced it (75 percent). The few Buddhists in the sample also show relatively high percentages. Both mystics and Buddhists display higher percentages on the average than either the nonreligious or the conventionally religious. The table also reports percentages for persons of "other" religious persuasions, but the numbers in these categories are either too small or the categories are too heterogeneous to draw meaningful inferences.

These data suggest two conclusions. First, they suggest that conventional religious loyalties probably do deter tendencies to believe in and to experience ESP. This seems evident from comparing all those with conventional religious preferences, of whom 32 percent are sure ESP exists and 55 percent think they've experienced it, with all those in the nonreligious categories, of whom 40 percent are certain of ESP's existence and 60 percent have experienced it. These differences are not large, of course, but they seem

Table 28. **ESP AND RELIGIOUS PREFERENCE
(Total Weighted Sample)**

Religion	Are sure ESP exists		Percent who Have experienced ESP	
Conventional:				
Catholic	34%	(218)	58%	(197)
Protestant	31%	(304)	53%	(268)
Jewish	20%	(20)	47%	(19)
Total	32%	(542)	55%	(484)
Nonreligious:				
Humanist	49%	(47)	71%	(42)
Agnostic	40%	(78)	59%	(68)
Atheist	39%	(23)	77%	(17)
None	38%	(119)	53%	(105)
Total	40%	(267)	60%	(232)
Eastern / mystical:				
Mystic	85%	(13)	75%	(12)
Buddhist	50%	(6)	60%	(5)
Total	74%	(19)	71%	(17)
Other:				
Mormon	53%	(17)	59%	(17)
Eastern Orthodox	50%	(6)	60%	(5)
Islamic	50%	(4)	75%	(4)
Other	71%	(49)	85%	(48)
Don't know	43%	(14)	50%	(12)
Total	61%	(90)	73%	(86)

Significance (left to right):
 $\chi^2 = 87.68, 27.15$; df = 42, 13; p = .001, .01

consistent with the idea that organized religion has spoken against rather than in favor of ESP. Second, the data give evidence that interest in ESP may have been reinforced by the new religious consciousness of recent years. Seventy-four percent of those identified with Eastern religions believe in ESP and 71 percent have had ESP experiences, the highest percentages for any of the broad religious categories.

The latter conclusion tends to be supported also by the relations between ESP items and attitudes toward new religious groups (those discussed in Chapter 1). Seventy-five percent of those who are strongly attracted to Transcendental Meditation, for example, are sure ESP exists, compared with 38 percent of those who are turned off by TM; and 81 percent of those strongly attracted to TM have experienced ESP, compared with 58 percent of those who say they are turned off by it. Similar relations exist between the ESP items and opinions of yoga (see Table 29).

These results give reason to associate interest in ESP with the new religious periphery and to suggest that ESP has probably been discouraged rather than encouraged by traditional religious commitments. Religious preference provides only a crude measure of a person's religious orientation, however. Merely to identify with a religion may say little about one's actual commitments. We turn, therefore, to an examination of religious belief.

RELIGIOUS BELIEF AND ESP

A central tenet of the Judeo-Christian tradition is faith in the existence of God. We asked respondents what their position was on this tenet, affording ourselves an opportunity to see if people with different views of the supernatural also differ in their responses to ESP. As shown in Table 30, they do, but not as we might have expected after our discussion of religious preference. Among those who definitely believe in God, 40 percent register certainty about the existence of ESP and 59 percent think they may have

Table 29. **ESP AND EASTERN RELIGIONS (Total Weighted Sample)**

| | Persons who | | | |
	Are sure ESP exists		Have experienced ESP	
Opinion of TM:				
Strongly attracted	75%	(29)	81%	(28)
Mildly attracted	58%	(91)	64%	(82)
Nothing either way	40%	(154)	62%	(144)
Turned off	38%	(40)	58%	(32)
Opinion of yoga groups:				
Strongly attracted	65%	(42)	77%	(42)
Mildly attracted	42%	(160)	57%	(146)
Nothing either way	40%	(216)	61%	(197)
Turned off	39%	(44)	51%	(42)

Significance (left to right) for TM:
$\chi^2 = 30.35, 4.01$; df = 9, 3; p = .001, .30
for yoga:
$\chi^2 = 15.80, 7.00$; df = 9, 3; p = .07, .07

Table 30. **ESP AND BELIEF IN GOD**
(Total Weighted Sample)

Belief in God	Percent who			
	Are sure ESP exists		Have experienced ESP	
Definitely believe	40%	(456)	59%	(409)
Lean toward believing	26%	(116)	44%	(99)
Lean toward not believing	17%	(30)	58%	(24)
Don't know whether God exists	33%	(99)	53%	(89)
Don't believe	34%	(44)	58%	(38)
Believe in something "beyond"	50%	(131)	68%	(122)

Significance (left to right):
$\chi^2 = 28.83, 13.49$; df = 15, 5; p = .02, .02

experienced it personally These percentages are *higher* than those for people who aren't certain about God but lean toward believing in Him; they are also higher than among those who lean toward not believing in God, than among those who don't believe in God, and than among those who take an agnostic view of God's existence. The only respondents with higher percentages believing in ESP and having experienced it are those who believe in something "more" or "beyond" but feel uncomfortable about the word "God."

This result conflicts with our previous finding that ESP is less common among the traditionally religious than among the nonreligious. The differences between believers and nonbelievers suggest that the religious may be *more* inclined to believe in ESP than the nonreligious. This possibility also gains support from another question which asked respondents to say how strongly they felt their lives to be influenced by God. The proportions who felt sure that ESP exists ranged from 40 percent for those who thought God determined their lives almost entirely and 40 percent for those who thought God had a strong influence on their lives, to 36 percent for those who thought God had a small influence on their lives and 31 percent for those who thought God had no influence on their lives. The proportions who felt they may have experienced ESP varied respectively from 62 percent to 54 percent.

To shed some additional light on the relations between religious belief and ESP, we turn next to a question which asked about belief in life after death (see Table 31). Once again, the data suggest that persons holding beliefs in the supernatural may be more positively inclined toward ESP than persons rejecting the supernatural, but they qualify somewhat the idea that traditional religious beliefs encourage ESP. Leaving aside those who believe in reincarnation, the highest proportion of believers in ESP is among those who believe in life after death with rewards but no punishments (48 percent), and the next highest proportion is among those who feel there must be life after death but haven't any idea what it may be like (42 percent). These percentages are significantly higher than for those unsure whether to believe in life after death or not (28 percent) and for those who do not believe in life after death (27 percent). The most traditional or orthodox view of life after death, however, finds only about as many believers in ESP (32 percent) as among those who reject life after death. As the table shows, the tendency to have experienced ESP follows a similar pattern. The data do add further support, it should be noted, to the idea that interest in ESP is positively associated with commitment to the new religions. Those who say reincarnation best expresses their views of life after death are most likely of all to believe in the existence of ESP (74 percent) and to say they may have experienced it (81 percent).

Table 31. ESP AND BELIEF IN LIFE AFTER DEATH (Total Weighted Sample)

Belief in Life after Death	Percent who			
	Are sure ESP exists		Have experienced ESP	
Life after death with rewards for some and punishment for others	32%	(170)	54%	(145)
Life after death with rewards but no punishment	48%	(27)	66%	(24)
Something after death but have no idea what it may be like	42%	(329)	61%	(299)
Not sure whether there is	28%	(161)	53%	(141)
No life after death	27%	(143)	59%	(118)
Reincarnation	74%	(45)	81%	(45)

Significance (left to right):
$\chi^2 = 53.87, 13.71$; df $= 15, 5$; p $= .001, .02$

What these results suggest is the need for an interpretation somewhat different from the one with which we began this chapter. Contrary to the idea that ESP may be perceived by the religiously devout as heresy or at least as a potentially threatening alternative to religious interpretations of extraordinary experiences, all but the most orthodox members of the religious public seem to be at least as positive toward ESP as the nonreligious. Indeed, greater degrees of faith in religious tenets having to do with the supernatural tend to be associated with greater probabilities of belief in ESP and experiences of ESP. For those with unorthodox, Eastern, or mystical religious orientations, the propensity to believe in ESP is even stronger.

RELIGIOUS EXPERIENCE AND ESP

The interpretation that seems most consistent with these results is that one kind of belief in supernatural phenomena reinforces another. The argument for this interpretation may be put in the following way. ESP and religion both affirm the existence of realities beyond the mundane existence of everyday life. The realities they point to are conceived somewhat differently, the one being limited mostly to extrasensory communication among people, the other positing a divine being. Hence, the two need not conflict. Instead, either one may break the shackles of daily life, opening up possibilities of other supraempirical realities as well. Having experienced one, a person may find others credible as well.

That religious orientations and ESP may directly reinforce one another was actually suggested by several respondents' experiences with ESP. For example, a Christian Scientist in the sample reported an experience which she considered to be ESP, but which also had deep religious significance for her:

When my son was very young, about two, I was working in the kitchen and we had a refrigerator with an outside hinge. He put his hand in the hinge and was squeezed in the hinge when I closed the door. I was terribly upset, of course, and picked up the screaming child and reached out in prayer to God. As I walked into the next room with him still screaming, I heard a voice as if it were spoken behind me saying, "You are not alone, divine love is ever-present." Then the urgency of the situation just vanished. The child began to laugh. The sun streamed into the room. The suffering and tragic experience were completely gone. There was never any trace on the child's hand of the accident.

Another respondent claimed to have become religious because of an ESP experience:

I was brought up in Russia where religion was banned, and I never learned to my knowledge any prayers. When I was about 13, I had a dream of a situation that actually occurred about three years later. I was at a railroad station on the way to the ship that took us out of Europe. In the dream, a pure white horse knocked me down flat, put a sheet of tarpaper over me, and told me to recite the Lord's Prayer, which I didn't know consciously. And in the dream, I actually recited it in old Slavonic, and when I woke up I knew it in Russian.

Such experiences may be atypical, but they illustrate the possibility that even the same experience can be interpreted both as an example of ESP and as a religious experience.

If the important connection between ESP and religion is an orientation that transcends everyday life, we should find strong relations between having actually had religious experiences and ESP. This possibility is examined in Table 32. There we have presented the relations between our ESP items and two questions about religious experience, the first asking about feelings of close contact with the holy or sacred, an experience that someone oriented to traditional religion might have; the second asking about feelings of harmony with the universe, a more mystical form of religious experience.

The data show persons having had religious experiences to be consider-

Table 32. ESP AND RELIGIOUS EXPERIENCE (Total Weighted Sample)

	Percent who	
Religious experience	Are sure ESP exists	Have experienced ESP
Ever been in close contact with the holy or sacred:		
Yes, it was important	47% (249)	71% (221)
Yes, not important	40% (217)	62% (195)
No, but like to	33% (225)	51% (208)
No, don't care	28% (203)	51% (165)
Experienced harmony with the universe:		
Yes, it was important	50% (212)	69% (195)
Yes, not important	40% (156)	63% (142)
No, but like to	39% (316)	54% (285)
No, don't care	25% (229)	52% (191)

Significance (left to right) for contact with the sacred:
   $\chi^2 = 34.00, 24.33$; df = 9, 3; p = .001, .001
for harmony with universe:
   $\chi^2 = 34.73, 14.72$; df = 9, 3; p = .001, .01

ably more likely to have had ESP experiences and to believe in ESP than those not having had religious experiences. For example, 47 percent of those having experienced close contact with the holy or sacred and regarding their experience as being of lasting importance in their lives felt sure that ESP exists. By comparison, only 28 percent of those never having had such an experience, and not caring that they hadn't, said they believed in ESP. The former were also 20 percent more likely than the latter to have had ESP experiences. Persons who have transcended the ordinary in one way, to put it simply, seem inclined to transcend it in other ways as well.

This conclusion can also be inferred simply from looking at the degree to which people are *concerned* about matters which transcend everyday life. Some people, of course, spend a great deal more time thinking about the so-called ultimate concerns of life—what the meaning and purpose of life is, who they are and how they came to be who they are, and so forth—than others do, whether they think about these concerns in religious terms or not. And these people also are more likely to believe in ESP and to have had ESP experiences than those more totally engrossed with everyday affairs (see Table 33). For example, 67 percent of those who think about the purpose of life a lot have experienced ESP, in comparison with 43 percent of those who never think about the purpose of life and don't consider it an important question. Even those who have thought about such questions in the past, but no longer do, seem more inclined toward ESP experiences than those who haven't considered these questions significant at all.

It is also the case, as should be expected by now, that people who consciously spend time in meditation, especially if they use some specific meditation techniques such as sitting or breathing or thinking in special ways, are much more likely to believe in and experience ESP than people who don't. Among meditators using special techniques, 73 percent are sure ESP exists. This compares with 38 percent among those who spend time thinking about their lives but don't actually practice meditation and 30 percent among those who don't meditate at all. The proportions having experienced ESP are 77 percent, 61 percent, and 47 percent respectively.[5]

5. These results are supported by those from two laboratory studies: K. Osis and E. Bokert, "ESP and Changed States of Consciousness Induced by Meditation," *Journal of the American Society for Psychical Research* 65 (January 1971): 17–65, a three-year study which found that self-transcendence and openness from meditation, as reported in questionnaires, was positively related to ESP experiences; and Gertrude R. Schmeidler, "High ESP Scores After a Swami's Brief Instruction in Meditation and Breathing," *Journal of the American Society for Psychical Research* 64 (January 1970): 100–103, a small study of six subjects who scored significantly higher on an ESP test after listening to a lecture on meditation and performing a breathing exercise.

Table 33. **ESP AND ULTIMATE QUESTIONS**
(Total Weighted Sample)

Ultimate questions	Percent who			
	Are sure ESP exists		Have experienced ESP	
Thought about the purpose of life:				
A lot	44%	(274)	67%	(237)
Some	37%	(366)	55%	(339)
In the past, but not now	30%	(95)	60%	(80)
Never, but think it important	31%	(112)	57%	(103)
Never, not important	32%	(47)	43%	(31)
Thought about how they came to be who they are:				
A lot	42%	(289)	68%	(256)
Some	38%	(294)	58%	(267)
In the past, but not now	40%	(115)	55%	(99)
Never, but think it important	20%	(99)	49%	(82)
Never, not important	34%	(98)	47%	(87)
Bothered wondering about the meaning of life:				
A lot	52%	(89)	72%	(81)
A little	38%	(243)	61%	(228)
In the past, not now	37%	(305)	56%	(268)
Never	34%	(278)	54%	(237)

Significance (left to right) for purpose:
$\chi^2 = 55.72, 12.72$; df = 12, 4; p = .001, .01
who you are:
$\chi^2 = 28.91, 17.68$; df = 12, 4; p = .01, .01
meaning:
$\chi^2 = 25.92, 8.17$; df = 9, 3; p = .01, .05

OTHER FACTORS

All the items about religion that we have examined have been associated significantly with belief in ESP and with ESP experiences, the majority suggesting that religious orientations reinforce tendencies to believe in and to experience ESP. But are the relations real or are they, perhaps, artifacts of other differences between those who are inclined positively toward ESP and those who are not—differences, for example, in age, education, sex, ethnicity, or other factors?

The answer to this question seems to be no, at least as far as most of the more obvious factors we might expect to be associated with ESP are concerned. Most of these factors are not significantly related to ESP at all. Ethnicity, for example, frequently has been associated with ESP in popular mythology, but when we compare people with ancestors from various countries—Africa, China, England, France, Germany, Ireland, Italy, Mexico, Poland, Russia, Scandinavia, and Scotland—with people not having ancestors from any of these countries, the only significant relationship we find is between having ancestors from Mexico and being more likely to have experienced ESP.[6] Education might also be thought to have an influence on ESP, but again the differences are small and form no consistent pattern: 39 percent of the college educated are sure ESP exists, as are 37 percent of the high school educated and 36 percent of the grade school educated; 60 percent of the first have experienced what they feel may have been ESP, compared with only 52 percent of the second, but 69 percent of the third.[7] Nor are there significant differences, as sometimes suggested, between men and women.[8] And we have already seen that the differences between younger and older people are small.

More generally, none of the usual background variables typically associated with other kinds of beliefs or attitudes shows any relationship with ESP.[9] Religious factors are the only items in our data that help to determine

6. None of the other relations were significant at or beyond the .05 level.
7. The lack of a relation between ESP and education seems consistent with findings reported by Carroll B. Nash and Catherine S. Nash, "Correlations between ESP Scores and Intelligence," *International Journal of Parapsychology* 6 (1964): 309–323, showing no relations between ESP performance and course grades or scholastic ability scores in a sample of 144 college students.
8. The chi-square value for the relation was .365 with 1 degree of freedom, significant at the .55 level; this lack of relationship is consistent with C. E. Green, "Spontaneous 'Paranormal' Experiences in Relation to Sex and Academic Background," *Journal of the American Society for Psychical Research* 43 (1966): 357–362, a study of 115 college students, showing no differences in self-reported ESP experiences between men and women.
9. Other variables examined and found unrelated to ESP experiences include occupation (χ^2 = 6.62, d.f. = 10, p = .76); work status (χ^2 = 8.92, d.f. = 7, p = .259); raised in rural,

who will be more likely and who will be less likely to believe in ESP and to experience ESP.

CONCLUSION

The results in this chapter have come from looking at only a couple of questions about ESP. Thus, we cannot be sure of the validity of the responses to these questions. If the responses are valid, they suggest relatively widespread belief in ESP in the Bay Area and a sizable proportion of people who had had experiences they thought may have been examples of ESP. If nothing more, these responses suggest that many people in the Bay Area seem open to the possibility that ESP may exist and to the possibility that they may have experienced it personally.

In examining the relations of belief in ESP and ESP experiences with a number of background characteristics of our respondents, such as ethnicity, education, sex, and age, we have found no significant relationships. The only characteristics we have been able to examine that seem to be consistently associated with ESP in the Bay Area have had to do with religion.

The results suggest that there is probably a positive relation in the Bay Area between religious experimentation and openness to ESP. We have seen that respondents who identify their religious preference as Eastern or mystical are more likely than average to believe in ESP and to say they may have experienced it. We have also seen this tendency among respondents who are attracted to TM or yoga, among respondents who are uncomfortable about the word "God" but believe in something more or something beyond, among respondents who believe in reincarnation, among respondents who say they have been in harmony with the universe, and among respondents who practice meditation.

The relations between conventional religious commitment and ESP seem to be more ambiguous. On the average, Protestants, Catholics, and Jews in the Bay Area were seen to be less inclined toward ESP than the nonreligious. But when responses to specific items about religious belief were examined, we saw that people who said they definitely believed in God and people who said they thought God had had a strong influence on their lives were somewhat more open to ESP than people who were unsure of God's existence or who thought God had had little or no influence on their lives. We also saw that people who believed in some form of life after death were

---

suburban, or urban area (χ^2 = .15, d.f. = 2, p = .93); church attendance as a youth (χ^2 = 2.42, d.f. = 3, p = .49); political position from liberal to conservative (χ^2 = 6.12, d.f. = 8, p = .634); and father's education (χ^2 = 3.36, d.f. = 7, p = .849).

generally more open to ESP than people who were unsure about life after death or who didn't think it existed.

Of the two kinds of questions—religious preference and religious beliefs—the latter is probably a more precise measure of religious commitment, since a number of those in the sample who listed their religious preference as Protestant, Catholic, or Jewish seemed to be only nominally committed to their faiths (see Chapter 8). If we were to conclude anything specific about the relations between conventional religious commitment and inclinations toward ESP in the Bay Area, therefore, it would probably be that there is a positive relation between the two. This conclusion may well be limited to certain kinds of conventional beliefs, however. We saw, for example, that people choosing the most orthodox response regarding life after death were somewhat less open to ESP than persons choosing slightly less orthodox responses. In any future research on the relations between conventional religious commitment and ESP, therefore, it would appear useful to distinguish empirically among alternative dimensions of belief.

In concluding, one note of caution is worth re-emphasizing. We cannot conclude from these results that people who are religious or who are somehow oriented toward the transcendent actually become more capable of receiving and sending extrasensory messages than other people. This may be a logical possibility, given some laboratory research suggesting that ESP abilities can be enhanced through experimentally induced changes in mental set. But the present data do not demonstrate whether or not this may be the case.

CHAPTER 4

Mysticism and Politics

Mysticism was another form of religious experimentation that came to be widely publicized during the late 1960s and early 1970s. Although mysticism was scarcely new to American culture, the visible influx of Eastern religious movements, together with the drug culture, gave it considerably more prominence than it had had in the past. This chapter examines one aspect of this recent experimentation with mysticism that has received frequent comment but thus far has failed to be informed by much factual evidence—its relation with political activism.

Because of their simultaneous appearance in the counterculture, mysticism and political activism have commonly been assumed to bear some relation to one another. The precise nature of this relation has been the subject of some disagreement, however. Some have suggested that mysticism and political activism have reinforced one another. Others have taken what is probably the more common view, suggesting a trade-off relation between the two. Mysticism, according to this view, leads to withdrawal from political activity.

There has been some anecdotal evidence from the counterculture in support of both these views. There have also been carefully-framed theoretical arguments, well preceding the counterculture, regarding the relations between mysticism and politics. In order to set the stage for our empirical inquiry, therefore, we shall begin by reviewing several of these theoretical arguments. These arguments will take us somewhat away from the contemporary period itself, but will illumine some of the specific links that have been posited between mysticism and politics. We shall then examine the empirical relations between a measure of mysticism and various measures of political action in the Bay Area. Finally, we shall consider briefly some of the differences, and some of the reasons for these differences, between the contemporary relations between mysticism and politics and those having existed at other times and places.

THE WEBERIAN ARGUMENT

For sociologists, one of the main sources of ideas about the relations between mysticism and other kinds of behavior has probably been the writings of Max Weber and his disciple, Ernst Troeltsch. Both gave mysticism an important place in their discussions of religion; Weber, as a negative case for understanding inner-worldly asceticism; Troeltsch, as one of the basic responses of Christendom, along with churchly religion and sectarianism, to the secular world. Their remarks on the relations between mysticism and politics, therefore, were rooted in more general theoretical concerns. However, it is clear that they regarded mysticism as associated more with political withdrawal than with political activity. At least six reasons for this conclusion can be identified in their discussions.

First, mysticism seeks salvation, not through worldly activity as the ascetic does, but through contemplation, which requires "the extrusion of all everyday mundane interests."[1] Even the world-*rejecting* ascetic works within the world, although his ultimate rewards lie in a different sphere. But the mystic transvalues ("flees" from) the world and seeks divine union. Thus, the world-fleeing mystic considers political activity as "a temptation against which he must maintain his state of grace" (p. 174). To the extent that mysticism takes a more inner-worldly orientation (Weber cites Tauler as an example), "the usual result is the acceptance of the secular social structure which happens to be at hand, an acceptance that is relatively indifferent to the world but at least humble before it" (pp. 175–176).

Second, the mystical value system idealizes "acosmic love" to the extent that it cannot countenance the realism of practical political affairs.[2] Like Trotskyites of the religious world, the mystic sees flaws in every practical social involvement and therefore remains aloof, critical, and uncompromising. Furthermore, the "completely unselective generosity" of the mystical love ethic precludes any activity—political, economic, or otherwise— necessitating rational (utilitarian) criteria of evaluation.

Third, the mystic is intensely private or personalistic. As Troeltsch puts it, "mysticism lays no stress at all upon the relation between individuals but

1. Max Weber, *The Sociology of Religion* (Boston: Beacon Press, 1963), p. 168. Succeeding quotations are also from this volume unless otherwise indicated.
2. Max Weber, *From Max Weber: Essays in Sociology*, ed. Hans Gerth and C. Wright Mills (New York: Oxford University Press, 1946), p. 340; see also Arthur Mitzman, *The Iron Cage: An Historical Interpretation of Max Weber* (New York: Grosset & Dunlap, 1969), pp. 196–230.

only upon the relations between the soul and God."[3] The terms "soul" and
"God" might be phrased more broadly so as to include more secular varieties of mysticism. But the implication of Troeltsch's statement for political involvement seems clear. Such a narrowly personalistic value-
orientation is hardly conducive to political involvement.

Fourth, in spite of its individualism, mysticism also tends to be characterized as highly interested in intimate social relations. Troeltsch squares
these two observations simply: "Even the mystic is human, and he feels the
need for the give-and-take of intimate fellowship with other souls" (p.
754). From a more Durkheimian perspective, the small *gemeinschaftliche*
community of mystics becomes crucial for maintaining the plausibility of
their faith in cosmic harmony. Only by restricting their social relations to
such intimate settings is it likely that social harmony can be maintained,
with which collective representations of universal harmony can find reso-
nance.[4] Political action, being more macroscopic and impersonal, is thus
excluded from the purview of the mystic.

Fifth, the mystic tends to be preoccupied with problems of ultimate
meaning. "Why" questions occupy his consciousness to the exclusion of
the "how to" questions of ordinary life. The ascetic need not concern
himself to so great an extent with ultimate questions because such questions
are answerable only to God, who, especially in the Calvinist tradition,
remains unfathomable. The mystic, in contrast, believes that illumination
into the mysteries of the ultimate is possible and that only by attaining
illumination will the rest of life become meaningful.[5] This difference is
magnified by the conception of God held by each, the former viewing God
as strictly transcendent and ultimately beyond "possession" by the individual, the latter regarding God as relatively more imminent and attainable.[6]
The mystic, therefore, may be too engaged with questions of ultimate
meaning to become involved in the practical struggles associated with
political affairs.

Finally, the mystic, being devoted to peace and brotherhood, "with-
draws from the pragma of violence which no political action can escape."[7]

From the perspective offered by Weber and Troeltsch, therefore, there
would seem to be ample reasons for us to suspect that the recent experimentation with mysticism in American culture, if anything, has probably been

3. Ernest Troeltsch, *The Social Teaching of the Christian Churches* (New York: Harper and
Row, 1960), p. 743. Subsequent quotations from Troeltsch are also from this volume.
4. Cf. Bryan Wilson, *Religious Sects: A Sociological Study* (London: World University
Library, 1970), pp. 118–140.
5. Mitzman, *The Iron Cage*, pp. 196–230.
6. Weber, *The Sociology of Religion*, p. 178.
7. Weber, *From Max Weber*, p. 336.

associated negatively with political activism. Judging from more contemporary studies, the emphasis upon contemplation, idealism, introspection, intimacy, ultimate meaning, and nonviolence seems to be as much a part of contemporary mysticism as of the historical forms upon which Weber and Troeltsch based their observations.[8] Some observers of the recent counterculture, in fact, have portrayed its mystical aspects and its political activities as deeply contradictory, even antagonistic.

OTHER ARGUMENTS

Still, other scholars have offered compelling reasons why mysticism might be expected to *encourage* rather than discourage political activity, basing their arguments on conceptions of mysticism much the same as those of Weber and Troeltsch.[9] We shall consider only two of these reasons, on which we shall subsequently be able to present some evidence.

The first reason why mysticism might be expected to be positively associated with political action is its tendency toward *moral relativism*. Weber and Troeltsch themselves, as well as others, have commented on this characteristic of mysticism.[10] The mystic tends to assume that ultimate authority resides within each person himself. Knowledge of the Absolute comes only through personal illumination. In consequence, moral standards tend to be defined relative to each individual's desires, needs, and conceptions of truth. Each lives by his own *gnosis* and refrains from attempting to formulate general rules of conduct for others. To be sure, mysticism can become just as intolerant and dogmatic as other religious orientations (Weber calls this "mystagogery"), but the more common tendency seems to be toward

8. Weber's discussion of the characteristics of mysticism agrees on most points with those of Evelyn Underhill, *Mysticism* (New York: E. P. Dutton, 1961); Georgia Harkness, *Mysticism: Its Meaning and Message* (New York: Abington Press, 1973); Hal Bridges, *American Mysticism: From William James to Zen* (New York: Harper and Row, 1970); Rudolph Otto, *The Idea of the Holy* (London: Oxford University Press, 1923); William James, *The Varieties of Religious Experience* (New York: New American Library, (1958); and M. Laski, *Ecstasy: A Study of Some Secular and Religious Experiences* (London: The Cresset Press, 1961).

9. Arguments to this effect have been put forth by Susanne K. Langer, *Philosophy in a New Key: A Study in the Symbolism of Reason, Rite, and Art* (New York: The New American Library, 1942); and by Abraham Maslow, *Toward a Psychology of Being* (London: D. Van Nostrand Company, 1962) and *Religions, Values, and Peak-Experiences* (New York: Viking Press, 1970). These have been discussed in Robert Wuthnow, *The Consciousness Reformation* (Berkeley and Los Angeles: University of California Press, 1976).

10. Weber, *The Sociology of Religion*, pp. 174 and 197; Troeltsch, *The Social Teaching of the Christian Churches*, p. 775; Baron Friedrich Hugel, *The Mystical Element of Religion as Studied in Saint Catherine of Genoa and Her Friends* (New York: E. P. Dutton, 1923), p. 138; Nathan Adler, *The Underground Stream: New Life Styles and the Antinomian Personality* (New York: Harper and Row, 1972); and G. Van der Leeuw, *Religion in Essence and Manifestation: A Study in Phenomenology* (New York: Harper and Row, 1963), p. 505.

tolerance of others' moral and ethical styles, however different they may be from one's own.

This tendency toward moral relativism also seems to derive from the mystic's propensity to merge the meanings of "right" and "wrong" into a larger unity. As Browning once wrote:

> Type needs antitype:
> As night needs day, as shine needs shade, so good
> Needs evil: how were pity understood,
> Unless by pain?[11]

Given this orientation, it becomes unclear to the mystic what, as "right," should be encouraged and what, as "wrong," should be discouraged; in brief, it becomes necessary to be tolerant.

Furthermore, mysticism, unlike many other religious orientations, tends to avoid those sharp divisions between the "saved" and the "damned" which have so often been used to legitimate the condemnation of peoples and life styles different from those of the saved.[12] In mysticism, salvation is not so much a decision or an act, but a gradual process, an ordered movement toward higher levels of reality.[13] Everyone contains the "Divine Seed" within him and has only to nourish it. Everyone has the necessary basis for choosing his own standards of behavior. Hence, there is a strong motivation toward tolerance, as Troeltsch puts it, toward "liberty of conscience," toward acceptance of religions, races and life styles different from one's own. Troeltsch, in fact, remarks that mystics have frequently been the champions of religious freedom and tolerance.[14]

According to this argument, mysticism might encourage political activity because the moral relativism inherent in mysticism is likely to conflict with the intolerance, injustice, and particularism of the rest of the society. Holding freedom and tolerance as values, the mystic has cause to engage in political dissent to bring about a more tolerant, just, and equitable society. Melford Spiro, in fact, has remarked on precisely this tendency among the members of the tiny *kammatic* sect in Burma: though deeply mystical, their moral relativism has caused them to engage repeatedly in political activism.[15] By the same token, the conflict between the moral relativism of the mystic and the less relativistic character of the society may lead the

---

11. Robert Browning, *Complete Poetical Works,* 12 vols. (New York: T. Y. Crowell, 1898).
12. For example, see Charles Y. Glock and Rodney Stark, *Christian Beliefs and Anti-Semitism* (New York: Harper and Row, 1966).
13. Underhill, *Mysticism,* pp. 81–82.
14. Troeltsch, *The Social Teaching of the Christian Churches*, p. 763.
15. Melford E. Spiro, *Buddhism and Society: A Great Tradition and Its Burmese Vicissitudes* (New York: Harper and Row, 1970), p. 96.

mystic only to become alienated. But at least a rationale for engaging in political action is there.

The second argument which has suggested the possibility of a positive relation between mysticism and political involvement is partly derivative from the first, but focuses more directly upon social structures themselves. This argument stresses the tendency for mysticism to encourage (for want of a better term) *liberalism*—that is, a critical, detached awareness of existing social arrangements, coupled with a desire for social change. The logic of this argument is as follows.

The mystic values an order of experience that transcends ordinary social reality. His "truth" comes from a "higher" authority than socially institutionalized sources.[16] Ordinary forms of reality, including social arrangements, are thought to be purely human constructions. Thus, social reality tends not to be perceived simply as "reality," and is no longer simply taken for granted, but is regarded as a human construction. The mystic comes to think of social forces as something problematic rather than simply "given."

From this awareness of social forces, the mystic may be led further to seeing social reality as confining. The manner in which society has been constructed may be regarded as a limiting factor preventing the attainment of higher-order mystical experiences. The blinders of socialization and culture may be considered the reason why it is so difficult to achieve mystical illumination. To paraphrase Norman O. Brown, society is "our construction, our constriction."[17]

One response to the feeling that society is constricting, of course, may be to withdraw from it. But, as Weber pointed out, the mystic to some extent always has to live within the social world. Hence, he may wish for, and even work toward, some transformation of the society, one means of which may be political action.

In sum, there are theoretical discussions suggesting both that mysticism and politics should be negatively related and that they should be positively related. To discover what the relation of the recent experimentation with mysticism has been with political activity, therefore, we clearly need to turn to the data.

EMPIRICAL MEASURES

There seem to be no universally agreed upon definitions of mysticism, just as there are no universally agreed upon definitions for the other kinds of

16. Weber, *The Sociology of Religion*, p. 170.
17. Norman O. Brown, *Love's Body* (New York: Vintage Books, 1966).

religious variables that sociologists have tried to study (such as "orthodoxy," "fundamentalism," or "devotionalism"). But neither is there total disagreement. Among those who have sought to conceptualize mysticism, including Weber and Troeltsch, most seem to have included indicators such as meditation, introspection, and intense transcendent experiences. Most have suggested that mysticism has been more characteristic of Eastern religions than of Western religions. Most have also stressed an interest in noncognitive ways of knowing, such as experiencing nature or experiencing the body. Mystics and students of mysticism would probably agree that indicators such as these fall short of actually capturing the essence of mysticism. But they would probably concede that such indicators may be useful for identifying relative *degrees* of commitment to mysticism.

The Bay Area survey had included a variety of questions aimed at measuring relative degrees of involvement with mysticism. Seven of these questions, in particular, seemed to be useful. They concerned meditation, mystical experiences such as experiencing harmony with the universe and being deeply moved by the beauty of nature, attraction to Eastern religions, emphasis on spending a lot of time getting to know the inner self and the body, and belief in the possibility of learning a lot about life from something such as walks in the woods. A factor analysis of these items showed they contained a single underlying factor.[18] And there seemed to be substantial warrant in the discussions of experts on mysticism, such as Weber and Troeltsch, Evelyn Underhill, Marghanita Laski, William James, and others, for considering each item an indicator of mysticism.[19] Consequently, the seven items were standardized, weighted according to their factor-score coefficients, and added to form a mysticism scale.

18. After factor analyzing the items, factor score coefficients (a measure of the degree to which each item predicts scores on the overall factor) were computed, and each item was weighted according to these coefficients (see Appendix Table A-3).

19. Justification for the inclusion of each item is found in Weber, Troeltsch, and a variety of other sources as follows. Meditation: Weber, *The Sociology of Religion*, p. 168; and Underhill, *Mysticism*, pp. 328–357. Attraction to Eastern religions: Weber, *The Sociology of Religion*, pp. 169 and 177; and Talcott Parsons, *The Structure of Social Action* (Glencoe, Ill.: Free Press, 1937). Getting to know the inner self: Weber, *The Sociology of Religion*, pp. 174–175; Troeltsch, *The Social Teaching of the Christian Churches*, p. 731; Underhill, *Mysticism*, pp. 298–327; Harkness, *Mysticism*, p. 15; and Bridges, *American Mysticism*, p. 3. Ecstatic experiences: Weber, *The Sociology of Religion*, p. 171; Troelsch, *The Social Teaching of the Christian Churches*, p. 730; Underhill, *Mysticism*, pp. 358–379; James, *The Varieties of Religious Experience*, p. 293; Otto, *The Idea of the Holy*; Elmer O'Brien, *Varieties of Mystic Experience* (New York: New American Library, 1964), p. 14; Laski, *Ecstasy*; Maslow, *Toward a Psychology of Being*; Harkness, *Mysticism*, p. 32; and Bridges, *American Mysticism*, p. 2. Learning from walks in the woods: Underhill, *Mysticism*, p. 206; Laski, *Ecstasy*; James, *Varieties of Religious Experience*, pp. 302–305; and Theodore Roszak, *The Making of a Counter-Culture* (Garden City, N.Y.: Doubleday, 1969), p. 149. Body awareness: Underhill, *Mysticism*, pp. 198–231; Roszak, *The Making of a Counter-Culture*, p. 129; and Laski, *Ecstasy*.

The Bay Area survey also included a number of political questions. To construct a measure of political action, a factor analysis was performed on all these items. This yielded three factors, one of which appeared to measure political action, another of which appeared to measure liberalism, and the third of which seemed to be a more generalized kind of social concern. A political action measure, then, was constructed by standardizing the items and weighting them according to their factor-score coefficients on the political action factor. The items weighted most heavily were attendance at political meetings, writing to political officials, and participation in demonstrations.[20] Since we were also interested in liberalism, as the foregoing discussion has indicated, a measure of liberalism was constructed in the same manner using the liberalism factor. The item contributing most to this scale was a nine-point continuum on which respondents had rated themselves from radical to liberal to moderate to conservative.[21]

The remaining variable we wished to measure was moral relativism. As a measure of this variable, the following items were standardized, weighted according to their factor-score coefficients, and added: approval of cohabitation, of homosexuality, of communes, and of legalized marijuana, likelihood of playing hooky from work, and likelihood of purchasing stolen goods.[22]

MYSTICISM AND POLITICS IN THE BAY AREA

The correlations between the mysticism scale and each political item in the Bay Area data, as well as correlations with the scales constructed from these items, are reported in Table 34.[23] In each instance there is a significant *positive* relation between the mysticism scale and each political indicator. For instance, there is a correlation of .297 between mysticism and having taken part in a demonstration, a correlation of .255 between mysticism and having attended political meetings, and a correlation of .207 between mysticism and wanting to help solve social problems. The correlation between the mysticism and the political activism scale is .332. In other words, all of the evidence seems to suggest that mysticism and politics in the Bay Area tend to be associated rather than conflictive.

Correlations such as these should not be accepted too readily, of course. The fact that mysticism and politics seem to go together may simply be a function of the kinds of people who scored high on both the mysticism and

20. See Appendix Table A-4.
21. See Appendix Table A-4.
22. See Appendix Table A-5.
23. Our use of correlations in this chapter rather than tabular analysis as in previous chapters is dictated primarily by the availability of sufficient numbers of items to construct continuous, normally distributed variables.

Table 34. **MYSTICISM AND POLITICAL ITEMS**

	Correlations with mysticism scale	Correlations controlling for age, education, and father's politics
Demonstrated	.297	.228
Written to officials	.150	.078*
Attended meetings	.255	.175
Radical or liberal	.274	.209
Support revolutionaries	.219	.168
Change government	.187	.167
Guaranteed wage	.135	.107
Value social change	.242	.209
Help solve social problems	.207	.183
Liberalism (Factor I)	.326	.269
Social concern (Factor II)	.224	.200
Activism (Factor III)	.332	.242

*Significance level = .01, all others = .001

political measures. For example, if mysticism and political activism were both characteristics of the counterculture in the Bay Area, then both may be more common among the young than among the old, among the educated than among the uneducated, and perhaps among those from liberal backgrounds (which have been shown to be conducive to countercultural involvement) than among those from conservative backgrounds. If these factors were taken into account, the positive correlations between mysticism and political action might be reduced or even reversed.

But Table 34 also reports correlations controlling for these possibilities. The correlations in the right-hand column show the relations between the mysticism scale and each political item controlling for the possible effects of age, education, and father's political position.[24] In every instance, the correlations remain positive and are statistically significant. For example, there is a correlation of .228 between mysticism and having taken part in a demonstration, a correlation of .175 between mysticism and attendance at political meetings, and a correlation of .183 between mysticism and wanting to help solve social problems. The correlation between the mysticism scale and the political activism scale is .242.

24. As in previous chapters, education is adjusted to compensate for the fact that younger people have not yet finished their education.

Since the data suggest positive relations between mysticism and political action, we turn next to an examination of the links between mysticism and politics. We suggested earlier that some scholars, who have hypothesized a positive relation such as that evident here, have argued that mysticism may produce moral relativism which, in turn, becomes a basis for political action aimed at making the society more relativistic and tolerant. We also suggested that moral relativism and other ideas associated with mysticism may lead to liberalism which, in turn, encourages political involvement. We haven't the means to test these arguments in any detail. But since we have been able to develop crude measures of moral relativism and liberalism, let us see whether or not they "interpret" the relation between mysticism and political action. Since the causal order among the variables cannot be determined with data such as ours, collected at only one time, we simply introduce the variables in the logical order in which they have been presented.

As shown in Diagram 1, there is a positive relation between mysticism and moral relativism, as hypothesized, and a positive relation between mysticism and liberalism, as hypothesized. There is also a positive relation between moral relativism and liberalism, and both moral relativism and liberalism are positively associated with political activism. Together, moral relativism and liberalism account for a little over half of the total relation between mysticism and political activism. In other words, the data suggest that a significant part of the reason why mysticism and political activism are positively related may be that mysticism engenders moral relativism and liberalism, both of which seem conducive to political involvement.

Diagram 1. Path Model for Mysticism, Moral Relativism, Liberalism, and Political Activism

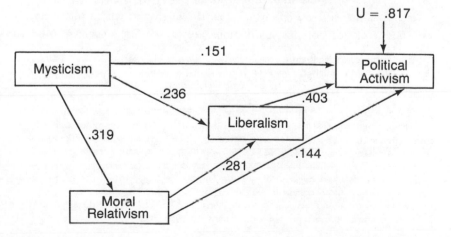

While these results are consistent with some of the arguments we have reviewed, they suggest, of course, that the relations between mysticism and politics in the Bay Area, to the extent that we have been able to measure them, seem to be different from those apparently having prevailed in the societies with which Weber and Troeltsch were concerned. This is not to say that Weber and Troeltsch were mistaken in their observations. But it does suggest that social conditions existing in different societies may affect the specific nature of the relations between mysticism and politics. Or, more specifically, if mysticism combines orientations that can lead to political withdrawal in some circumstances and to political action in other circumstances, then some attention needs to be given to these different circumstances. We can perhaps gain further insight into the contemporary relations between mysticism and politics, therefore, by briefly comparing them with those having existed in other contexts, paying special attention to the social circumstances affecting these relations.

A BRIEF CROSS-CULTURAL COMPARISON

Looking at mysticism historically and comparatively suggests that much of the variation in its relation with politics may be a function of two factors: the availability or unavailability of political channels, and the degree of institutional differentiation. These factors have proven helpful in the past for understanding differences in political activities in different societies.[25] And in the case of mysticism, they also seem to play an indirect role by influencing the character of the dominant religion.[26]

The availability or unavailability of political channels refers to the likelihood of ordinary citizens being able to influence either the selection of political elites or the formulation of social policy by these elites.[27]

Institutional differentiation refers to the degree to which relatively independent or autonomous institutions are present in a society. Modern

25. For example, see William Kornhauser, *The Politics of Mass Society* (Glencoe, Ill.: Free Press, 1959); Neil J. Smelser, *Theory of Collective Behavior* (New York: Free Press, 1962); and Talcott Parsons, *The System of Modern Societies* (Englewood Cliffs, N.J.: Prentice-Hall 1971).
26. See Robert N. Bellah, *Beyond Belief* (New York: Harper and Row, 1970), pp. 20–50.
27. It must be noted that the accessibility of political elites not only influences but is, in turn significantly influenced by religious action, as has been argued with reference to ascetic Protestantism by Michael Walzer, *The Revolution of the Saints: A Study in the Origin of Radical Politics* (New York: Atheneum, 1965), and by David Little, *Religion, Order, and Law: A Study in Pre-Revolutionary England* (New York: Harper and Row, 1969). But in the case of mysticism, which has everywhere been relatively minor in comparison with the larger religious institution (as Troeltsch notes), it seems appropriate to regard the availability of political channels more as a precondition than as a consequence of mysticism.

societies tend to be characterized by relatively high degrees of differentiation, while traditional societies tend to exhibit less differentiation and may be dominated by one or a few institutions, such as the family or the polity.

At the level of the individual, institutional differentiation is manifested as role differentiation—that is, the number of relatively autonomous sectors in which a person's behavior is divided, such as behavior in the roles of family member, employee, church member, and so on. It is important, as we shall see shortly, to recognize that members of the same society, as well as whole societies, may differ with respect to the number of differentiated roles into which their activities are divided.

Cross-classifying these two variables yields four societal configurations: (1) The combination of no political channels and low institutional differentiation yields what might be called "totalitarian" social conditions.[28] Not only is the average citizen cut off from decision-making powers, but the polity is infused in all areas of life. No autonomous institutions exist to shield the individual from political elites. Behavior cannot be compartmentalized into separate spheres or into "public" and "private" sectors. (2) The combination of no political channels and high institutional differentiation, which we might call "bureaucratic" social conditions, differs from the first chiefly in that the individual is "protected" from political elites to a greater extent.[29] The economy especially is likely to be better differentiated. In consequence, roles can be compartmentalized such that only a portion of one's behavior need have political implications. (3) The combination of available political channels and high institutional differentiation yields "pluralistic" conditions in which members of society are able to enter into the decision-making process but are prevented from focusing exclusively upon politics, or from exerting undue pressure upon political elites, by virtue of involvement in separate institutional roles. (4) The combination of available political channels and low institutional differentiation produces a "mass" society in which direct and encompassing pressure can be levied by the members of the society upon political elites.

Our hypothesis is that the relations between mysticism and politics have assumed different forms under these different combinations of social conditions. As far as the contemporary relations between mysticism and politics are concerned, we are suggesting that these relations have taken the form they have at least partly because of the character of the larger society. Let us

28. This classification draws heavily on Kornhauser, *The Politics of Mass Society*, although only parts of his model most relevant to the politics-mysticism relation have been introduced here.

29. Some justification for the use of the term "bureaucratic" can be found in S. N. Eisenstadt, *The Political Systems of Empires* (New York: Free Press, 1969), but the choice of exact descriptors is obviously somewhat arbitrary.

review briefly the relations that have existed in each of the four kinds of societies.

Mysticism Under Totalitarian Conditions. The characteristic political response of mysticism under conditions of inaccessible political elites and relatively little institutional differentiation seems to have been retreatism. The Islamic nations from approximately the 11th to the 16th centuries, the period when the great Sufi orders flourished, were typical of such conditions. A differentiated economy had not yet developed, nor had religion and polity become clearly differentiated. Political channels were relatively closed, especially to the mystic, because of the close connection between orthodox Islam and politics. The mystical Sufi *khānqāh* or converts typified retreatism, ardently rejecting all forms of worldly activity. Even so, the Sufi mystics frequently became targets of repression at the hands of the orthodox *ulama* and the more dogmatic *Shi'a*. As repression increased, especially during the 12th and 13th centuries, the Sufi monasteries became closed circles of initiates who withdrew from all secular activities.[30]

Also illustrative of totalitarian structural conditions were the Roman Empire, India especially from 100 to 400 A.D., and China during the Sung dynasty.[31] In each instance the dominant mystical orientation appears to have been withdrawal, as in the case of the Essenes and the Therapeutae in the Roman Empire and the Buddhist monasteries or *sangha* in China and India.[32]

The significance of accessible or inaccessible political channels seems especially evident in the development of Buddhism in India. Buddhism tended to champion quietistic withdrawal from the beginning, but ironically it attracted persons who were actively engaged in economic and social affairs, at least throughout the third century B.C., during which it enjoyed the patronage of Emperor Ashoka (accessible political channels). But with the Brahmanic counter-reformation, which cut off these channels, Buddhism became increasingly monastic and withdrew from active public involvement.[33]

The significance of an absence of differentiated institutions in such

30. A. J. Arberry, *Sufism: An Account of the Mystics of Islam* (London: George Allen and Unwin, 1950); and H. A. R. Gibb, *Mohammedanism* (London: Oxford University Press, 1962).

31. Parsons, *The System of Modern Societies.*

32. Ernst Muller, *History of Jewish Mysticism* (Oxford: East and West Library, 1946); John B. Noss, *Man's Religions*, 3rd ed. (New York: Macmillan, 1963); Charles Dreckmeier, *Kingship and Community in Early India* (Stanford: Stanford University Press, 1962); and Sukumar Dutt, *Buddhist Monks and Monasteries of India: Their History and Their Contribution to Indian Culture* (London: George Allen and Unwin, 1962).

33. Dreckmeier, *Kingship and Community in Early India.*

societies seems to be that this absence exacerbates withdrawal tendencies among mystics. Especially where religion and polity remain undifferentiated, mysticism poses a threat, not only to formalized religious teachings and practices, but to political authority as well. Consequently, mysticism is more likely to become the target of forceful oppression. In response to oppression, the mystical tendency is to withdraw. And since there is a relative absence of role differentiation, withdrawal takes place not only with regard to religious or political matters but from all secular affairs.

Mysticism and Bureaucratic Societies. The mystic's response to worldly affairs under conditions of unavailable political channels and relatively *high* institutional differentiation is what might best be termed "segmented service"—that is, involvement in worldly activity but limited to those activities that can be carried out within the confines of the religious institution. Mystics fail to become involved directly in political affairs, but seem to be less withdrawn than under totalitarian conditions. Charitable activities, teaching, and church reform become common activities of the mystic.

Differentiation between religion and the polity appears especially significant in producing segmented service rather than retreatism. As a separate institution, religion can incorporate mysticism into its structure without mysticism posing a political threat. The typical mode of accommodating mysticism under these conditions seems to be compartmentalization. The dominant religion itself provides the seedbed which nourishes mysticism, although internal controls tend to be applied to guard against it spreading too widely.

The late medieval period in Europe, during which separate institutions were already becoming relatively well differentiated, and during which political access had not yet become widespread, found mysticism primarily within monasteries and religious orders. In the Low Countries, the dominant center of mysticism was not in the well-known, independent Brethren of the Common Life, but in the Cistercian and Benedictine monasteries which produced figures such as Beatrice of Nazareth (13th c.), St. Lutgard of Tongres (13th c.), and Louis de Blois (16th c.). The Carthusian order also played a prominent role in the fourteenth century, fostering mystics such as Denis van Leeuwen, Lawrence Surius, and Richard Beaucousin, as did to a lesser extent the Franciscan and Carmelite orders.[34] In Italy, which in the tenth century was already becoming a more differentiated society, the Benedictine order functioned as a strong bastion of mysticism. In twelfth-century France, the Franciscan order and especially the abbey of St. Victor

34. Stephanus Axters, *The Spirituality of the Low Countries* (London: Aquin Press, 1954).

in Paris were the chief centers of mysticism.[35] In the Rhineland section of Europe in the thirteenth century, the Dominican monasteries came to be another center of mysticism.[36] And in the fourteenth and fifteenth centuries, the English Carthusian charterhouses provided another environment in which mysticism flourished.[37] "If mysticism and monasticism are not as inseparable as asceticism and cenobilitism," writes one observer, "they are, at least, practically mutalizing and reinforcing."[38]

Under these structural conditions, the extreme world-fleeing orientation of mysticism still seems somewhat evident. But some form of service to the larger religious institution seems to be more typical. During the twelfth and thirteenth centuries, for instance, Hugo St. Victor and Bonaventura took their mystical teachings into the schools of the church. Richard Rolle, the most widely known English mystic of the late medieval period, engaged in charitable works within the church. Catherine of Siena (14th c.) was in frequent contact with the Pope and made numerous tours throughout Italy to secure support from the clergy and laity for the Crusades. Ruysbroeck (14th c.) in Brussels, although profoundly mystical, served for some twenty-five years as chaplain to the clergy of St. Gudule. And Catherine of Genoa (15th c.) served for years as superintendent of the sick, and later as rector of the Genoese hospital.

It is also interesting to note that throughout the medieval period there was an increasing attempt among mystics to differentiate theologically between the contemplative and the active life in such a way that both were required for true spiritual purification. This reorientation can be seen particularly in St. Catherine, Ruysbroeck, and in the *Theologia Germanica* of the late fourteenth century.

It is well to observe that even though a higher degree of worldly activity seems evident under these conditions than under those where there is less institutional differentiation, this worldly activity still tends to be conducted quite apart from actual political involvement. That this is perhaps in large measure due to the absence of political channels is illustrated by an important "deviant case"—namely, Bernard of Clairveux, who, having personal access to the king of France, did not hesitate to become an outspoken critic of his policies.[39]

Mysticism in Pluralistic Societies. Under conditions of relatively high institutional differentiation and accessible political channels, mysticism seems to

35. Ray C. Petry, *Late Medieval Mysticism* (Philadelphia: Westminster Press, 1965).
36. David Knowles, *The English Mystical Tradition* (London: Burns and Oates, 1961), p. 34.
37. Eric Colledge, *The Medieval Mystics of England* (New York: Charles Scribner's Sons, 1961).
38. Petry, *Late Medieval Mysticism,* p. 20.
39. George W. Forrell, *Christian Social Teachings* (Garden City, N.Y.: Doubleday, 1966).

be associated with what might be termed "individuated participation" in political affairs—that is, participation by some individual mystics in politics, but no apparent tendency for mysticism more generally to be associated either with political involvement or withdrawal. On the one hand, mysticism may encourage political activism. John Woolman, successor to George Fox, was in the forefront of the anti-slavery movement in America. Toyohiko Kagawa was not only one of the most prominent Japanese mystics of the early twentieth century but was an ardent labor organizer as well. On the other hand, quietistic withdrawal from worldly affairs seems just as likely. Father Augustine Baker in revolutionary England illustrated well this ambiguity. A distinguished lawyer, he vacillated between periods in political office and periods spent in mystical withdrawal from worldly affairs, never able to fully integrate the two.[40]

The individuated form of mystical response to politics under "pluralist" conditions was especially evident among the American transcendentalists. Bronson Alcott represented the extreme quietistic response; George Ripley, Orestes Brownson, and Isaac Hecker combined the utopian communalism of Brook Farm with a more outspoken form of radical criticism of the polity; Thoreau actively engaged in civil disobedience in protest against the Mexican war; and Emerson found himself torn between all these alternative responses.

The reason for the individuated pattern of response seems to be found within the structure of "pluralist" society itself. Political channels are available and are not ordinarily dominated by established religion, so that the mystic tends not to be excluded out of hand from political participation. But the high degree of role differentiation present in pluralist society precludes any *necessary* connection between mysticism and politics. The high degree of differentiation between private and public life makes it possible for mysticism and politics to be largely compartmentalized from one another. An intense mystic like Hammarskjöld can lead a highly political public life but keep his private convictions to himself. Still, like non-mystics who remain apathetic toward politics, many mystics tend to remain apathetic too.

Mysticism in Mass Society. Structural conditions of a "mass society" character—that is, accessible political channels but relatively low institutional differentiation—may be characteristic of whole societies or may characterize some segments of societies more than others. For example, young people in an otherwise pluralist society may experience conditions of mass society to a greater extent than older people. This may occur because younger people tend to be less attached to the system of differentiated roles

40. Knowles, *The English Mystical Tradition*, pp. 151–187.

in the economy, the family, the church, and the community. Virtually all of their roles may be played within their own peer group, especially if they are isolated from the larger society—for example, as on many college campuses.

Structural conditions in a mass society appear optimum for a positive relation between mysticism and political activism. Not only is it possible to engage in political activity, but the alienative tendencies which seem to be inherent in mysticism seem unlikely to be compartmentalized strictly within the religious role and seem likely to "spill over" into political action. One clear example of this tendency appears to have been the *Wandervogel* movement that emerged in Germany after World War I. Under the mass society conditions prevailing in Germany at this time, this strongly mystical movement soon became politicized and served as an important seedbed for the nascent *Hitlerjugend*.[41]

Mass society conditions seem clearly to have characterized the counterculture of the late 1960s in which both mysticism and political activism flourished. Not only was it possible for mystics to engage in political activities, but persons within the counterculture seem to have experienced a relative absence of role differentiation, performing many of their roles among their own peer group and on campuses rather than in the differentiated institutions of the established society. Lacking clearly compartmentalized roles, it seems (as we have seen from the Bay Area data) that many who became involved with mysticism also became involved with political activism.

The Bay Area data, in fact, provided some direct evidence on the influence of differentiated roles and their absence. We were able to classify respondents according to the number of differentiated social institutions to which they were attached: the family (in that they were married); the economy (in that they placed great importance on job security and at least a fair amount of importance on high pay); the church (in that they were active in a church and placed at least a fair amount of importance on church activities); and the community (in that they hadn't moved within the past two years). These indicators allowed respondents to be classified on an index from 0 to 6, where 0 indicated low role differentiation, and 6 indicated high role differentiation. These were by no means adequate indicators, but they did give a crude indication of whether people were relatively more or less attached to a spectrum of conventional social institutions.

As Table 35 shows, those who most closely approximated pluralistic social conditions (in the sense that their roles were divided among a variety

41. Howard Becker, *German Youth: Bond or Free* (New York: Oxford University Press, 1946).

Table 35. MYSTICISM AND POLITICAL ACTIVISM BY ROLE DIFFERENTIATION

| | Role Differentiation | | | | | | |
	Low 0	1	2	3	4	5	High 6
Correlations between mysticism and activism	.47 (60)	.41 (145)	.37 (254)	.20 (248)	.17 (178)	.17 (87)	* (28)

*Not significant at .05 level.

Table 36. SUMMARY OF STRUCTURAL CONDITIONS AFFECTING THE RELATION BETWEEN MYSTICISM AND POLITICAL ACTION

Type	Political channels	Differentiation	Response of dominant religion	Form of political action
Totalitarian	–	–	repression	withdrawal
Bureaucratic	–	+	compartmentalization	segmented service
Pluralistic	+	+	coexistence	individuated participation
Mass	+	–	acceptance	activism

of major social institutions) were considerably less likely to show a positive relation between mysticism and political action than those who approximated mass society conditions (i.e., who were relatively detached from major social institutions). The correlations range from insignificance among those scoring 6 on the index (.17 among those scoring 5) to .47 among those scoring 0.[42]

To summarize, we have suggested that much of the historical and cross-cultural variation in the relations between mysticism and politics may be explainable by the combinations of available or unavailable political channels and weak or strong institutional differentiation. Table 36 summarizes the hypotheses we have suggested involving these social conditions.

CONCLUSION

The data from the Bay Area have shown positive relations between our measure of mysticism and our measures of political action. These positive relations seem consistent with some of the anecdotal accounts of mystics and political activists in the recent counterculture. But the prevailing imagery has probably tended to regard mysticism and political activism more as contradictory than as mutually compatible. The Bay Area data also indicated that these relations were not simply a function of mystics being younger, better educated, or from more liberal backgrounds than others.

The data we have examined in this chapter have clearly not allowed us to "test," either directly or adequately, any of the more general theories that students of religion have outlined regarding the possible relations between mysticism and politics. We did present some evidence, however, suggesting that one of the reasons why mysticism was positively associated with political action in the Bay Area may have been that mysticism tends to be associated with a morally relativistic outlook which, in turn, tends to be associated with an interest in politics as a way of reforming nonrelativistic social conditions. We also suggested that mysticism may be associated with a critical, "liberal" attitude toward social arrangements which, again, may be associated with political activities aimed at social reform.

The data from the Bay Area do not "refute" any of the arguments we reviewed from Weber and Troeltsch leading us to suspect negative relations between mysticism and politics. But the fact that the relations in the Bay Area seemed to be different from those which Weber and Troeltsch had observed in other societies led us to suggest that something further might

42. See Appendix Table A-6 for evidence that the interactive relation shown in Table 35 is significant; in other words, that the relation between mysticism and political action is significantly stronger under mass society conditions than under pluralistic conditions.

be learned about the contemporary relations between mysticism and politics by considering some of the broader social conditions possibly affecting these relations.

In particular, we suggested that positive relations between mysticism and political action in the Bay Area may have been facilitated by an availability of political channels, so that mystics *could* engage in political activity if they wished, and by relatively low institutional role differentiation, making it less likely for mystical religious ideas to be kept totally compartmentalized from political activities. From briefly comparing societies differing with regard to these two social conditons, we hypothesized that mysticism has probably been associated with political retreatism in societies lacking both political channels and institutional differentiation; that it has probably been associated with "segmented service" within the religious institution in societies lacking political channels but having greater institutional differentiation; that its political implications have probably been more a matter of individual predisposition in societies having both political channels and high institutional differentiation; and that it has probably been most likely to be associated with political activism in societies having political channels but lacking clear institutional differentiation of roles. These hypotheses remain very tentative, of course, since the societies illustrating the various social conditions have also differed in many other ways, some of which may have also affected the character of mysticism and its political implications.

In concluding, the discussion in this chapter has probably raised at least one more general question about the relation of religious belief systems to political action that also needs to be addressed briefly. The argument that mysticism's relation to political action will likely be different in different social settings can perhaps be regarded as merely another way of stating the assertion, so common among some social scientists, that belief systems really have little bearing on social actions, compared with the influence of more "objective" social conditions. But posing the matter in such terms necessarily oversimplifies the problem. A more fruitful perspective on belief systems and social action, we submit, is to recognize that any long-enduring belief system, such as mysticism (or ascetic Protestantism, for that matter), necessarily combines paradoxical and even contradictory assumptions. Mysticism seems to be intensely individualistic *and* communalistic, world-fleeing *and* acutely aware of the social influences of this world, rigidly ethical against political violence *and* morally relativistic, fatalistic with respect to society *and* fully aware of the dependence of society upon human constructions. By the same token, inner-worldly asceticism seems to be at once individualistic (as Weber stressed) *and* highly collectivistic, predestinarian *and* committed to the concept of free will, particularistic with regard to salvation *and* universalistic with regard to ethics, committed to the value of work *and* antagonistic to the pursuit of material success. Paradox seems to be an inveterate characteristic of belief systems. Therein, in fact, probably lies much of their strength and longevity. Because of the contradictory assumptions which tend to be welded together in belief systems, their effects probably cannot be fully specified from an examination of their cognitive elements alone. It seems necessary to ask, under what social conditions do different cognitive elements become *activated*? Once this has been determined and properly specified, it then becomes appropriate to examine the extent to which these assumptions reinforce and legitimate specific courses of social action.

In the case of contemporary mysticism, therefore, we have argued that more needs to be said than just reporting its perhaps anomalous (at least from a Weberian perspective) effect of encouraging political activisim. This effect may make sense in light of mysticism's moral relativism and generalized liberalism. But these elements would probably not predominate under totalitarian, bureaucratic, and perhaps not even under pluralistic conditions. The mass conditions seemingly present in at least some parts of American society have probably helped to lay the foundation for these aspects of mysticism to be activated as legitimations of political involvement.

CHAPTER 5

The Ethics of Peaking

Thus far, we have examined a variety of the phenomena that have been associated in one way or another with the new religious experimentation of recent years. Intense religious or transcendent experiences—what Abraham Maslow called "peak experiences"—seem to have been another of these phenomena.[1] Many of the new religious movements, including ones from both Eastern and Christian traditions, have been portrayed as advocates of the experiential dimension of religious commitment. Interest in peak experiences also seems to have been generated by the drug culture and by experimentation with other means of attaining altered states of consciousness.

Peak experiences, of course, are not necessarily religious, and they are by no means new. They are of immediate interest to us here as one of the ways that the new religions may be influencing the culture, if, indeed, they have been a source of the current interest in peak experiences. But because peak experiences are a more general phenomenon, we shall not attempt to limit our attention to those forms of experience specifically associated with the new religions. We shall be interested in examining some of the personal and ethical values that are seemingly reinforced by peak experiences more generally.

Many claims have been made about the nature of peak experiences and about their consequences. But, for the most part, these claims have been derived either from volunteered accounts or from clinical studies. Little effort has been made to examine them in broader, predefined samples from the general population. As a result, one finds frequent contradictions in the

1. Abraham Maslow, *Toward a Psychology of Being* (Princeton, N.J.: D. Van Nostrand, 1962) and *Religions, Values, and Peak-Experiences* (New York: Viking Press, 1970). Maslow characterizes peak experiences as "the most wonderful experience or experiences of your life, happiest moments, ecstatic moments, moments of rapture."

literature on peak experiences. There are conflicting claims, for example, about how rare or how common peak experiences are, about whether they are more common among self-actualizing persons or among persons with disturbed personalities, and about whether these experiences produce any significant social consequences or whether their consequences are strictly personal. This chapter uses the data from the Bay Area to supply some evidence on these questions.

THE INCIDENCE OF PEAK EXPERIENCES

The literature on peak experiences has been sharply divided as to how common these experiences are. Those who have given accounts of peak experiences have often described them as once-in-a-lifetime events per-ceived as happening only to a few especially fortunate persons. Yet it is conceivable that many people may have had such experiences and simply not bothered to record them. Maslow has suggested, in fact, that nearly everyone probably has had peak experiences of one sort or another and could probably describe them if investigators were to ask the right questions.

To find out how common or uncommon peak experiences were in the Bay Area, people in the survey were asked questions about three kinds of peak experiences. The first asked if people had "ever had the feeling that you were in close contact with something *holy or sacred*." The second asked about having "experienced the *beauty of nature* in a deeply moving way." And the third asked about "feeling that you were in *harmony with the universe*." Respondents were asked to state whether or not they had had each kind of experience. Those who had had each experience were also asked whether or not it had had a deep and lasting influence on their life. Those who had not had each experience were asked whether or not they would have liked to.

Table 37 shows the responses to these questions, indicating that these three kinds of peak experiences seem to be common to a wide cross-section of people in the Bay Area. One person in two had experienced contact with the holy or sacred, more than eight in ten had been moved deeply by the beauty of nature, and close to four in ten had experienced being in harmony with the universe. Of these, more than half in each case had had peak experiences which they said had had deep and lasting effects on their lives.

It is also of interest to note that people who had not had these peak experiences tended more often than not to say they would like to have them. More than three-fourths of those not having had a peak experience in nature said they would like to, as did about half of those not having had a mystical or a religious peak experience.

These results seem to suggest that peak experiences are not just the domain of mystics or artists or people with unusual talents for having such

Table 37. **FREQUENCY OF PEAK EXPERIENCES (Total Weighted Sample)**

| Response | Kind of experience: | | |
	Contact with the sacred	Beauty of nature	Harmony with the universe
Yes, and it has had a lasting influence on my life	27%	49%	22%
Yes, but it hasn't had a lasting influence on my life	23%	33%	17%
No, but I'd like to	25%	14%	34%
No, I don't care whether I ever do	25%	4%	27%
Total	100%	100%	100%
Number	(1000)	(1000)	(1000)

experiences, as has been suggested on occasion. The fact that so many people in the Bay Area say they have had these three kinds of experiences suggests that Maslow may have been right: if questions were asked about a variety of peak experiences, virtually everyone would probably have had at least one. In the present case, just asking about nature experiences and religious experiences showed that all but 12 percent had had at least one of these experiences.

We did not ask how often people had had peak experiences, but there is some indication that peak experiences may be relatively frequent occurrences, judging from the answers people gave about when they had had their last peak experience. Among those who had had a deep and lasting experience of the sacred, 47 percent had had such an experience within the past year, and 75 percent had had such an experience within the past five years. Among those having had a deep and lasting experience with nature, 70 percent had had one within the past year, and 90 percent had had one within the past five years. And those having had a lasting experience of harmony with the universe were even more likely to have had such an experience recently: 76 percent had had one within the past year, and 92 percent had had one within the past five years.

To gain some additional insight as to what these experiences were like, we also conducted depth-interviews with a small subsample of respondents. Their comments indicated that peak experiences tend to occur under the most diverse circumstances. For example, these are some of the descriptions given by those who had had peak experiences from nature:

Sometimes when I've been driving through the desert, I've just pulled off the road and walked out into the desert and just sat down and listened and felt part of it all. A very quiet peaceful feeling comes over me. It only happens when I'm completely alone in nature out of the sight of any man-made things.

When I'm out in the wilds it makes me realize in a deeper sense that I am as much a part of nature as the lakes and trees are a part of nature. It seems like the natural place to be, rather than in an office building.

The first time I saw the Grand Canyon it really bowled me over. I was awed at the way everything fit together somehow. That kind of experience helps you put things in perspective.

When we were traveling to Oregon for my grandmother's funeral, I saw a rainbow that was so unbelievably close it was as if it came right through the car. Physically I felt frightened at first and then enormously elated. I felt very much that it was a sign or a symbol of something. I'm still kind of coming to terms with it.

I'm very much turned on by the beach at night. All you can see is the waves. I have an affinity for the water and for the night. It takes me back to where I belong. I guess it's the slow smooth rhythm. The ocean makes me feel like I'm home.

These accounts give evidence of the diversity of peak experiences, yet they also suggest some similarities in the feelings they elicit. It seems important to note especially the intense feelings of meaning or, as Herbert Fingarette has put it, feelings that everything somehow "hangs together," that seem to result from these experiences.[2]

Such feelings are also evident in the accounts of those having experienced being in harmony with the universe:

I just feel that I'm here and am part of the universe. If I use what I've been given and what I've learned in some good way, I am in harmony with the universe. It writes the script for me, you might say.

The birth of my first child. I don't see how you could ever feel separate from anything when that happens. I treasure it and think of it at quiet times, and it has made my life more meaningful.

When I do meditation it kind of reassures me that the Absolute exists. Doing meditation has given me a number of experiences in which I have felt more sensitive to the universe. You don't see things around you as objects to be used by you, but you feel a part of them. You begin to appreciate the life-giving force, the energy that lives within them. You begin to have a higher regard for all living things.

Not everyone who was interviewed, of course, had had such dramatic or vivid experiences as these or ones with such long-lasting effects. As already seen in Table 37, nearly half of those who had had each experience claimed it had not had a lasting effect on their lives.

In sum, even though most people in the sample seem to have had peak experiences at one time or another, it also appears that some may be more "into" what Maslow called "peaking" than others. If so, the data afford an opportunity to explore what people may be like who are most heavily

2. Herbert Fingarette, *The Self in Transformation: Psychoanalysis, Philosophy and the Life of the Spirit* (New York: Harper and Row, 1963).

oriented toward peak experiences. Do they manifest distinctive patterns of life or are they like everyone else?

PEAKING AS A WAY OF LIFE

Maslow has suggested that "peakers" (that is, people who have intense peak experiences and who are oriented toward valuing these experiences) tend to exhibit a distinctive style of life—namely, that of the self-actualizing person. For example, Maslow has written that the person who has had intense peak experiences tends to be "more apt to feel that life in general is worthwhile, even if it is usually drab, pedestrian, painful, or undergratifying, since beauty, excitement, honesty, play, goodness, truth and meaningfulness have been demonstrated to him to exist."[3] Some clinical evidence, chiefly with patients having been the subjects of psychedelic-induced peak experiences, tends to confirm Maslow's suggestion, finding that peak experiences tend to produce greater feelings of self-confidence and a deeper sense of meaning and purpose.[4]

But not everyone has agreed that peaking is associated with a more fully functioning style of life. Some have regarded these experiences more as a sign of some state of meaninglessness, anomie, or pathology. One psychologist, for example, has suggested that mystical experiences may be associated with pathological regression.[5] In a similar vein, another has suggested that persons having mystical and similar kinds of experiences have been extremely antinomian personalities throughout history, unable to cope with their problems or with the problems of living in a larger social context.[6]

From the available literature, therefore, we may be led on the one hand to expect peakers to be self-actualizing persons, and on the other hand to expect them to be psychologically deprived if not actually pathological. Another expectation, of course, is that they may be no different from anyone else. Much of Marghanita Laski's provocative material on ecstasy, for example, suggests that ecstatic experiences simply happen to people as "bolts from the blue." They neither expect nor particularly desire these experiences, and although they may treasure them, they may be changed little by

---

3. Maslow, *Toward a Psychology of Being,* p. 95.
4. C. J. Savage, R. Fadiman, R. Mogar, and M. Allen, "The Effects of Psychedelic Therapy on Values, Personality, and Behavior," *International Journal of Neuropsychiatry* 2 (1966): 241–254; and R. Mogar, "Current Status and Future Trends in Psychedelic (LSD) Research," *Journal of Human Psychology* 2 (1965): 147–166, reprinted in Charles T. Tart (ed.), *Altered States of Consciousness* (Garden City, N.Y.: Doubleday, 1972), pp. 391–408.
5. R. Prince, "Mystical States and the Concept of Regression," *Psychedelic Review* 8 (1966); reprinted in John White (ed.), *The Highest State of Consciousness* (Garden City, N.Y.: Doubleday, 1972), pp. 114–134.
6. Nathan Adler, *The Underground Stream: New Life Styles and the Antinomian Personality* (New York: Harper and Row, 1972).

having had them.[7] These different views, therefore, give radically different clues as to what the broader meaning and consequences of the current interest in peak experiences may be.

Our data, designed primarily for testing other kinds of propositions, did not afford an opportunity to examine the personalities or life styles of peakers in detail. They do shed some light on the alternative hypotheses just mentioned, however. Among the questions germane to this controversy, one asked simply whether people were finding their lives very meaningful, fairly meaningful, not meaningful, or whether they didn't think about meaning. Another question, designed to see how introspective people were about their lives, asked how much, if any, they thought about the purpose of life: a lot, some, some in the past but none now, or never. Along the same lines as this question, another one asked if people actually spent times meditating about their lives, either using formal meditation techniques or not using such techniques. Another question asked how settled people were as to whether they felt they knew the answer to the age-old question, what is the purpose of life? Finally, a brief attempt was made to find out how self-assured people felt about themselves by asking them to say how much or how little of each of a dozen kinds of talents they had; for example, the ability to make things, the ability to organize well, intelligence, self-confidence, and so forth.

The data indicate that peakers do differ on these kinds of questions from nonpeakers. Peakers apparently find their lives more meaningful, feel more assured of themselves, and think about questions of meaning and purpose more often than nonpeakers. The data in Table 38 show these relations. The table shows how people having had each of the three kinds of experiences differ from those who haven't. Five groups are compared: those having had each experience in a deep and lasting way within the past year; those having had each experience in a deep and lasting way but not within the past year; those having had the experience but not in a deep and lasting way; those who haven't had the experience but would like to; and those who haven't had and wouldn't care to have the experience. The table shows the percentage of each group who have the characteristics listed in the left-hand column.

Each of the three peak experience questions shows virtually the same results. Those who have had each experience, and especially those who say they have had it in a deep and lasting way, are more likely than others to feel that their lives are very meaningful, to think a lot about the purpose of life and to meditate about their lives, to feel they know what the purpose of life is, and to feel assured about their own capabilities. For example, 68 percent

7. M. Laski, *Ecstasy: A Study of Some Secular and Religious Experiences* (London: The Cresset Press, 1961).

Table 38. PERSONAL CORRELATES OF PEAK EXPERIENCES (Total Weighted Sample)

	Response to each peak experience item:				
	Yes, within 1 year	Yes, not within 1 year	Yes, but not lasting	No, but would like to	No, and wouldn't care to
Experience: Contact with the sacred					
Life very meaningful	68%	46%	46%	39%	36%
Think about purpose a lot	54%	41%	28%	24%	19%
Meditate	82%	78%	71%	66%	55%
Know purpose of life	65%	44%	30%	18%	21%
Self-assured*	47%	39%	39%	22%	31%
Number	(127)	(141)	(231)	(252)	(242)
Experience: The beauty of nature					
Life very meaningful	55%	40%	39%	41%	36%
Think about purpose a lot	39%	29%	26%	23%	12%
Meditate	80%	72%	62%	53%	40%
Know purpose of life**	33%	35%	31%	25%	23%
Self-assured*	45%	28%	28%	24%	26%
Number	(342)	(147)	(325)	(137)	(46)
Experience: Harmony with the universe					
Life very meaningful	63%	54%	46%	37%	40%
Think about purpose a lot	49%	54%	26%	24%	22%
Meditate	86%	91%	79%	66%	47%
Know purpose of life**	39%	50%	29%	25%	33%
Self-assured*	55%	38%	36%	26%	26%
Number	(169)	(53)	(168)	(335)	(266)

* Average score of 1 or 2 on 4-point scale.   **Not significant at .05 level (chi square).

of those who have experienced contact with the sacred within the past year say their lives are very meaningful, compared with 46 percent of those who have had such an experience but not within the past year or not with lasting effects, 39 percent of those who haven't had such an experience but would like to, and 36 percent of those who haven't had such an experience and don't care to.

An important observation to be made from these data is that peak experiences seem not to be just isolated phenomena, but seem to be part of a broader style of life, a reflective, inner-directed, self-aware, self-confident style. Although the data do not say for sure, Maslow's view that peakers tend to be self-actualizing persons seems to be consistent with the data.

As further evidence for this conclusion, Table 39 divides the sample into three groups: "high peakers," "average peakers," and "nonpeakers." This division is made simply on the basis of the range of peak experiences each person had had, high peakers being those having had all three kinds in a deep and lasting way, average peakers having had only one or two in a deep and lasting way, and nonpeakers having had none of the three experiences in a deep and lasting way. Again, it is evident that the high peakers are most likely, and nonpeakers least likely, to feel that their lives are meaningful, to think about the purpose of life, to meditate, to feel that they know what the purpose of life is, and to feel assured of their own talents.[8]

THE ETHICAL EFFECTS OF PEAKING

If peaking is part of a more general, reflective style of life, perceived as being meaningful and as having a purpose, does this pattern of life have consequences for the way in which a person lives and relates to others? Maslow has suggested that it has extremely important consequences. He has argued that the self-actualizing person, as someone who is more at peace with himself or herself than the average person, should be able to rise above many of the petty concerns that are culturally ingrained on a wide scale, and pursue values that are more humanly beneficial.   •

One such trait that Maslow suggests is manifested among peak experiencers is a sub-average concern for material possessions. The peak experience presumably lifts persons to an expanded state of consciousness, as we suggested in discussing its relations with ESP, creating distance from the pursuit of material goods. In addition, the introspective style of life of the peak experiencer is itself in some respects alien to the more rationalistic and technological assumptions characterizing the materialist.[9] Other writers have made similar arguments, claiming, for instance, that LSD experi-

8. All the relations shown in Table 39 are significant at or beyond the .05 level.
9. See Maslow, *Toward a Psychology of Being*, p. 22.

Table 39. **PERSONAL CORRELATES BY PEAK EXPERIENCE TYPOLOGY (Total Weighted Sample)**

	Percentage having each characteristic listed at the left among those who are:		
	High peakers	*Average peakers*	*Non-peakers*
Life very meaningful	65%	48%	35%
Think about purpose a lot	59%	33%	19%
Meditate	88%	75%	55%
Know purpose of life	46%	36%	22%
Self-assured	53%	36%	26%
Number	(96)	(496)	(397)

ences decrease interest in material possessions and that mystical experiences historically have been associated with a renunciation of material values. [10]

The arguments for why peak experiences should be associated with devaluation of material pursuits seem compelling. However, they had been made mostly in the absence of solid evidence. Often the evidence cited consists only of extreme cases in point, such as the lives of Buddha, Schweitzer, or Thoreau. The question remains open as to whether peak experiences are related to a rejection of material values in any statistically significant sense or whether this conclusion has resulted from selective observations.

Our data afford an exploratory test of the relation between peaking and material values. Respondents were asked to sort 17 cards, each containing a value, into four piles ranging from great importance to no importance. Then they were asked to choose the three cards containing the values which were most important of all to them. Three of the values concerned material possessions: having a beautiful home, a new car, and other nice things; having a high-paying job; and having job security. Table 40 shows the relation between these values and being a high, average, or nonpeaker. All of the comparisons tend to support the hypothesis. Nonpeakers tend to be most likely to attach importance to these values, followed by average peakers, with the high peakers being least likely to consider them important. Thus, only 11 percent of the high peakers include any of these among their most important values, compared with 28 percent of the average peakers, and 49 percent of the nonpeakers. [11]

A second consequence of peak experiences that the literature has em-

10. See Mogar, "Current Status and Future Trends in Psychedelic (LSD) Research"; and C. Owens, "The Mystical Experience: Facts and Values," *Main Currents in Modern Thought* 23 (1967), reprinted in John White (ed.), *The Highest State of Consciousness*, pp. 135–152.
11. All the relations shown in Table 40 are significant at or beyond the .05 level.

Table 40. **MATERIALISTIC VALUES BY PEAK EXPERIENCE TYPOLOGY (Total Weighted Sample)**

	High peakers	Average peakers	Non-peakers
Percent giving *great importance to:*			
Beautiful home, new car, nice things	4%	14%	18%
Having a high-paying job	3%	20%	24%
Having job security	30%	42%	48%
Percent listing one of above among three most impor-tant values	11%	28%	49%
Number	(96)	(496)	(397)

phasized is that they may encourage people to be less status-conscious.[12] Again, the argument has been that peak experiences help people rise above such concerns, causing them to believe that social status is not important. But, again, no systematic data have been presented to substantiate or refute this argument.

Included in the survey were two questions concerning status consciousness: valuing becoming famous and valuing having a lot of friends. As Table 41 reports, the data are somewhat inconsistent but in general tend to support the notion that peakers are somewhat less concerned with having high status than nonpeakers. Only 4 percent of the total sample placed great importance on becoming famous; however, this proportion drops to only 1 percent among high peakers and rises to 5 percent among nonpeakers. The other item—having a lot of friends—shows virtually no differences between high, average, and nonpeakers. When asked to list their three most important values, however, high peakers were considerably less likely than the nonpeakers to choose one of these two items; only 9 percent do, compared with 19 percent of the average peakers, and 30 percent of the nonpeakers.[13]

12. Mogar, "Current Status and Future Trends in Psychedelic (LSD) Research."
13. The relations between peaking and valuing becoming famous and listing one of the status values among the top three (shown in Table 41) are significant at the .05 level; the relation with valuing a lot of friends is not significant.

Table 41. **STATUS CONSCIOUSNESS BY PEAK
EXPERIENCE TYPOLOGY
(Total Weighted Sample)**

	High peakers	Average peakers	Non-peakers
Percent giving *great importance to:*			
Becoming famous	1%	4%	5%
Having a lot of friends	33%	33%	34%
Percent listing one of above among three most important values	9%	19%	30%
Number	(96)	(496)	(397)

A third possible correlate of peak experiences about which the data afford some information is social concern—that is, concern with such matters as helping others or helping to eradicate social problems. Maslow, along with several other students of peak experiences, has argued that by making people more confident about themselves peak experiences may free people to become more concerned about the needs of others. Again the present data lend some support to this notion. Three of the values that respondents were asked to choose among were: working for major changes in our society; helping solve social problems such as poverty and air pollution; and giving time to help people who are in need. Table 42 shows that all three of these values are more likely to be valued highly by the high peakers than by the nonpeakers. For example, 79 percent of the high peakers include one of these among their most important values, in comparison with 52 percent of the other respondents.[14]

On the whole, these results from the Bay Area suggest that peak experiences seem not to be events affecting only people's private lives; they also seem to be related to how people orient themselves to the culture and to the society in which they live. What the present data don't show, of course, since they were collected at only one point in time, is which comes first— having peak experiences or being disinterested in material possessions and social status and interested in social concerns. More than likely, however, even experimental data would show that the relation works in both direc-

14. All the relations shown in Table 42 are significant at or beyond the .05 level.

Table 42. **SOCIAL CONCERN BY PEAK EXPERIENCE TYPOLOGY (Total Weighted Sample)**

	High peakers	Average peakers	Non-peakers
Percent giving great importance to:			
Working for social changes	46%	30%	21%
Helping solve social problems	56%	37%	29%
Helping people in need	68%	49%	41%
Percent listing one of above among three most important values	79%	52%	52%
Number	(96)	(496)	(397)

tions. Peak experiences would probably tend to nourish these other values as well as being nourished by them. Another question left open, though, is whether or not the above relations may be spurious. For instance, it may be that high peakers are less materialistic, less status-conscious, and more socially concerned simply because they are young, or educated, or female, or because of some other factors.

While the present data do not permit ruling out entirely the possibility that the above relations may be spurious, they do permit some of the factors conceivably capable of explaining away these relations to be examined. For any third factor to be the "true cause" of the above associations, it would have to be related, first, to the likelihood or unlikelihood of being a high peak experiencer. Thus, some factors can be ruled out by virtue of not being related in this way.

Table 43 shows the relations between the peak experience typology and a variety of background characteristics that might be expected to be related to having peak experiences. Being young, for example, might be expected to show a relation with having peak experiences, since many of the new religions that appeal predominately to the young (as seen in Chapter 1) seem to stress the experiential dimension of religion. Females have often been thought to be more attuned to the experiential than males. The educated, perhaps being more aware of new religions and possibly more exposed to drugs, art, and other potential sources of peak experiences, might develop

Table 43. BACKGROUND CHARACTERISTICS BY PEAK EXPERIENCE TYPOLOGY (Total Weighted Sample)

	High peakers	Average peakers	Non-peakers
Age:*			
16 through 30	29%	34%	32%
31 through 50	36%	34%	38%
51 and over	36%	32%	30%
Number	(96)	(496)	(397)
Sex:*			
Female	65%	55%	57%
Male	35%	45%	43%
Number	(96)	(496)	(397)
Education:**			
Some college	65%	54%	45%
High school or less	35%	46%	55%
Number	(85)	(410)	(324)
Marital status:*			
Never married	23%	28%	26%
Married	77%	72%	74%
Number	(96)	(496)	(397)
Employment status:*			
In labor force	64%	62%	63%
Not in labor force	36%	38%	37%
Number	(96)	(496)	(397)

*Not significant at .05 level (chi square).

**Age 16 to 22 excluded; i.e., figures include only those old enough to have gone to college.

a greater propensity to have peak experiences than the uneducated. People not integrated into conventional family patterns or into the labor force might be expected to have peak experiences more commonly than average simply because they have more time for such pursuits. Of these factors, however, only education appears to be significantly related to peak experiences. Whereas 65 percent of the high peakers have been to college, only

45 percent of the nonpeakers have. On all the other items, high peakers, average peakers, and nonpeakers show virtually the same percentages. While it may be that other factors about which data were not obtained are related to peak experiences, those items examined here indicate that only education seems to be a possible third factor that could account for the relations between peak experiences and the above values.

It is plausible that education may be such a third factor, for the educated would probably be in the best position to devote themselves to activities such as helping others, rather than pursuing status or material goods. The relations shown in Table 44, however, indicate that education does not explain away the effects of peak experiences. Both among those with some college education and among those without any college education, being a high peaker is associated with lower degrees of emphasis on material possessions and on status and with a greater emphasis on social concerns than among either the average peakers or the nonpeakers.[15]

CONCLUSION

With the data from the Bay Area, we have been able to engage in little more than an exploratory investigation of peak experiences. Nevertheless, the fact that these data, unlike almost all past information on peak experiences, have come from a systematic sample of people in a general community has shown some interesting results. We have seen, first, that peak experiences seem to occur widely in the Bay Area. Virtually everyone in the sample appeared to have had them of one kind or another. The data also indicated that peak experiences seemed to be about equally common among the young and the old and among men and women. They did appear to be somewhat more common among the educated than the uneducated. But this may have been a function of the way in which the present questions were worded.

The data have also suggested that peak experiences do not appear to be mere chance occurrences that have little to do with the rest of a person's life. Instead, they appear to be but one, although a significant, aspect of a reflective style of life. The Bay Area data have given no hint that peak experiences are, as some have suggested, more common among pathological types of personalities. Rather, having peak experiences seems to be associated with introspective, self-aware, self-assured personalities.

With regard to the ethical implications of peaking, the data have suggested that peak experiencers do, as Maslow suspected, exhibit some important differences in values from nonpeakers. In the Bay Area, they

15. All the relations shown in Table 44 are significant at or beyond the .05 level.

Table 44. **MATERIALISM, STATUS CONSCIOUSNESS, AND SOCIAL CONCERN BY PEAK EXPERIENCE TYPOLOGY, CONTROLLING FOR EDUCATION (Total Weighted Sample)**

	High peakers	*Average peakers*	*Non-peakers*
Materialism (percent listing one among three most important values):			
Some college or more	16%	26%	47%
Number	(55)	(216)	(139)
High school or less	5%	32%	49%
Number	(30)	(188)	(176)
Status conscious-ness (percent listing one among three most important values):			
Some college or more	3%	16%	31%
Number	(55)	(216)	(139)
High school or less	15%	19%	28%
Number	(30)	(188)	(176)
Social concern (percent listing one among three most important values):			
Some college or more	79%	53%	54%
Number	(55)	(216)	(139)
High school or less	65%	50%	48%
Number	(30)	(188)	(176)

appear to be less materialistic, less status-conscious, and more socially concerned than nonpeakers.

This last finding may be especially worthy of further attention. Although a great deal of interest has been shown in peak experiences in recent years, practically all of this interest has been devoted to describing the purely psychological (and physiological) characteristics of these experiences. Scarcely any attention has been given to their social significance. Certainly, it seems important to understand the psychological and physiological processes that take place during the course of these experiences. The significance of peak experiences somehow seems greater to us, if it can be shown that they have therapeutic effects for individuals; for example, that they can be used to cure states of depression, that they can make people happier, that they can enable people to better cope with anxiety and frustration, or that they can simply make people more aware of their own human potential.

But, at the same time, the social potential of peak experiences should not be neglected. If they have none, this should be documented. However, if these experiences do encourage people to be less concerned about status and possessions and more concerned with helping others, as the Bay Area data have suggested, this possibility needs to be explored. It needs to be understood so that its potential for relieving such problems as social disintegration, prejudice, or poverty can be made known. This is especially the case at present, since much of the energy spent during the 1960s in pursuit of social and political reforms appears to have survived only in more religious, more introspective pursuits.

This concludes our inquiries about the various experimental phenomena, popularly associated in recent years with the new religions, on which the Bay Area data have provided some evidence. Much of what we have learned deserves further comment in order to place it in some larger context. This can best be done, however, after first examining some of the data concerning the religious mainstream.

II. THE RELIGIOUS MAINSTREAM

CHAPTER 6

The Counterculture
and Conventional Religion

The chapters in the foregoing section were concerned with various aspects of the recent religious experimentation on which the Bay Area data provided some information. The chapters in this section concern the religious mainstream. The aim of these chapters is to examine several of the developments having taken place in mainstream religion during the recent period in which the new religions emerged. This chapter investigates the extent of declines in commitment to organized religion during the 1960s and early 1970s and attempts to formulate a theory accounting for these trends.

RECENT TRENDS IN ORGANIZED RELIGION

During the past quarter century, a reversal seems to have taken place in the direction of American religious commitment. This reversal has been commented upon frequently in the literature on religion and seems to be well-evidenced from empirical indicators. During the 1950s, a so-called religious revival was widely commented upon as the major religious development of the decade.[1] Virtually all religious indicators, except perhaps theologically conservative belief, demonstrated growth during this period (although it remains unclear whether this was an extension of longer-range growth or was unique to the post-war period).[2] During the 1960s and early 1970s, in comparison, the majority view among students of religion and among the general public seems to have been that commitment to or-

1. Among other discussions, see Charles Y. Glock and Rodney Stark, *Religion and Society in Tension* (Chicago: Rand McNally, 1965), Chapter 4.
2. See Seymour Martin Lipset, "Religion in America: What Religious Revival?," *Columbia University Forum* 2 (1959): 12.

ganized religion for the most part was declining, even though there was apparently some growth in conservative churches and, of course, in the new religious movements.[3]

The direction of these religious trends can be seen by examining some of the standard indicators on which annual records have been kept, such as religious contributions, religious degrees, religious book publishing, church construction, church attendance, and religious belief. These indicators give different estimates of the absolute strength of organized religion, but they largely tend to document similar trends.

One religious statistic on which annual records have been kept over the past several decades, and one often used as a rough indication of commitment to organized religion, is religious contributions. The data on religious contributions from 1950 to 1973 are reported in Figure 1.[4] In absolute amounts, contributions to organized religion climbed steadily from $1.1 billion in 1950 to $4.8 billion in 1973, a substantial increase even when adjusted to compensate for inflation. In comparison with the rest of the economy, religious contributions also rose, but only till 1961, reaching a high of 0.65 percent of the national personal income for that year. After 1961, religious contributions declined steadily as a proportion of personal income, averaging about 0.48 percent during the early 1970s.

Another indicator of commitment to organized religion on which annual figures have been kept is the number of college degrees granted in religion each year. Figure 2 reports the numbers granted each year between 1950 and 1972.[5] The numbers grew each year until 1960, from about 6,300 to 9,000. Between 1960 and 1967 they declined, dropping to about 8,100. After 1967, the trends were generally upward, reaching almost 9,500 in 1972. As a proportion of all college degrees granted, those in religion increased each year between 1950 and 1955, from 1.45 percent to 2.68

3. Discussions in the sociology of religion of this decline include Harvey Cox, *The Secular City* (London: S.C.M., 1965); Charles Y. Glock (ed.), *Religion in Sociological Perspective: Essays in the Empirical Study of Religion* (Belmont, Calif.: Wadsworth, 1973), especially Chapter 20; and Robert Wuthnow and Charles Y. Glock, "Religious Loyalty, Defection, and Experimentation among College Youth," *Journal for the Scientific Study of Religion* 12 (June 1973): 157–180. For a dissenting view, see Andrew M. Greeley, *The Denominational Society: A Sociological Approach to Religion in America* (Glenview, Ill.: Scott, Foresman, 1972); and Andrew M. Greeley, *Unsecular Man: The Persistence of Religion* (New York: Schocken, 1972). Evidence on public perceptions of declining strength in the churches has been discussed in N. J. Demerath, III, "Trends and Anti-Trends in Religious Change," in Eleanor Bernert Sheldon and Wilbert E. Moore (eds.), *Indicators of Social Change: Concepts and Measurements* (New York: Russell Sage, 1968), pp. 349–448. The apparent growth of religious commitment during the 1960s in the small conservative churches has been discussed in Dean M. Kelley, *Why Conservative Churches are Growing* (New York: Harper & Row, 1971).
4. These data are from the *Yearbook of American Churches*, 1960–1973; and the *Statistical Abstract of the United States*, 1952–1974.
5. Source: *United Nations Statistical Yearbook*, 1953–1972.

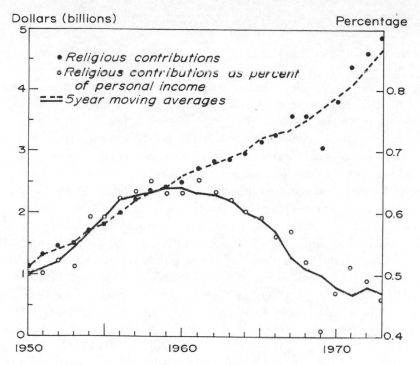

Figure 1. Trends in Religious Contributions

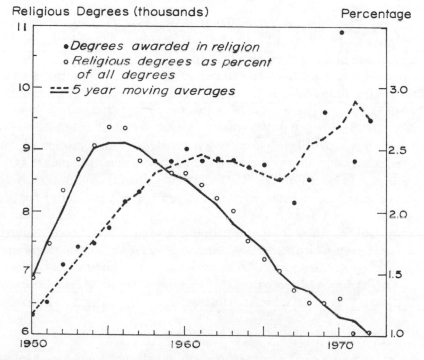

Figure 2. Trends in Religious Degrees

percent. But since 1955 the proportions have decreased continuously to
1.00 percent in 1972, lower than the 1950 figure. In other words, the
growth in religious education has failed to keep pace with that in other areas
of higher education, and even in absolute terms it suffered a substantial
setback during the 1960s.

Figures on religious book publishing, reported annually by UNESCO,
afford another crude longitudinal indicator of religious commitment in the
culture. These figures manifest somewhat different patterns, although the
overall trend appears much the same as that for religious contributions and
religious degrees (see Figure 3).[6] The number of religious books published
each year increased pretty much continuously from 1950 until the middle
1960s, from around 700 to more than 2,000 in 1967. During the late
1960s and early 1970s, however, these trends faltered. By 1972, after
several years of drastic fluctuation, the number was back approximately to
where it had been in 1964. As a proportion of all books published, the
trends for religious books divide roughly into three periods. From 1950 to
1958, the proportions increased; from 1958 to about 1968, they decreased
gradually; and from 1968 to 1972, they decreased more precipitously.
Overall, therefore, the data on religious books also suggest that something
happened during the 1960s to make religious trends different from what
they had been in the 1950s.

Another set of statistics often used as an indicator of religious strength is
the annual value of expenditures for the construction of new church buildings, which in turn reflects membership size, contributions, endowments,
economic conditions, and other factors.[7] Figure 4 shows what the trend in
these expenditures looks like when adjusted to take inflation into account.
There is a progressive increase from about half a billion dollars in 1950 to
more than $1.2 billion in 1965 (based on 1967 prices), although the rate of
growth is considerably less after 1960 than before. From 1965 onward, the
trend is reversed. Construction expenditures drop steadily, dipping to $644
million in 1973 (at 1967 prices). While construction expenditures doubled
during the fifties, therefore, they fell by approximately half during the late
sixties.

Probably the most familiar of all religious indicators is weekly church
attendance, on which comparable data have been made available for several
decades by the Gallup poll.[8] The evidence on church attendance shows
trends similar to those seen from the other indicators already examined (see
Figure 5). There was a substantial increase in weekly church-going between

6. Source: *UNESCO Statistical Yearbook*, 1967–1973.
7. Source: *Yearbook of American Churches*, 1960–1973.
8. George H. Gallup, *The Gallup Poll: Public Opinion, 1935–1971*. (New York: Random
House, 1972).

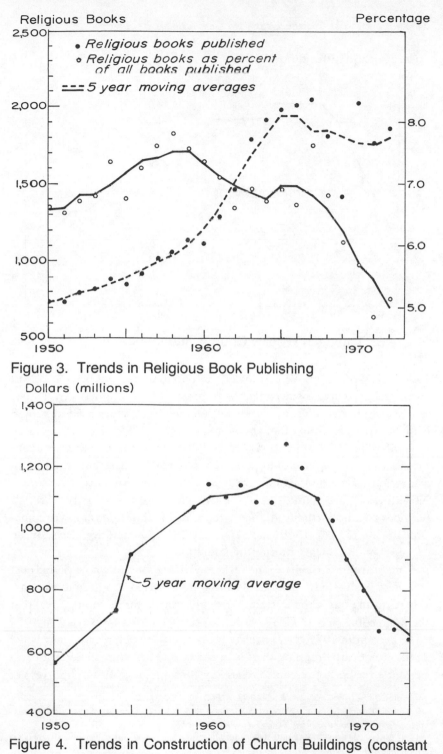

Figure 3. Trends in Religious Book Publishing

Figure 4. Trends in Construction of Church Buildings (constant dollars, 1967 = 1)

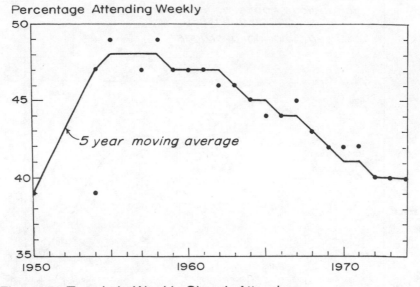

Figure 5. Trends in Weekly Church Attendance

1950 and 1955, from 39 percent of the population to 49 percent. Until 1961, the percentages stayed relatively constant, varying between 47 percent and 49 percent. Then, between 1961 and 1974, church-going fell off little by little, leveling off at about 40 percent.

Perhaps no ready conclusions can be drawn from these indicators about the exact pattern of recent religious trends. As others have noted, different dimensions of religious commitment probably vary differently over time.[9] Nonetheless, these indicators uniformly show the nonlinearity of recent religious trends. Virtually all show a tapering off of religious growth sometime during the late 1950s and very early 1960s; a majority also show an appreciable downswing during the late 1960s.

Data on religious beliefs, though unavailable for the whole period just considered, also show that the 1960s were a period of religious decline. Figures from polls of the Detroit metropolitan area, for example, reveal that the proportion "sure of God's existence" dropped from 68 percent in 1959 to 48 percent in 1971.[10] On a related belief, Gallup poll results show belief in life after death dropping sharply in the late 1960s from 76 percent to 53 percent after having remained relatively constant since 1944.[11] Surveys of

9. Glock and Stark, *Religion and Society in Tension,* Chapter 2.
10. Otis Dudley Duncan, Howard Schuman, and Beverly Duncan, *Social Change in a Metropolitan Community* (New York: Russell Sage, 1973).
11. Gallup, *The Gallup Poll;* and Hazel Gaudet Erskine, "The Polls: Personal Religion," *Public Opinion Quarterly* 29 (1965): 145–157.

college students also indicate that religious commitment declined during the 1960s after having risen throughout the 1940s and early 1950s.[12]

To summarize, the period during which the new religious movements flourished was one in which commitment to the religious mainstream seems to have withered, not to the point of collapse by any means, but certainly to a noticeable degree in comparison with the growth it had previously experienced. By the late 1960s or early '70s, every available indicator of organizational strength in the churches seems to have resided at a lower level than a decade previously. Why? What caused the abrupt reversal of religious trends during the 1960s?

POSSIBLE EXPLANATIONS

Approached sociologically, religious trends such as those just observed have usually been accounted for by reference to some dimension of the modernization process—for example, industrial expansion, gradual upgrading in education and diffusion of scientific knowledge, urbanization, or professionalization.[13] Implicit in these explanations has been the assumption that societies gradually become more and more secular or "disenchanted" as they modernize. A sudden downtrend in religious commitment, therefore, would cause one to suspect that some prior relatively abrupt spurt had occurred in the modernization process.

But the downward trend of the 1960s in religion does not seem explainable in terms of ordinary modernization-secularization theories. In contrast to the nonlinear or discontinuous patterns in religious indicators since 1950, most indicators of modernization—GNP, industrial productivity, energy consumption, enrollment in higher education, scientific publications, expenditures on science, and basic inventions—have shown nearly

12. Dean R. Hoge, *Commitment on Campus: Changes in Religion and Values over Five Decades* (Philadelphia: Westminster, 1974).

13. A. MacIntyre, *Secularization and Moral Change* (London: Oxford University Press, 1967), emphasizes the role of industrial expansion in religious change, as does Peter L. Berger, *The Scared Canopy: Elements of a Sociological Theory of Religion* (Garden City, N.Y.: Doubleday, 1969). Gradual upgrading of education and diffusion of science have been stressed by Vernon Pratt, *Religion and Secularization* (London: Macmillan, 1970); and by Charles Y. Glock, "Consciousness and Youth," in Charles Y. Glock and Robert N. Bellah (eds.), *The New Religious Consciousness* (Berkeley and Los Angeles: University of California Press, 1976), Chapter 15. The role of urbanization has been discussed in J. Milton Yinger, "Religion and Social Change: Problems of Integration and Pluralism among the Privileged," *Review of Religious Research* 4 (1963): 129–148; and in Andrew J. Weigert and Darwin L. Thomas, "Secularization and Religiosity: A Cross-National Study of Catholic Adolescents in Five Societies," *Sociological Analysis* 35 (1974): 1–23. The role of professionalization has been emphasized in Guy E. Swanson, "Modern Secularity: Its Meaning, Sources, and Interpretation," in Donald R. Cutler (ed.), *The Religious Situation* (New York: Beacon Press, 1968), pp. 350–361.

constant growth rates for at least the past 50 years.[14] Modernization processes may have contributed to the spread of nonreligion in the 1960s, but additional influences must have also been involved.

Explanations of a more *ad hoc* character have also been applied to these trends in religion. The civil rights movement, the activism of the clergy against the Vietnam war, the size of the churches, the nature of their beliefs, and ecumenism have all been put forth as possible reasons why the churches began losing influence. But *ad hoc* explanations fail to illuminate much about the process by which the shifts in religious commitment may have come about. Who, specifically, defected from the churches? Why, specifically, did they defect? What were the social processes by which *ad hoc* events in the society came to influence the churches?

Ad hoc explanations fail to answer questions such as these. Moreover, they may, in fact, be somewhat misleading, insofar as they suggest that the recent shifts in religious commitment were due to idiosyncratic features of the period. To the contrary, sudden reversals in the direction of religious trends have probably been more the rule than the exception in religious history. For example, the seventeenth century has often been regarded as a time of gradual erosion in biblical faith and ecclesiastical authority, but the Great Awakening of the early eighteenth century marked a distinct reversal of these trends.[15] By the same token, the Great Revival of the early nineteenth century initiated a relatively sudden realignment of American religious power. Relatively precipitous shifts away from religious commitment have also been observed—for example, during World War II.[16] To focus only on the *ad hoc* conditions of the past few years, therefore, while possibly illuminating, fails to advance us toward an understanding of the more *general* processes that may be common in episodes of abrupt religious change. For this reason, we shall attempt to develop an explanation for the spread of nonreligion in the 1960s that may be applicable to other instances of abrupt discontinuity in religious history as well. This explanation derives from a classic paper by the sociologist Karl Mannheim on the "problem of generations."[17]

14. Time-series analyses of trends in these variables have been presented in Robert L. Hamblin, R. Brooke Jacobsen, and Jerry L. L. Miller, *A Mathematical Theory of Social Change* (New York: Wiley, 1973).

15. Sydney E. Ahlstrom, *A Religious History of the American People* (New Haven: Yale University Press, 1972).

16. Rodney Stark, "Age and Faith: A Changing Outlook or an Old Process," *Sociological Analysis* 29 (1968): 1–10.

17. Karl Mannheim, *Essays on the Sociology of Knowledge* (New York: Oxford University Press, 1952). For other recent discussions of Mannheim's theory, see Sheila Allen, "Class, Culture and Generation," *Sociological Review* 21 (1973): 437–446; T. Allen Lambert, "Generations and Change: Toward a Theory of Generations as a Force in Historical Process,"

MANNHEIM'S THEORY OF GENERATION UNITS

Mannheim's ideas seem admirably suited to the problem of religious trends, for he assumes the presence of long-term evolutionary processes, such as secularization, but also attempts to interpret shifts in the rate and direction of these processes. The key to his discussion is the "generation unit": a biological age group that (a) shares a "common location in the social and historical process" which limits it to "a specific range of potential experience, predisposing it for a certain characteristic mode of thought and experience, and a characteristic type of historically relevant action," (b) has a "common destiny" or interest just as that of a socioeconomic class, and (c) exhibits "identity of responses, a certain affinity in the way in which all move with and are formed by their common experiences." A generation unit, therefore, is more than simply a biological age group and more than simply an age "cohort," as the term has come to be used.[18] It is not just an aggregate of age-similar individuals, but a social unit bound together by a common location in the social structure, a common cultural system, self-consciousness as a social unit, and social interaction and solidarity among its members. While it may emerge in response to prior societal changes, once developed it becomes a vehicle for mobilizing and transmitting change. Mannheim explicitly regards its emergence as a harbinger of discontinuity in the social process.

Applied to religion, the generation unit theory suggests that changes in the rate or direction of religious trends, *ceteris paribus,* are most likely when prior social or cultural developments impinge upon one age group more than another, resulting in feelings of social solidarity within that age group. In modern societies, there is an ever-present potential for disjunctures between age strata due to high levels of differentiation between the family and the economy.[19] The differences between the values learned while growing up in the family and those confronted in the workplace make the

---

Youth and Society 4 (1972): 21–45; Robert H. Lauer, "The Generation Gap as Sociometric Choice," *Youth and Society* 5 (1973): 227–241; and George H. Strauss, "Two Perspectives on High School Student Politics: Political Objects versus Political Actors," *Youth and Society* 4 (1974): 360–376.

18. The concept of "cohort" has been discussed in a very informative paper by Norman B. Ryder, "The Cohort as a Concept in the Study of Social Change," *American Sociological Review* 30 (1965): 843–861. Mannheim's concept of "generation unit" implies both less and more. Analyses of cohorts typically focus on whole age strata, whereas a generation unit involves only part of an age stratum, that part which responds to events in a similar way. The generation unit is also a somewhat self-conscious collectivity which shares unique symbols of self-identity, whereas the cohort need have no such bonds of conscious solidarity.

19. This point is the focus of S. N. Eisenstadt's very useful book, *From Generation to Generation,* 2nd ed. (New York: Free Press, 1971).

transition from youth to adulthood an arduous and often stressful task to accomplish. The formation of youth subcultures and the frequent presence of conflict between young people and their elders have been attributed in part to the stressfulness of the maturation process in modern societies. Thus, it might be added to Mannheim's discussion that any events placing extra strain on the transition from family values to economic values are likely to increase the chances of distinct generation units forming. Wars, in that they disrupt the entry of young people into the economy, or mobility (geographical and occupational), in that it necessitates socialization into occupational values different from those of one's parents, are examples of such events.

By inference, Mannheim's discussion also suggests why events such as wars and migrations, on the surface having nothing to do with religion, may result in religious change and, indeed, often have.[20] The age strata set off from one another by such events do not react to them simply as individuals but develop identities as social units. Forming such an identity requires cultural symbols, not the least of which are religious. Indeed, one widely recognized characteristic of religion is that it helps establish and maintain feelings of collective identity and solidarity. Distinct shifts in religious trends may be the result, therefore, of one or several age strata attempting to differentiate themselves from other age strata, either by rejecting or reaffirming traditional religious symbols or by developing entirely new religious symbols.

THE COUNTERCULTURE AS A GENERATION UNIT

The counterculture of the 1960s appears, upon consideration, to have manifested all the characteristics of a generation unit outlined in Mannheim's discussion. The conditions commonly identified as sources of the counterculture—the Vietnam war, growth in mass communications, sustained affluence, upgrading of educational requirements, and the politicization of the university, among others—affected younger age strata considerably more than older strata.[21] The historical confluence of these events

20. Among other studies dealing with such instances, see H. G. Barnett, *Innovation: The Basis of Cultural Change* (New York: McGraw-Hill, 1953); and E. J. Hobsbawm, *Primitive Rebels: Studies in Archaic Forms of Social Movement in the Nineteenth and Twentieth Centuries* (New York: Free Press, 1962).
21. Among the more convincing accounts of the social and cultural origins of the counterculture, see Seymour Martin Lipset, *Student Politics* (New York: Basic Books, 1967); Kenneth Keniston, *Young Radicals: Notes on Committed Youth* (New York: Harcourt Brace, and World, 1968); Kenneth Keniston, *Youth and Dissent: The Rise of a New Opposition* (New

welded young people into a self-conscious generation unit in relation to the rest of society. Terms such as "flower children," "age of Aquarius," and "counterculture" reflected this self-consciousness.[22] A distinct subculture, providing symbols of common identity and purpose, similar to what has been referred to in other contexts as "class consciousness," also emerged.[23] The hallmarks of this subculture included drug use, sexual experimentation and communal living, political disenchantment, an interest in exploring the inner self, fascination with the occult, distinctive dress and language, and anti-technological or "naturalistic" values.[24] All of these became accepted with increasing frequency among young people during the '60s and early '70s, to the point that a large minority—if not a majority—came to be identified with at least some aspects of the counterculture.[25] On and around the nation's campuses, conformity to the norms of this subculture

York: Harcourt Brace Jovanovich, 1971); Henry Malcolm, *Generation of Narcissus* (Boston: Little, Brown, 1971); Richard Flacks, *Conformity, Resistance, and Self-Determination: The Individual and Authority* (Boston: Little, Brown, 1973); Talcott Parsons, "Youth in the Context of American Society," in Erik H. Erikson (ed.), *The Challenge of Youth* (Garden City, N.Y.: Doubleday, 1963), pp. 93–119; Seymour Martin Lipset, *Rebellion in the University* (Boston: Little, Brown, 1972); John M. Meyer and Richard Rubinson, "Structural Determinants of Student Political Activity: A Comparative Interpretation," *Sociology of Education* 45 (1972): 23–46; and Erik H. Erikson, "Reflections on the Dissent of Contemporary Youth," *Daedalus* 99 (1970): 154–178.

22. These are emphasized in Edgar Z. Friedenberg (ed.), *The Anti-American Generation* (Chicago: Transaction Books, 1971).

23. The best statement of this similarity is that of Milton Manoff and Richard Flacks, "The Changing Social Base of the American Student Movement," *Annals of the American Academy of Political and Social Science* 395 (1971): 55–67.

24. On drug use, see Lewis Yablonsky, *The Hippie Trip* (New York: Pegasus, 1968). On sexual experimentation and communal living, see Herbert A. Otto, "Communes: The Alternative Life-Style," *Saturday Review* (April 24, 1971): 16–21; Rosabeth Moss Kanter, *Commitment and Community: Communes and Utopias in Sociological Perspective* (Cambridge: Harvard University Press, 1972); and Arlene S. Skolnick and Jerome H. Skolnick, "Rethinking the Family," in Arlene S. Skolnick and Jerome H. Skolnick (eds.), *Family in Transition: Rethinking Marriage, Sexuality, Child Rearing, and Family Organization* (Boston: Little, Brown, 1971). On political disenchantment, see Lipset, *Rebellion in the University*. On exploring the inner self, see Donald Stone, *The Human Potential Movement* (Ph.D. dissertation, University of California, Berkeley, 1976); and Kurt W. Back, *Beyond Words: The Story of Sensitivity Training and the Encounter Movement* (Baltimore: Penguin Books, 1972). On the occult, see Chapter 2 of the present volume. On values, see Charles A. Reich, *The Greening of America* (New York: Bantam Books, 1971); Theodore Roszak, *The Making of a Counter-Culture* (Garden City, N.Y.: Doubleday, 1969); Theodore Roszak, *Where the Wasteland Ends* (Garden City, N.Y.: Doubleday, 1972); and William Braden, *The Age of Aquarius: Technology and the Cultural Revolution* (New York: Pocket Books, 1971).

25. For statistical evidence to this effect, see Daniel Yankelovich, *The Changing Values on Campus: Political and Personal Attitudes of Today's College Students* (New York: Washington Square Press, 1972); Daniel Yankelovich, *The New Morality: A Profile of American Youth in the 70s* (New York: McGraw-Hill, 1974); and Robert Wuthnow, *The Consciousness Reformation* (Berkeley and Los Angeles: University of California Press, 1976).

came to be regarded not merely as a matter of personal choice but as a criterion for allocating status and rewards within this generation unit.[26]

There are several reasons for suggesting that the downward shift in religious commitment during the '60s was at least partly, if not largely, attributable to the emergence of this generation unit. Both occurred to a greater extent among young people than among older people (as we shall see shortly), and both took place at approximately the same time. The counterculture gradually became focused less on specific political issues, such as the Vietnam war, and more on general values, i.e., on the possibilities of creating a "new consciousness." Part of the counterculture was aimed specifically at finding alternatives to established religion, whether in Marxism, mysticism, or other philosophies.[27] But perhaps more importantly, many of the more visible characteristics of the counterculture were activities to which established religion, either explicitly or implicitly, had long been opposed, as evidenced in studies of religious commitment and political radicalism, civil rights militancy, anti-war activism, civil libertarianism, homosexuality, drug use, and alternative life styles.[28] The alarmed reaction

26. For a discussion of the importance of status-role identification in the student movement, see Klaus R. Allerbeck, "Some Structural Conditions for Youth and Student Movements," *International Social Science Journal* 24 (1972): 257–270.

27. See especially, John Charles Cooper, *Religion in the Age of Aquarius* (Philadelphia: Westminster, 1971); and Charles Y. Glock and Robert N. Bellah (eds.), *The New Religious Consciousness.*

28. Studies documenting relations between religious commitment and political radicalism include Harold C. Meier and William Orzen, "Student Legitimation of Campus Activism: Some Survey Findings," *Social Problems* 19 (1971): 181–192; and Wuthnow and Glock, "Religious Loyalty, Defection, and Experimentation among College Youth." Research on religion and civil rights militancy includes Gary T. Marx, *Protest and Prejudice* (New York: Harper and Row, 1969); Jeffrey K. Hadden, *The Gathering Storm in the Churches* (Garden City, N.Y.: Doubleday, 1969); and Kenneth W. Eckhardt, "Religiosity and Civil Rights Militancy," *Review of Religious Research* 11 (1970): 197–203. On religion and anti-war activism, see Harold E. Quinley, *The Prophetic Clergy: Social Activism among Protestant Ministers* (New York: Wiley, 1974); John F. Connors, III, Richard C. Leonard, and Kenneth E. Burnham, "Religion and Opposition to War among College Students," *Sociological Analysis* 29 (1968): 211–219; and Vincent Jeffries and Clarence E. Tygart, "The Influence of Theology, Denomination, and Values upon the Positions of Clergy on Social Issues," *Journal for the Scientific Study of Religion* 13 (1974): 309–324. On religion and civil libertarianism, see Samuel A. Stouffer, *Communism, Civil Liberties, and Conformity* (Garden City, N.Y.: Doubleday, 1955); Rodney Stark, Bruce D. Foster, Charles Y. Glock, and; Harold E. Quinley, *Wayward Shepherds: Prejudice and the Protestant Clergy* (New York: Harper and Row, 1971); Gertrude J. Selznick and Stephen Steinberg, *The Tenacity of Prejudice* (New York: Harper and Row, 1969); and Robert Wuthnow, "Religious Commitment and Conservatism: In Quest of an Elusive Relationship," in Charles Y. Glock (ed.), *Religion in Sociological Perspective*, pp. 117–132. On religious orientations and homosexuality, see Jon P. Alston, "Review of the Polls: Attitudes toward Extramarital and Homosexual Relations," *Journal for the Scientific Study of Religion* 13 (1974): 479–481. On religion and drug use, see Wuthnow and Glock, "Religious Loyalty, Defection, and Experimentation among College Youth"; and Charles Y. Glock and Robert Wuthnow, "The Religious Dimension," in Rocco Caporale and Antonio

of the churches to these various challenges has been well documented. [29]

To the extent that a relation between religious trends and the emergence of the counterculture can be posited, it also appears warranted to suggest that the dominant direction of influence was from the counterculture to religion rather than from religion to the counterculture, especially during the late '60s and early '70s. Evidence has been presented elsewhere showing the role of longer-term shifts in religious meaning systems as facilitators of the recent social experimentation. [30] But the relatively sharp reversal of trends in organized religious commitment during the past decade seems explicable only as a consequence, in part, of the more general countercultural unrest that preceded and accompanied it. The counterculture was never as concerned with organized religion as organized religion came to be with the counterculture. For particular participants in the counterculture, participation may have been preceded by disaffection with the churches, of course; but even at the individual level, evidence suggests, as we shall see in Chapter 7, that the dominant source of religious disaffection for many young people may have been prior identification with the counterculture. [31]

FIVE HYPOTHESES

To establish that the countercultural generation unit was, in fact, a source of the shift in religious trends during the '60s would require panel data, at minimum, preferably from a cohort of young people just beginning to

Grumelli (eds.), *Emerging Dimensions of Religious Consciousness* (Berkeley and Los Angeles: University of California Press, 1977). On religious commitment and alternative life styles, see Robert Wuthnow and Charles Y. Glock, "The Shifting Focus of Faith: A Survey Report," *Psychology Today* 8 (1974): 131–136.

29. See, for example, Donald Heinz, "Religious Signals from the Counter-Culture," Report to the National Council of Churches Committee on Faith and Action, 1975; Barbara Hargrove, "Ministers at the Margin," in Glock and Bellah (eds.), *The New Religious Consciousness*, Chapter 8; D. P. Costello, "From Counter-Culture to Anti-Culture," *Commonwealth* 96 (1972): 383–386; J. R. Moore, "Literature of Countercultural Religion," *Christianity Today* 16 (1972): 14–16; and R. C. Ouradnik, "Middle-Class Quest for Alternatives," *Christian Century* 91 (1974); 366–369.

30. Wuthnow, *The Consciousness Reformation*.

31. It should be noted that at least two approaches may be taken to the religious trends of the past two decades. One, which was adopted widely during the late '50s and early '60s, is to regard the growth of religion during the '50s as an anomaly warranting explanation. In the light of longer-range trends in religion, this approach appears to be inappropriate. The growth during the '50s seems to have been simply an extension of longer-range growth; for example, church membership as a proportion of the population grew steadily ever since the Civil War until about 1960 when, significantly, it ceased to grow. The second approach, which appears preferable, is to regard the sudden downward shift during the '60s as more the phenomenon warranting explanation. In focusing on the countercultural generation unit, we are, of course, opting for the latter approach.

mature during the early '60s, a cohort that could be followed throughout the '60s to determine the effects of differential involvement in the counterculture on religious development. The opportunity to collect such data no longer exists. An alternative procedure, however, is to divide the interpretation just outlined into more specific, interrelated hypotheses readily testable with available data. Largely through the informative discussions of Matilda White Riley and her collaborators on the nature of age strata, it is possible to identify at least five testable hypotheses implicit in the foregoing discussion.[32]

First, if the increased secularization during the '60s is partly attributable to the emergence of a countercultural generation unit among the young, the extent of religious decline should be greater among younger age strata than among older strata.

Second, the pattern of cross-sectional age differences in religious commitment in the late '60s and early '70s should differ from that prior to the '60s. Indicators of religious commitment showing youth relatively more committed than older people prior to the '60s should show these differences either reduced, eliminated, or reversed subsequent to the '60s, while indicators initially showing less commitment among youth should show these differences to have increased subsequent to the '60s.

Third, current age differences in religious commitment should not be attributable entirely to life cycle differences, but should partly reflect differences in countercultural involvements.

Fourth, current age differences in religious commitment should be attributable to specific involvement in countercultural activities, taking into account differences in exposure to social and cultural trends other than the counterculture, such as rising levels of education, urbanization, and professionalization, or perhaps longer-term tendencies toward liberalism or nonreligion.

Finally, and most importantly, overall period differences in religious commitment since 1950 or thereabouts should not be explicable solely in terms of general secularizing trends, such as modernization, but should be partly attributable to the rise of countercultural events.

TESTING THE HYPOTHESES

Several sources of longitudinal data on religious commitment by age strata are available for testing the hypothesis that greater declines in religious commitment have occurred among youth than among older people. For example, Gallup Poll data on church attendance between 1957, when all

32. Matilda White Riley, Marilyn Johnson, and Anne Foner, *Aging and Society, Volume 3: A Sociology of Age Stratification* (New York: Russel Sage, 1972).

Percentage Attending Weekly

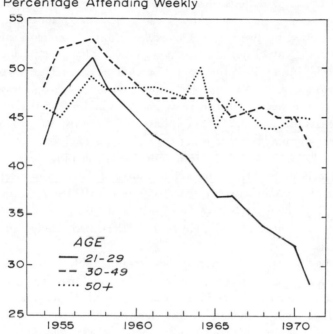

Figure 6. Weekly Church Attendance by Age Strata, 1954–1971

age strata were at a high point in attendance, and 1971, the last year for which comparable age categories were used, show that persons age 21 to 29 registered a decline of 23 percentage points, while those age 30 to 49 declined only 11 points, and those age 50 and over declined only four points (see Figure 6).[33] Evidence from surveys of the Detroit area also confirms the hypothesis. Between 1959 and 1971, the proportion of those age 21 to 34 attending church weekly declined 27 points, compared to 14 points for persons over age 35. The proportion very sure of God's existence dropped 24 points for the younger group but only 15 points for the older group. Other questions were more stable, but showed similar patterns: belief in God declined 7 points for the younger people and 1 point for the older people; belief in life after death dropped 4 points among youth but rose 2 points among their elders; and the proportions reporting that they ask often "what God would want me to do" declined 3 points among the young but increased 5 points in the older group.[34]

33. Gallup, *The Gallup Poll.*
34. I would like to thank Otis Dudley Duncan and Beverly Duncan for making these data available to me. A recent cohort analysis of religious belief in 1957 and in 1968 from Gallup polls also supports these results. See Bradley R. Hertel and Hart M. Nelsen, "Are We Entering a Post-Christian Era? Religious Belief and Attendance in America, 1957–1968," *Journal for the Scientific Study of Religion* 13 (1974): 409–421.

The second hypothesis—that recent differences in religious commitment between age strata should be greater than those prior to the '60s—is also supported by these data. On weekly church attendance nationally, persons age 21 to 29 were 2 percentage points higher than people over age 50 in 1957, but by 1971 they were 17 points lower (see Figure 6 again). In the Detroit area, those age 34 and under were only 3 percent less likely to attend church weekly than those over age 34 in 1959, but they were 16 percent less likely in 1971. On certainty of God's existence, young people were initially only 1 point lower than older people, but were 10 points lower by 1971. They were 2 percent more likely than older people to believe in God in 1959, but 4 percent less likely in 1971. Both groups were equally likely to believe in life after death in 1959, but in 1971 young people were 6 percent less likely to believe. And on asking God's advice, they were initially 12 points less likely, but by 1971 the differences had increased to 20 points.

The Bay Area data also support these results. Table 45 shows significant differences on each indicator of religious belief and practice between those under age 35 and those over 35. Partitioning the likelihood-ratio chi-square for each relation demonstrates that the other age breaks shown add no significant variation.[35] Thus, the proportions who definitely believe in God, for example, are virtually the same for those age 16 through 25 as for those age 26 through 35, but between those age 26 through 35 and those age 36 through 50 there is a difference of approximately 20 percentage points, while there are virtually no differences again among the three older age groups. Comparing alternative cutting points (see the bottom of Table 45) also demonstrates that age 35 (rather than ages 25, 30, 40, or 45) is the most desirable cutting point for maximizing variation in all but one of the seven items.[36]

35. The likelihood-ratio chi-square, unlike the more commonly used Pearson chi-square, can be partitioned; i.e., chi-square values for contingency tables presenting the same data but having some of the categories collapsed in certain instances can be compared through subtraction, and the resulting difference yields an estimate of the significance of the differences between the tables. Thus, in Table 45 we have presented the likelihood-ratio chi-square value for the relation between belief in God and age, where age is divided into five categories ($\chi^2 = 52.49$, d.f. = 4) and the comparable chi-square value where age is dichotomized ($\chi^2 = 51.40$, d.f. = 1). Subtracting chi-square values (52.49–51.40) and degrees of freedom (4–1) yields a resultant chi-square value of 1.09 for 3 degrees of freedom which is significant only at the .80 level. Hence, we conclude that no significant information is added by having five categories of age rather than two. Substantively, we conclude that the only significant difference in belief in God is between those under and those over age 35. 36. This is determined simply from comparing the chi-square values themselves, since the degrees of freedom equal 1 in all cases. For example, the chi-square value for the relation between belief in creation and age, where age is dichotomized at age 35, is 24.97, whereas this value is only 17.11 when age is dichotomized at age 30, 15.64 when age is dichotomized at age 40, and so forth. Thus, we conclude that age 35 is the point at which the differences in belief in creation between the young and the old are maximized.

The sharp break between those under and those over age 35 in these data, while similar to that in the recent Gallup and Detroit data, differs, as hypothesized, from the findings of studies conducted during the late '50s and early '60s, which typically show minor differences, if any, between persons over and under age 30 or 35 on such items as church attendance, belief in God, and other dimensions of religious commitment.[37] It also differs from the more gradual relations that would be expected due to maturation.[38] Instead, it is suggestive of a cohort difference attributable to events having taken place during the '60s. People who were over age 35 in 1973 would have, for the most part, reached adulthood and completed their period of primary socialization prior to the '60s. Those who completed college at the modal age of 21 or 22, for instance, would have done so before 1960. Respondents age 35 and under in 1973, in contrast, would have reached adulthood after 1960 and would have experienced part of their primary socialization during the '60s. Thus, both the cross-sectional age differences and the over-time data suggest that something was taking place during the '60s which created a shift in the character of religious commitment. To be certain, however, it is necessary to extend the analysis.

Our third hypothesis was that the age differences we have just been examining should be partly attributable to young people having been more involved in countercultural activities than older people, rather than being solely a product of young people being at a different stage in their life cycle than older people. The latter possibility warrants serious consideration since a variety of compelling arguments have been put forth suggesting strong relations between religious commitment and maturation. Older people with families allegedly show greater interest in religion than younger people without families because religious programs and religious symbols have tended to be geared to the family.[39] Responsibility for

37. Relations between church attendance and age have been reported in Bernard Lazerwitz, "Some Factors Associated with Variations in Church Attendance," *Social Forces* 39 (1961): 301–309; Michael Argyle, *Religious Behavior* (London: Routledge and Kegan Paul, 1958); and Harold L. Orbach, "Aging and Religion: A Study of Church Attendance in the Detroit Metropolitan Area," *Geriatrics* 16 (1961): 530–540. Relations between belief in God and age can be found in Matilda White Riley and Anne Foner, *Aging and Society, Volume 1: An Inventory of Research Findings* (New York: Russell Sage, 1968). Evidence on other dimensions of religious commitment by age has been presented in Yoshio Fukuyama, "The Major Dimensions of Church Membership," *Review of Religious Research* 2 (1961): 154–161; Serge Carlos, "Religious Participation and the Urban-Suburban Continuum," *American Journal of Sociology* 75 (1970): 742–759; and Hazel Gaudet Erskine, "The Polls: Personal Religion," *Public Opinion Quarterly* 29 (1965): 145–157; see also Rodney Stark and Charles Y. Glock, *The Poor in Spirit: Sources of Religious Commitment* (forthcoming).

38. An illuminating discussion of the major patterns that would be expected between religion and age due to maturation has been presented in Howard M. Bahr, "Aging and Religious Disaffiliation," *Social Forces* 49 (1970): 60–71.

39. See Charles Y. Glock, Benjamin B. Ringer, and Earl R. Babbie, *To Comfort and to Challenge* (Berkeley and Los Angeles: University of California Press, 1967).

Table 45. RELIGIOUS COMMITMENT BY AGE (Unweighted Bay Area Sample)

Age:	Post-Sixties cohort 16–25	26–35	Pre-Sixties cohort 36–50	51–65	Over 65	X^{2*}	df	p
Religious belief								
(a) Definitely believe in God	42%	43%	64%	69%	65%	52.49	4	.001
						51.40	1	.001
(b) Believe in creation	50%	46%	64%	66%	65%	26.28	4	.001
						24.97	1	.001
(c) Value following God's will a fair amount	46%	48%	63%	75%	68%	49.65	4	.001
						44.96	1	.001
Religious practice								
(d) Active in a church	34%	32%	45%	42%	43%	11.08	4	.025
						10.27	1	.001
(e) Attend church at least several times a month	19%	18%	29%	30%	28%	14.27	4	.006
						13.92	1	.001
(f) Value taking part in church a fair amount	29%	30%	44%	44%	46%	22.23	4	.001
						22.10	1	.001
(g) Pray at least several times a week	35%	35%	54%	63%	65%	58.18	4	.001
						54.83	1	.001
Number	(410)	(233)	(152)	(131)	(74)			

| Item | *Likelihood ratio X^2 for alternative cutting points ($df = 1$)* | | | | |
	Age 25	Age 30	Age 35	Age 40	Age 45
(a)	20.45	53.74	51.40	35.69	28.84
(b)	4.94	17.11	24.97	15.64	8.25
(c)	20.00	36.25	44.96	33.05	27.31
(d)	2.19	4.80	10.27	3.27	2.34
(e)	4.08	9.45	13.92	9.40	8.69
(f)	9.14	19.56	22.10	14.94	11.41
(g)	21.45	42.25	54.83	43.74	31.97

*Top figure = likelihood ratio chi-square for 5 age categories; bottom figure = same for age dichotomized at age 35.

socializing children, moreover, has been suspected to encourage commitment to traditional values generally, including religion.[40] Being out of school has been associated with higher levels of religiosity than being in school, stemming apparently in part from job responsibilities that stimulate conformity to more conventional values.[41] Settling down as a stable community resident has also been thought to encourage loyalty to traditional activities, including church participation.[42] Furthermore, family, job, and community ties may promote more general resistance to change *qua* change.[43] In this regard, Norman Ryder concludes that "the potential for change is concentrated in the cohorts of young adults who are old enough to participate directly in the movements impelled by change, but not old enough to have become committed to an occupation, a residence, a family of procreation or a way of life."[44] Finally, the subjective concerns associated with life cycle differences (work plans, identity problems, worries about illness and death) may also be responsible for different levels of religious commitment among the young and the old. The generation unit theory does not deny the importance of such life cycle differences, but postulates, in addition to them, significant differences due to the cohort in which one is raised.

This hypothesis can best be tested by combining it with our fourth hypothesis: that age differences in religious commitment at present should be partly a product of involvement in countercultural activities, taking into account differences between young and old people on such "trend factors" as rising levels of education, increasing urbanization, long-range tendencies toward liberalism or nonreligion, and so forth. This too is an important consideration, since youth, being generally better educated and apparently

40. Sidney L. Pressey and Raymond G. Kuhlen, *Psychological Development through the Life Span* (New York: Harper and Row, 1957).

41. On the differences between those in school and those out of school on religious commitments, see Kenneth A. Feldman, "Change and Stability of Religious Orientations during College, Part II: Social-Structural Correlates," *Review of Religious Research* 11 (1970): 103–127. On employment and conventionality, see Ludwig Von Mises, *Bureaucracy* (New Haven: Yale University Press, 1956), and Ely Chinoy, *Automobile Workers and the American Dream* (Boston: Beacon Press, 1955).

42. See especially the informative discussion of Harold Wilensky, "Work, Careers, and Social Integration," *International Social Science Journal* 12 (1960): 543–560; some suggestive insights are also presented in Gibson Winter, *The Suburban Captivity of the Churches* (New York: Macmillan, 1962). The negative relation between age and geographic mobility is a well established generalization in demography; see William Peterson, *Population* (Toronto: Macmillan, 1969).

43. This argument has probably been stated most clearly in Angus Campbell, *The American Voter* (New York: Wiley, 1960).

44. Norman B. Ryder, "The Cohort as a Concept in the Study of Social Change," *American Sociological Review* 30 (1965): 843–861.

more aware of current events than many older people, are likely to be more exposed to such trends.[45]

To test these two hypotheses, relations among five variables need to be examined: age, exposure to trends, life cycle, countercultural involvement, and religious commitment. Measures of each of these variables, with the exception of age, which is simply measured in years, are constructed by combining a variety of items having high face validity and strong inter-relations with one another to form scales. The items in each scale and the correlations between each scale and its component items are shown in Table 46.

The relations among the variables are shown in Diagram 2. Our expecta-tion is that there should be a strong relation between age and countercul-tural involvement and between countercultural involvement and religious commitment, such that countercultural involvement "explains away" the differences in religious commitment due to age. Furthermore, this should hold true taking into account the effects of trend exposure and life cycle.[46]

The results confirm our expectations. Virtually no differences in religious commitment due to age remain, as indicated by the coefficient of the path from age to religion (-.034), when countercultural involvement, trend exposure, and life cycle differences are taken into account. Practically all the effects of age, moreover, are explained away by the differences in counter-

45. One study, for example, found people under age 30 generally more aware of contempo-rary issues than people over age 30 and was able to explain this difference as a function of the higher educational levels of the young; see Norval D. Glenn, "Aging, Disengagement, and Opinionation," *Public Opinion Quarterly* 33 (1969): 17–33. It should be noted that young people may also be more *receptive* to the new ideas to which they are exposed, since they are still in the process of forming their basic values; see Einsenstadt, *From Generation to Generation*, and Erikson, *The Challenge of Youth*.

46. We assume a recursive pattern in Diagram 2—that is, a model in which each variable from left to right is assumed to bear a causal influence on all subsequent variables—for the following reasons. The independent status of age should be apparent. A causal influence from trend exposure to life cycle can be posited, since the rate at which life cycle tasks are accomplished depends partly on choice (e.g., deciding when to marry or when to have children), which in turn depends on family background characteristics such as those in-cluded in the trend variable (e.g., education or social class background). Causal influences from trend exposure and life cycle to countercultural involvement can be assumed because these factors influence both exposure to countercultural ideas and opportunities to become involved in countercultural activities. Religious commitment can be assumed to be influenced by trend exposure and life cycle on the same grounds. Finally, the dependence of religious commitment on countercultural involvement can be posited on the grounds that the counterculture emanated primarily from sources other than the churches, the latter generally taking a follower role in these events, especially during the late '60s and early '70s. This position is widely reflected in the literature on the counterculture. Over a longer period, of course, the direction of causality between religion and social unrest may have been more ambiguous and even have been reversed. I have dealt extensively with this possibility in *The Consciousness Reformation*.

Table 46. **SCALES AND ITEMS**

Item	Item-to-Scale Correlations
Trend exposure	
Father graduated from college	.624
Respondent had some college	.641
Father was politically liberal	.505
Less than weekly church attendance as youth	.563
Life cycle	
Has been married	.788
Has children	.765
Hasn't moved in past two years	.467
Not attending school	.644
Not bothered about career plans	.500
Countercultural involvement	
Favor legalizing marijuana	.808
Been "high" on drugs	.720
Approve of an unmarried couple living together	.765
Favor more freedom for homosexuals	.751
Taken part in a demonstration	.614
Religious commitment	
Definitely believe in God	.763
God created the first man and woman	.710
Following God's will is of fair importance	.775
Active in a religious group	.694
Attend church several times a month	.699
Church participation is of fair importance	.778
Pray several times a week	.757

cultural involvement, as indicated by the strength of the relation between age and involvement (-.283) and between involvement and religion (-.471). The effects of trend exposure and of life cycle differences in the model are quite small.[47] In other words, the current generation gap in religious commitment between the young and the old in the Bay Area appears to be the result of younger people having been more involved in the

47. The overall effect of each variable is determined by multiplying the coefficients for each indirect path between it and religious commitment and then adding the effects of all direct and indirect paths. The "error terms" for each variable are: trend exposure, .990; life cycle, .787; countercultural involvement, .872; and religious commitment, .843.

Diagram 2. **Counterctultural Involvement as the Link between Age and Religious Commitment, Controlling for Differences in Trend Exposure and Life Cycle**

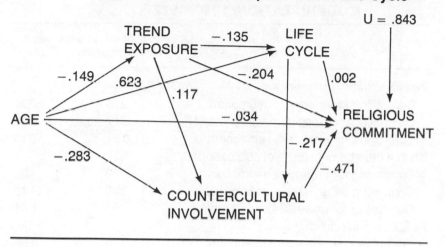

counterculture than older people, rather than the result of other kinds of differences between the young and the old.

The final hypothesis to be tested is that *trends* in religious indicators, like age strata differences, should be due partly to trends in countercultural events rather than being solely the product of more conventional secularizing trends. Although somewhat crude, data on the number of protest demonstrations per year from Taylor and Hudson's *World Handbook of Political and Social Indicators* and data on the number of references to drugs per year in the *Reader's Guide* provide longitudinal measures of countercultural activity. Data on energy consumption, gross domestic product, enrollment in higher education, and book publishing provide indicators of other secularizing trends. And annual data for the items discussed toward the beginning of this chapter afford longitudinal measures of religious commitment.[48] The method of analysis is multiple regression, entering pairs of trend and countercultural variables stepwise to determine the increment in explained variation due to each countercultural variable for each religion variable.

As shown in Table 47, countercultural events account for significant variation in religious commitment beyond that explained by the trend variables. On the average, the increment in the proportion of variation

48. Charles Lewis Taylor and Michael C. Hudson, *World Handbook of Political and Social Indicators* (New Haven: Yale University Press, 1972); and Arthur S. Banks, *Cross-Polity Time-Series Data* (Cambridge: Massachusetts Institute of Technology Press, 1971).

Table 47. **INCREMENT IN EXPLAINED VARIATION IN RELIGIOUS TRENDS DUE TO COUNTER-CULTURAL TRENDS, CONTROLLING FOR MODERNIZATION, 1950–1972**

	Explained variation due to:	
Religious Trend	*Demonstrations*	*Drugs*
Weekly church attendance		
Controlling for energy consumption	.216	.004
Controlling for gross domestic product	.517	.003
Controlling for university enrollment	.181	.016
Church membership (as % of population)		
Controlling for energy consumption	.299	.188
Controlling for gross domestic product	.239	.148
Controlling for university enrollment	.155	.041
Religious contributions		
Controlling for energy consumption	.170	.158
Controlling for gross domestic product	.074	.123
Controlling for university enrollment	.144	.071
Church construction		
Controlling for energy consumption	.977	.189
Controlling for gross domestic product	.971	.214
Controlling for university enrollment	.984	.099
Religious books (as % of all books)		
Controlling for energy consumption	.339	.198
Controlling for gross domestic product	.372	.263
Controlling for university enrollment	.524	.605
Religious degrees (as % of all degrees)		
Controlling for energy consumption	.027	.063
Controlling for gross domestic product	.127	.081
Controlling for university enrollment	.040	.023

explained is approximately 18 percent. Even with these crude measures of countercultural activity, therefore, support is lent to the hypothesis.

CONCLUSION

Our efforts to test the idea that the emergence of a self-conscious generation unit contributed importantly to the religious downswing of the '60s have admittedly been less conclusive than would be desired. It cannot be certain, for example, that the age break examined in the Bay Area data corresponds to the differential shift observed in the over-time data, nor can it be supposed that the Bay Area data are representative of the nation at large. It should be noted, however, that the Bay Area, as a focal point of the counterculture, has afforded a highly appropriate context for observing the specific functioning of a generation unit. Our efforts to control for the effects of maturation and of differential exposure to other trends have also been limited to the extent that other variables may have been discovered that would have been capable of explaining away the effects of countercultural involvement. In testing five hypotheses involving several data sets, however, no evidence has been found that contradicts the interpretation offered.

Evidence has been presented that the rate of secularization since the 1950s has been more pronounced among younger than among older age strata in the Detroit area and nationally on both religious practice and religious belief.[49] It has been shown perforce that a "generation gap" exists in religious data collected in the early '70s, whereas none existed in data collected in the late '50s and early '60s.[50] The Bay Area data demonstrate that differential involvement in the countercultural generation unit of the '60s largely accounts for this generation gap, taking into account the effects of life cycle factors and exposure to longer-term trends. It has also been seen that longitudinal indicators of countercultural activity account for significant variation in longitudinal indicators of religious commitment beyond that accounted for by indicators of modernization.

An important implication of these results is that long-range predictions about religious trends based on data from the past decade, as made frequently in the popular literature, are likely to be highly misleading. Implicit in such predictions is an assumption that current trends are rooted in longer-range, more continuous processes of modernization, and therefore may be expected to continue in the future at a similar rate. If, instead, they are the product of a specific generation unit, they may be of indeterminate duration. As successive age strata mature, not having experienced the countercultural contagion of the '60s, there may well be a return to more traditional religious commitments. Indeed, there has already been some evidence to this effect.

A more general implication is that generation units may be an important

49. The fact that the younger cohort was considerably larger during the 1960s than during the 1950s in proportion to older cohorts also magnifies its importance; see Matilda White Riley, Marilyn Johnson, and Anne Foner, *Aging and Society, Volume 3: A Sociology of Age Stratification.*

50. Otis Dudley Duncan's term "cohort chasm" is actually more precise here than the more popular term ("Measuring Social Change via Replication of Surveys," in Kenneth C. Land and Seymour Spilerman (eds.), *Social-Indicator Models* (New York: Russell Sage, 1975), pp. 105–127.

key to understanding discontinuities in the secularization process that cannot be explained by more established theories emphasizing continuous, long-term religious evolution. Although the emergence of generation units may be dependent upon exogenous historical events, the process by which religious effects result would appear from Mannheim's disucssion to follow relatively predictable patterns. Fluctuations in religious trends need not be discounted as embarrassing departures from sociological principles, but can be understood as the product of social factors. As the recent trends in religious commitment suggest, discontinuities in religious configurations may be expected when age strata are differentiated sufficiently by changes in the social structure to develop a self-conscious collective identity requiring legitimating and integrating symbols.

While it would take us too far afield to extend the present interpretation to other periods of history, it might be fruitful to suggest some of the directions that such an inquiry might take. Whitney Cross's thoughtful examination of the "burned-over district" in New York state in the early nineteenth century, for example, suggests that the second Great Awakening, perhaps the most influential of all religious movements in American religious history, was importantly a generational as well as a regional and economic phenomenon.[51] Religious fervor spread first among young people migrating westward, apparently serving in part to crystallize their collective identity vis-à-vis older age strata who remained on the eastern seaboard. Although it may be maintained that migration, not age cleavage, was the essential precondition for the Second Great Awakening, it seems sufficient to suggest that the effects of migration would likely have been less dramatic had older strata migrated westward too.

Similar interpretations may be, and have been, extended to quasireligious and surrogate religious phenomena. One historian, for example, has attributed the growth of the Comintern in Germany after 1918 to an influx of young people who had been molded into a distinct generation unit by the disruptions of World War I and the economic recession that followed.[52] Other discussions that suggest the relevance of a generational approach to religious cycles include those of shifts in Ireland having taken place subsequent to the rebellion of 1916 and in recent years, the period of rapid secularization in post-revolutionary France, the Protestant Reformation, and the religious growth experienced in the United States during the early part of the twentieth century.[53]

51. Whitney R. Cross, *The Burned-Over District: The Social and Intellectual History of Enthusiastic Religion in Western New York, 1800–1850* (New York: Harper and Row, 1950).
52. R. F. Wheeler, "German Labor and the Comintern: A Problem of Generations?," *Journal of Social History* 7 (1974): 304–321.
53. On Ireland, see Norman F. Cantor, *The Age of Protest: Dissent and Rebellion in the Twentieth Century* (New York: Hawthorn Books, 1969), and Sue Jenvy, "Sons and Haters: Ulster

At the most general level, whether the sources are generational or otherwise, abrupt fluctuations in religious trends such as those experienced during the 1960s should be acknowledged as the rule, not the exception, in religious change. Theories of religious change cannot rest content to focus only on the more continuous effects of modernization or gradual evolutionary processes within religious institutions.[54] Perhaps Robert Nisbet, in criticizing the evolutionary perspective more generally, has said it best: "Change in any degree of notable significance is intermittent rather than continuous, mutational, even explosive, rather than the simple accumulation of internal variations."[55]

To summarize, the recent period during which countless new religious experiments achieved notoriety was also one in which considerable losses were registered by the churches, whether the losses are measured in terms of attendance, belief, contributions, or by other indicators. Our argument has been that these losses can be explained to a significant degree as the result of young people being thrust together by a variety of historical events into a countercultural generation unit whose values and life styles did not include, and were often in active opposition to, participation in organized religion. The new religions formed a part of the counterculture, of course. But the losses experienced by the churches cannot be attributed solely to the gains of the new religions. They must be traced to the counterculture in its broadest sense and ultimately to the strains giving rise to the counterculture. It was the young who felt the impact of these strains most severely. And it was they who led the exodus from the churches.

Many of these young people, of course, were students, and all available evidence suggests that rates of religious defection among students have been exceptionally high. Chapter 7 examines this defection, affording a further test of the argument we have advanced to account for the recent trends in mainstream religion.

Youth in Conflict," *New Society* 21 (1972): 5–127. On post-revolutionary France, see George Brandes, *Main Currents in Nineteenth-Century Literature, V: The Romantic School in France* (New York: Macmillan, 1906). On the Protestant Reformation, see Pitirim A. Sorokin, *Society, Culture and Personality* (New York: Harper and Row, 1947). And on the United States, see Will Herberg, *Protestant, Catholic, Jew: An Essay in American Religious Sociology* (Garden City, N.Y.: Doubleday, 1955).
54. Cf. Kenneth E. Bock, "Evolution, Function and Change," *American Sociological Review* 28 (1963): 229–237.
55. Robert A. Nisbet, *Social Change and History* (New York: Oxford University Press, 1969), pp. 281–282.

CHAPTER 7

Religious Defection
on Campus

(GLEN MELLINGER, CO-AUTHOR)

This chapter examines the sources of religious defection among college students, using panel data from two cohorts of male students at the university of California, Berkeley. We shall focus on two forms of religious defection: apostasy from organized religion and experimentation with Eastern or mystical religions. Of these two, religious apostasy has been more significant in terms of numbers, although it has received less publicity than the more exotic forms of religious experimentation. In the early 1970s, over half the students on certain elite campuses claimed to be without religious beliefs; nationally at least 20 percent of all college students denied any religious affiliation, and the number who remained only nominally religious ranged considerably higher.[1] Experimentation with Eastern religions and with mysticism, while less impressive numerically, was also much in

1. See Robert Wuthnow and Charles Y. Glock, "Religious Loyalty, Defection, and Experimentation among College Youth," *Journal for the Scientific Study of Religion* 12 (June 1973): 157–180; and *Gallup Opinion Index*, "Religion in America," (1975) Report No. 114.. Evidence on religious changes among college students has also been presented in Daniel Yankelovich, *The New Morality: A Profile of American Youth in the Seventies* (New York: McGraw-Hill, 1974). The Yankelovich research has shown that the proportion of college youth identifying with people of their religion dropped 17 percentage points between 1969 and 1973 and that noncollege youth registered a drop of 18 points during the same period. Data on longer-range trends in the religious commitments of students has been published in Dean R. Hoge, *Commitment on Campus: Changes in Religion and Values over Five Decades* (Philadelphia: Westminster Press, 1974). Evidence on more recent developments among some of the students studied in Hoge's earlier research can be found in Dean R. Hoge, "Changes in College Students' Value Patterns in the 1950s, 1960s, and 1970s," *Sociology of Education* 49 (April 1976): 155–163. A report on the detailed religious characteristics of the students in the Berkeley samples and on trends and changes in these characteristics has been published elsewhere; see Robert Wuthnow and Glen Mellinger, "Religious Loyalty, Defection, and Experimentation: A Longitudinal Analysis of University Men," *Review of Religious Research* 18 (1977).

evidence on campuses, drawing a large share of its recruits, as we have seen, from well-educated young people while they were still in school.

Building on the results presented in Chapter 6, the argument we wish to examine in the present chapter is that student participation in the counter-culture of the late 1960s and early '70s was a major source of religious apostasy and experimentation. As we have suggested, religion was never the central focus of the counterculture, but many of the major themes of the counterculture were contradictory to the political and moral orientations with which the churches had become associated during the religious revival of the '50s.

Students of the '50s, like their elders, manifested generally high levels of involvement in organized religion. Perhaps this was due to Cold War insecurities, as some have argued. But it was probably also a function of college students being *"gloriously contented* both in regard to their present day-to-day activity and their outlook for the future," as one observer of the times put it.[2] The first awareness that all was not well came, on many campuses, from students having participated in summer civil rights campaigns in the South. Many of these students had become critical of the churches for their silence on civil rights. It was also from this involvement that early campus unrest appeared, as at Berkeley where the Free Speech Movement grew directly from efforts to organize students returning from the South into protest squadrons for the Republican Convention in San Francisco.[3] As the '60s progressed, a whole series of cultural reorientations spread across college campuses. Anti-Communist sentiments eroded and criticism of business and technology increased, both trends running counter to church orientations of the '50s. Antiwar demonstrations and confrontations with police conflicted with norms of conformity to law and order that had seemed predominant in the churches, as did covert experimentation with drugs. And perhaps most importantly for the majority of students, new standards of sexual conduct came into favor, often in direct violation of church preachments. The counterculture elicited outspoken criticism from many church leaders (although there were certainly those in sympathy with it), supporting the view that the counterculture may have contributed

2. Philip E. Jacob, *Changing Values in College: An Exploratory Study of the Impact of College Teaching* (New York: Harper and Row, 1957), p. 1. Hoge's research has documented the relatively high levels of religious commitment among college students during the 1950s relative to previous and subsequent levels (Dean R. Hoge, *Commitment on Campus*). The Gallup data considered in Chapter 6 also suggest that young people's religious commitments were high, even in comparison with older people's, during the 1950s.

3. For a more detailed discussion, see Robert N. Bellah, "The New Consciousness and the Berkeley New Left," in Charles Y. Glock and Robert N. Bellah (eds.), *The New Religious Consciousness* (Berkeley and Los Angeles: University of California Press, 1976), pp. 77–92.

significantly to students' exodus from organized religion and their experimentation with new religions.

The data to be analyzed in this chapter afford longitudinal evidence of religious shifts among students while in college, where the effects of countercultural participation should presumably have been greatest. In addition, they provide evidence on religious changes in the years immediately following graduation, allowing us to assess whether countercultural participation during college also fostered religious defection and experimentation after college or whether students reverted back to conventional religion after leaving the campus milieu. Data will also be presented on the religious identities of students upon entering college in comparison with the religions in which they were raised, allowing us to examine whether parental and background characteristics known to have been conducive to participation in the counterculture were also conducive to religious defection and experimentation. These characteristics include religious background, socioeconomic status, parents' childrearing values, parents' politics, and the intellectual sophistication of the student. The effects of these characteristics on religious shifts during and after college will also be considered.

The data were collected as part of a larger study of changing values being conducted by the Institute for Research in Social Behavior in Berkeley.[4] They are panel data from two cohorts of male students at the University of California, Berkeley, a sample of 960 freshmen initially interviewed in Fall 1970 and a sample of 986 seniors initially interviewed in Spring 1971. Second waves of data were collected from each sample approximately two and a half years later with mailed questionnaires. Seventy-eight percent and 75 percent of those initially in the respective samples responded to both waves of the study. These data, of course, do not permit generalizations to be made about female students. The reason for limiting the samples to males was that the larger study was chiefly interested in occupational plans. It was assumed that quite different processes might operate among females than among males. To include both sexes, therefore, would limit what could be learned about either.

Students' religious identities were classified into four categories: Christian (Protestants and Catholics), nonreligious (atheists, agnostics, and students without religious beliefs), Eastern mystical (Hindus, Buddhists,

4. These data were collected under a grant from the National Institute of Mental Health (MH-21425) to the Institute for Research in Social Behavior, Berkeley, directed by Dean Manheimer, Glen Mellinger, and Robert Somers, to study "Changing Life Styles and Values among University Males." For further information on the sample, see D. I. Manheimer, G. D. Mellinger, R. H. Somers, and M. T. Kleman, "Technical and Ethical Considerations in Data Collection," *Drug Forum* 1 (July 1972): 323–333.

mystics, and adherents of other Eastern philosophies), and other (Jews, believers in Eastern Orthodoxy, Mormons, members of cults, and students failing or unwilling to identify their religious beliefs). This division affords a crude indication of the extent to which each respondent remained loyal to traditional religion, had abandoned religion altogether, or had become identified with some new religion. The data on religious identity was obtained with identical questions at both the first and second time periods for both the freshmen and senior cohorts. The religion in which the student had been raised was also asked and classified as Christian, nonreligious, or other.

Before turning to the data themselves, we should note that the problems of accurately analyzing changes in panel data are exceedingly complex, there currently being a variety of ways in which such changes can be examined, none of which is entirely satisfactory. The approach that presently seems to have gained the greatest support is to identify the sources of change in the following way. First, measure some phenomenon (here, religion) at two time periods and see how well the first set of responses predicts the second set of responses. Taking this relation into account, then examine how some other phenomenon (say, grade point average) measured at the first time period has affected the phenomenon of interest (religion) measured at the second time period.[5] In the present case, if there were a significant relation between grade point average at Time-1 and religion at Time-2, taking into account the relation between religion at Time-1 and religion at Time-2, we would say that grade point average was a cause of change in religious identity. This procedure essentially shows whether or not something at one time period produces subsequent *changes* in something else. But it avoids some of the statistical problems that arise from more direct approaches.

In the pages that follow, we shall consider a number of factors to see whether they cause change in religious identity at different times. We shall

5. See Peter M. Blau and Otis Dudley Duncan, *The American Occupational Structure* (New York: Wiley, 1967), for a discussion of the advantages of this method. This so-called "lagged dependent variable" procedure has generally been employed with continuous, linear variables using regression techniques. Since our own data involve nominal variables, we use a log-linear technique developed by Leo A. Goodman, "Causal Analysis of Data from Panel Studies and Other Kinds of Surveys," *American Journal of Sociology* 78 (March 1973): 1135–1191. The Goodman procedure as employed here is as follows: let variable (1) be religion at time t, variable (2) be religion at time t-1, and variable (3) be some test variable measured at time t-1; then the difference between the likelihood-ratio chi-square values for model H_1 which specifies relations between variables (1) and (2) and between variables (2) and (3) and model H_2 which specifies relations between variables (1) and (2) and variables (2) and (3) and variables (1) and (3) for appropriate degrees of freedom yields an estimate of the significance of the test variable's effect on change in religion. The figures for these tests are presented in the Appendix.

discuss which ones are statistically significant and which ones are not. To maintain the readability of the chapter, we have placed the statistics themselves in the Appendix. For those factors that do seem to cause significant changes in religious identity, we shall present some simple percentage tables to illustrate what their effects are.

The discussion focuses on religious changes during three periods: before the student enters college, as measured by comparing the religion one was raised in with his religion as a freshman, using data from the freshman cohort; during college, by comparing the religious identities of the freshman cohort as freshmen with their religious identities two and a half years later; and after college, by comparing the religious identities of the senior cohort as seniors with their religious identities two and a half years after graduation. For each of these time periods, we shall be most interested in discovering the differences between students who remain loyal to Christianity, students who become apostates from Christianity, students who are nonreligious to begin with and who stay nonreligious, and students who are experimenting with Eastern mysticism.

RELIGIOUS DEFECTION BEFORE COLLEGE

Although a great deal of attention has been given to religious shifts among students during college, it has become increasingly evident that the major religious changes probably occur before students ever enter college or at least during the very early weeks of college.[6] This is evidenced in the Berkeley data, where over half (58 percent) of those having grown up as Protestants or Catholics report some other religious preference by the Fall of their freshman year. Hence, it is important to discover the sources of this early religious experimentation.

We would expect one of the most powerful of these influences to be the religious convictions of the student's parents, and indeed they are.[7] The importance of religious convictions to their mothers and fathers, as perceived by the student, is the only information we have on parents' religious commitments, but this factor has important consequences. This is shown in Table 48, in which we compare the four types of students of greatest interest to us: *Christians* (raised as a Protestant or Catholic and still one as a

6. See Hoge, *Commitment on Campus*; and Jeffrey K. Hadden and Robert R. Evans, "Some Correlates of Religious Participation among College Freshmen," *Religious Education* 60 (July-August 1965): 277–285.
7. The significance tests for the items examined in this section are presented in Appendix Table A-7.

freshman); *apostates* (raised as a Protestant or Catholic but nonreligious as a freshman); *nones* (raised nonreligious and nonreligious as a freshman); and *mystics* (identified with Eastern mysticism as a freshman regardless of religious background). The table shows that 76 percent of the Christians say religious convictions were important to their mothers, compared with 50 percent of the apostates; over half of the Christians say religion was important to their fathers, compared with only a quarter of the apostates. A substantial share of religious defection, therefore, appears to reflect the religious disinterest of many students' parents. Among those raised nonreligious, only a few, as should be expected, say religion was important to their mothers (13 percent) or to their fathers (4 percent). Mystics, it turns out, are more likely to have had religious parents than apostates, but are somewhat less likely to have had religious parents than those who remained Christians.

After religious background, socioeconomic status has probably been considered one of the most important influences on religious commitment in general. Among young people, a higher status background should have promoted early exposure to the cultural innovations that were taking place in the 1960s and, therefore, have produced more religious defection than a lower status background. Some evidence to this effect has been documented, in fact, by national polls of students. One conducted in 1970, for example, found that 68 percent of the students whose parents had annual incomes of $15,000 or more felt religion was no longer relevant to their lives, in comparison with 44 percent among students whose parents earned less than $7,000 annually.[8] Studies have also shown that disaffection with other kinds of conventional values has been more characteristic of students from relatively advantaged families than from less advantaged families.[9]

Four indicators of social class background are available in our data: family income, father's education, mother's education, and father's occupation. We compared students whose families earned incomes of $20,000 or more with those whose families earned less, students whose fathers had college degrees with those whose fathers did not, students whose mothers had college degrees with those whose mothers did not, and students whose fathers worked in professions with those whose fathers worked in other occupations. Three of these indicators turned out to be unrelated to religious changes. Only father's occupation produced significant effects: significantly fewer of the Christians than of the apostates had fathers in profes-

8. *Gallup Opinion Index*, "Religion in America," (1972), Report No. 70.
9. See Robert Wuthnow, *The Consciousness Reformation* (Berkeley and Los Angeles: University of California Press, 1976).

sions. As between apostates and the nonreligious, there were no significant differences. Mystics, however, were much more likely to have fathers in professions than any of the others (see Table 48).

These results give some support, insofar as father's occupation is concerned, to the idea that religious experimentation may be located among students from economically and educationally advantaged families who, as a result of these advantages, may have been more exposed to recent cultural shifts than others. But this support is weak. It appears that socioeconomic status more generally conceived may have only a little to do with the choice to defect from religion or to experiment with new religions once the influence of the religion in which a student has been raised is taken into consideration. We should note, however, that Berkeley students tend generally to be recruited from relatively well-to-do families. On campuses with greater variation in students' socioeconomic backgrounds, the effects of such backgrounds might well be more significant.

Like the effects of social class, those of parents' values also seem to be relatively insignificant among the Berkeley students. It is sometimes argued that the recent countercultural unrest in general and religious disaffection in particular have resulted from the permissive child-rearing values of middle-class parents. By encouraging early independence and freedom of self-expression, this argument suggests, middle-class parents have unwittingly encouraged their children to experiment with life styles differing radically from their own. There is no support for this argument in our data. Students were asked (in the absence of information from parents themselves)

Table 48. SOURCES OF DEFECTION BEFORE COLLEGE (Berkeley Males)

| | Religious types: | | | |
	Christians	Apostates	Nones	Mystics
Percent whose:				
Mother valued religion	71%	50%	13%	61%
Father valued religion	58%	25%	4%	50%
Father worked in a profession	26%	38%	37%	61%
Mother gave lots of love	38%	24%	18%	39%
Father gave lots of love	33%	16%	11%	33%
Verbal SAT above average	37%	58%	44%	50%
Math SAT above average	45%	58%	53%	61%
Number	(211)	(187)	(116)	(18)

to give their perceptions of the importance their parents attached to a variety of child-rearing values, including "actively taught and encouraged me to be independent, do things on my own" and "encouraged me to develop my own opinions and express them even when he or she didn't agree." These questions were asked separately about the students' mothers and fathers. In neither case were the responses associated with students' religious identities as freshmen, taking into account their religious backgrounds.

Nor is there any support for a related argument that religious experimentation has been a reaction to middle-class parents who, being relatively affluent and preoccupied with careers and social obligations, were perceived by their offspring as overly materialistic. Students who said their mother or father "gave me material things to make up for the time and attention I didn't get" were neither more nor less likely to have defected from religion or to have engaged in religious experimentation than students who did not characterize their parents this way (again taking into account religious background).

The one child-rearing characteristic that is associated significantly with early religious defection is the amount of love and affection bestowed on the child by his parents, as perceived by the student (see Table 48 again). Thirty-eight percent of the Christians said the statement "gave me lots of love and affection" described their mother well, compared with 24 percent of the apostates and 18 percent of the nonreligious. The differences for fathers bear a similar pattern. For both parents, mystics and Christians give virtually identical responses. Thus, the perception that one's parents loved him and were affectionate toward him seems to deter defection from Christianity, and when defection does occur, it seems to promote religious experimentation rather than sheer nonreligiosity.

Another important source of student involvement in countercultural activities has been political socialization. Student radicalism, in fact, has sometimes seemed to be merely an extension of the liberal values of these students' parents.[10] Such values merit consideration as a possible source of religious defection and experimentation as well. Political liberalism has been associated with a greater willingness to countenance new and diverse ideas, including religious ideas, and perhaps to adopt them personally. Students on the modern campus would seem more likely to defect from traditional religion and to take part in the new religions they were exposed to when they had been reared in a liberal rather than a conservative envi-

10. See Seymour Martin Lipset, *Rebellion in the University* (Boston: Little, Brown, 1972), and Kenneth Keniston, *Youth and Dissent* (New York: Harcourt Brace Jovanovich, 1971).

ronment, merely because of greater tolerance in their families toward social experimentation.

These assertions notwithstanding, our data give no indication that religious changes before college are more likely among students from politically liberal backgrounds than among those of more conservative parentage. Students were asked to place each of their parents' political orientations on a nine-point continuum from radical to very conservative. Neither mother's nor father's political position is significantly related to students' religious identities as freshmen, holding constant their religious backgrounds. Parents' politics may have an indirect influence by affecting their own religious commitments, which in turn, as we have seen, condition the religious choices of their children. But the immediate sources of early religious defection and experimentation seem to lie most clearly in the religious characteristics of the student's background rather than the other values he may have acquired from his parents.

One additional characteristic to be considered as a possible source of student religious experimentation is the student's level of intellectual sophistication. This level may be partly a function of parental background, of course, but it warrants examination in its own right. Higher levels of intellectuality generally correspond with greater awareness of current ideas and events. Hence, they increase the chances of being exposed to the recent cultural reorientations that have detracted from the legitimacy of traditional religion and have legitimated experimentation with nonconventional religious forms. Greater intellectual sophistication may also increase the likelihood of being exposed to new religious practices themselves.

Three estimates of students' intellectual abilities upon entering college were obtained: high school grade point average, Standardized Aptitude Test (SAT) scores in verbal reasoning, and SAT scores in mathematical skills. Of these, greater confidence can probably be placed in the latter two than in the former, since grading policies differ markedly from one high school to the next, whereas SAT scores are based on uniform information. Both SAT scores are significantly related to religious identity, controlling for religious background, although high school GPA is not. Looking at Table 48 again shows that apostates are 19 percent more likely than Christians to have scored above average on the verbal test and 13 percent more likely to have scored above average on the mathematics test. Those raised nonreligious are more likely to score high on both tests than those raised as Christians, but fewer score high than among the apostates, suggesting that there may be something about religious rebellion rather than mere secularity that tends to be associated with academic performance. On both tests the mystics are more likely than either the Christians or the nonreligious to have received high scores.

These results suggest that intellectual sophistication may be a source of defection from Christianity to nonreligious or mystical orientations while students are still in high school or upon their entry to college. It should be observed, however, that these measures of intellectual sophistication are taken late in the students' high school careers. It is possible, therefore, that the religious defection among these students may have occurred earlier in their youth, when their academic performance was at a higher or lower level. For this reason, it cannot be said for sure that academic ability is the *cause* of religious defection. It may be that religious defection is the source of higher academic performance.

Summarizing briefly, religious defection before college appears to be most clearly a function of the degree of religious commitment to which students were exposed in their homes. There is some evidence as well that religious defection is more characteristic of students from higher status than from lower status backgrounds, but this evidence is qualified. Nor does religious defection among these students seem to be associated with exposure to supposedly middle-class values of independence and self-expression or with materialistic child-rearing orientations. Of the other items tested, perceptions of love and affection from parents and students' levels of intellectual sophistication prove to be significant factors, while parents' political attitudes are unrelated to religious defection.

RELIGIOUS DEFECTION DURING COLLEGE

Research on religious changes during college predates the counterculture of the '60s and '70s, beginning in the early part of the century along with studies aimed at discovering the effects of liberal higher education on students' values more generally. In most of this literature it has been assumed that college instruction makes students more open-minded (or, as some have put it, "enlightened") and therefore less willing to adhere to traditional religious dogma. Substantial evidence has accumulated showing that religious indifference or antagonism toward religion has not been uncommon on campuses, especially those of higher quality, and that this indifference or antagonism increases as students progress from their freshman to their senior year. On the surface, these results suggest that college training itself may be an important source of religious defection, apart from (or even instead of) involvement in specifically countercultural activities, as we have argued. Since experimentation with new religions presupposes some open-mindedness and tolerance of the nonconventional, as shown in Chapter 1, the same argument might be applied to it. Before turning to the effects of countercultural involvement, therefore, it seems necessary to give some attention to the effects of college training.

This is not the place to engage in an extensive review of the literature on college effects, but it should be pointed out that students of this literature have criticized it with increasing severity on several counts.[11] First, changes in values during college have usually been attributed to the college environment, but these changes are ones that might have occurred even if students had not been in college, simply because of maturation.[12] Second, the effects of the historical period during which the college effects were examined has usually not been taken into account. The frequently observed fact that students' values appear more liberal at the end of the research than at the beginning may be the result of more pervasive liberalizing trends in the culture, for which there has also been evidence. Third, research on college effects has often relied on methods too crude to draw accurate conclusions. For example, some research has suggested that students from conservative backgrounds abandon their childhood values when placed in a liberal college context more often than students from liberal backgrounds; it would be wrong to infer that conservatism somehow causes change, though, because conservatives have more of a *chance* to become liberals than students who are already liberal.

The Berkeley student data overcome these difficulties in large measure. Students who dropped out of college as well as those who remained in school were followed up with mailed questionnaires, providing a comparison group for determining whether religious changes are really a product of the college context or whether they occur equally outside this context. Dropouts, it should be noted, provide a good comparison group for students, since the two tend to be similar in many respects when they first enter college, at least more similar than young people never having gone to college. In the present data, religious changes among students and dropouts can also be compared with changes among graduating seniors over the same time period to determine whether or not college has any effects apart from the historical period. Furthermore, the methods we are using to assess the sources of change tend to be less constrained by statistical difficulties than most of the methods employed in previous studies of college effects.

11. Several excellent reviews have been published; for example, Kenneth A. Feldman, "Change and Stability of Religious Orientations during College. Part I. Freshman-Senior Comparisons," *Review of Religious Research* 11 (Fall 1969): 40–60; Kenneth A. Feldman, "Change and Stability of Religious Orientations during College. Part II. Social-Structural Correlates," *Review of Religious Research* 12 (Winter 1970): 103–128; and Clyde A. Parker, "Changes in Religious Beliefs of College Students," in Merton P. Strommen (ed.), *Research on Religious Development* (New York: Hawthorn Books, 1971), pp. 724–776.

12. Besides Feldman's review articles, see J. W. Trent and L. L. Medsker, *Beyond High School* (Berkeley: Center for Research and Development in Higher Education, University of California, 1967); and W. T. Plant and C. W. Telford, "Changes in Personality for Groups Completing Different Amounts of College over Two Years," *Genetic Psychology Monographs* 74 (1966): 3–36.

Looking first at dropouts and students, we see virtually the same religious changes in each group. If anything, there is more religious defection among dropouts, contrary to what we would expect if college training itself were a major source of religious defection. Among the dropouts, 25 percent of those who were Christians as freshmen have become nonreligious after two and a half years, in comparison with 21 percent among the continuously enrolled students. And fewer of the dropouts (3 percent) than of the continuous students (5 percent) who were initially nonreligious convert to Christianity. Some of the dropouts transfer to other colleges, of course, but it appears doubtful that these transfers would be more exposed to secularizing influences in their college environments than their counterparts at Berkeley. It seems more likely that the religious shifts among both dropouts and students can be traced to factors other than those unique to the campus.[13]

Another approach for discovering whether religious defection comes from going to college or simply from growing up has been to compare college students with college alumni. Research taking this approach has generally found religious commitment considerably higher among alumni than it had been when these alumni were in college, suggesting that maturation after college produces a return to religious loyalties. But since these increases have usually been based on comparisons between attitudes of students and attitudes of these students some fifteen years after graduation, it is difficult to know how to interpret them, except to conclude the obvious fact that long-term maturation partly reverses the effects of going to college. Were measures taken sooner after graduation, it would be easier to decide whether the college milieu itself generates religious defection in students, some of whom immediately return to religion upon leaving college, or if defection, owing more to maturation during early adulthood, continues unabated after graduation.

In our data we can compare religious defection during college with religious defection after college by looking at changes occurring among the freshman students who were continuously enrolled at Berkeley during the subsequent two and a half years and contrasting them with those changes occurring among the seniors during the two and a half years following graduation. Since both changes were measured between 1970 and 1973, we have the added advantage of not having to worry about differences in historical time periods. This comparison again casts doubt on the assumption that the campus environment per se contributes to secularity among

13. That there are no statistical differences in the religious changes of continuous students and of dropouts is demonstrated by comparing the likelihood-ratio chi-square values for log-linear models which do and which do not include the student-dropout distinction as a variable. This difference is 4.9 for 3 degrees of freedom, significant only at the .20 level.

students. Although more youth defect from Christianity to nonreligion during college than after (21 percent versus 15 percent), the numbers who defect after college continue to be sizable. Nor does the campus seem especially capable of preventing the nonreligious from becoming religious; about equal proportions in both cohorts shift from nonreligiosity to Christianity (5 percent and 6 percent of the nonreligious repsectively). These similarities lend support to the idea that religious defection may be rooted in general cultural patterns of the period or in maturation rather than in the college experience itself.

If college training were responsible for religious defection and experimentation, we would also expect better students to defect and experiment more often than poorer students. Better students would presumably be exposed to the general intellectual ferment of the campus more than poorer students and might also be more closely identified with it, having been more rewarded by it. The objective measures at our disposal for distinguishing between better and poorer students among freshmen, it will be recalled, are those used by the university itself to predict subsequent college performance—high school GPA, math SAT scores, and verbal SAT scores. In addition, two less objective measures are available—whether a student thinks of himself as an intellectual ("enjoys intellectual activities and has a wide range of interests in history, literature, philosophy, and so on") and whether he plans to attend graduate school. None of these items is significantly related to religion at the second time period, controlling for the students' religious identities as freshmen.[14] Thus, further doubt is cast on the assumption that the intellectual climate of the college context itself is a significant source of religious defection and experimentation.

Before turning to the effects of countercultural involvement, one other alternative explanation for religious defection warranting examination is the idea that shifts in religious identity stem from psychological stress. It has been argued that new religious movements often appeal to persons experiencing some form of social or psychological deprivation, and, indeed, we have seen some evidence to this effect among residents of the Bay Area.[15] In the present instance, we might expect stress to be high among experimenters with mysticism. As between Christians and the nonreligious, expectations are less clear, although one might suspect higher levels of stress among students who in any way changed their religious identities than among students who did not.

14. Tests of significance for the items discussed in this section are presented in Appendix Table A-8.
15. For a theory of religious movements linking them to various forms of stress or deprivation, see Charles Y. Glock and Rodney Stark, *Religion and Society in Tension* (Chicago: Rand McNally, 1965), Chapter 13.

Our measures of stress are relatively straightforward—whether students had been bothered by unhappiness, hopelessness, nervousness or tenseness, worry, or loneliness. None of these items is significantly related to religion at the second time period, taking into account the students' religious identities as freshmen.

The single explanation receiving unqualified support by the data is that religious defection and experimentation during college is rooted in the counterculture. By virtually any measure of countercultural involvement, students who dropped out of religion altogether during college or who took up Eastern identities are more likely to have been involved in the counterculture as freshmen than students who remained traditional Christians. Table 49 shows the proportions involved in countercultural activities among *Christians* (Protestants or Catholic at both Time-1 and Time-2), *apostates* (Protestants or Catholics at Time-1 but nonreligious at Time-2), *nones* (nonreligious at both Time-1 and Time-2), and *mystics* (Eastern or mystical at Time-2 regardless of affiliation at Time-1). The table shows that apostates are more likely than Christians to have (as freshmen) been in demonstrations, done community organizing, favored cohabitation, approved of premarital sex, considered marijuana important to their life style, and thought about living in a commune—all familiar themes of the counterculture. Those who were initially nonreligious are more likely than either the Christians or apostates to have done or said these things as freshmen. And mystics tend to be highest of all on most of these indicators.

Table 49. SOURCES OF DEFECTION DURING COLLEGE (Berkeley Males)

	Christians	Religious types: Apostates	Nones	Mystics
Percent who:				
Had been in a demonstration	18%	23%	38%	40%
Had done community organizing	19%	27%	33%	37%
Favored living together before marriage	43%	59%	82%	70%
Approved of premarital sex	25%	49%	70%	57%
Said marijuana was important to their life style	3%	13%	21%	30%
Said they'd like to live in a commune	19%	25%	42%	47%
Number	(135)	(49)	(303)	(30)

It should be added that none of the conditions (except father's religiosity) contributing to religious experimentation before college—socioeconomic background, love and affection from parents, parents' politics, intellectual sophistication, and so on—is significantly related to the religious identity of these students, controlling for their religious identities as freshmen. Thus, the importance of countercultural involvement as an explanation for religious defection and experimentation during college is further enhanced.

In sum, religious changes occurring during college turn out to be rooted in sources different from those occurring before college. Not surprisingly, they are no longer linked to parental values. But they are not chiefly a function of the intellectual training gotten on campus either. Rather, they are decidedly connected with involvement in the counterculture. Before commenting further on the importance of this involvement, however, the sources of religious defection after college need to be discussed.

RELIGIOUS DEFECTION AFTER COLLEGE

The data on religion among seniors and three years later provide a further test of the foregoing conclusions. They show whether involvement in the counterculture during college continues to influence religious changes after college. They also allow the effects of different life styles after college to be examined to see if any cause a return to traditional faith. Since somewhat more of the senior cohort were involved in experimentation with Eastern religions, they also provide some additional evidence on the sources of experimentation with these new identities and on defection from them.

The data show again that countercultural involvement is a significant source of religious defection and experimentation. Indicators such as having identified with new life styles as a senior, having used drugs in college, having lived with a girlfriend as a senior, having been in favor of living together before marriage, having been critical of conventional morals, and having given approval to nonviolent methods of protest tend uniformly to be associated with students' religious identities after college, controlling for their religious identities as seniors.[16]

Table 50 shows the differences in these items among six religious types: *Christians* (Protestants or Catholics at both times), *apostates* (Protestants or Catholics as seniors but subsequently nonreligious), *nones* (nonreligious at both times), *converts* (nonreligious as seniors but Protestants or Catholics subsequently), *mystics* (Eastern mystics at the second time period), and

---

16. Significance tests for the sources of religious defection discussed in this section are shown in Appendix Table A-9.

Table 50. **COUNTERCULTURAL INVOLVEMENT AND RELIGIOUS SHIFTS AFTER COLLEGE** (Berkeley Males)

			Religious types:			
	Christians	Apostates	Nones	Converts	Mystics	Former Mystics
Percent who had:						
Identified with new life styles	14%	23%	36%	13%	72%	61%
Used drugs	52%	70%	83%	87%	100%	96%
Been living with a girlfriend	5%	0%	15%	0%	28%	22%
Favored living together before marriage	53%	70%	89%	74%	94%	92%
Been critical of conventional morals	10%	22%	35%	30%	62%	55%
Approved of nonviolent confrontation	34%	52%	65%	56%	75%	69%
Number	(117)	(23)	(320)	(23)	(32)	(49)

former mystics (Eastern mystics as seniors but no longer identified as such). By any of the indicators except cohabitation, apostates are more likely than Christians to have been involved in the counterculture during college. Those who were nonreligious as seniors and who continued to be nonreligious are more likely than either Christians or apostates to have been involved in the counterculture. Converts were not as likely to have been involved in the counterculture as the nonreligious, but they were more likely to have been involved than the Christians. On most of the items, they resemble the apostates. The highest percentages on all the items are among the mystics, nearly all of whom at least gave lip-service to the counterculture while in college. Former mystics also tend to have been heavily involved in the counterculture, although the percentages for them are generally somewhat smaller than those for the current mystics. Countercultural involvement, therefore, discriminates between all these major religious styles.

The other background items examined previously cannot be examined as fully in the senior cohort, since data were not obtained on parental religiosity or child-rearing values. Indicators of socioeconomic status again turn out to be insignificantly related to religious identity, as does the single available measure of intellectual sophistication (college GPA). Measures of psychological stress also show no significant relations. The only difference from the previous findings is that parents' political orientations are now significantly related to religious experimentation. A look at the percentages, however, shows that differences in political background between Christians and apostates are small (25 percent and 27 percent respectively had liberal mothers and 18 percent and 20 percent respectively had liberal fathers) as are the differences between mystics and former mystics (59 percent versus 56 percent for mother and 42 percent versus 53 percent for father). The main differences appear to be between the nonreligious and converts, only 18 percent of the latter having had liberal mothers and 10 percent having had liberal fathers, in comparison with 40 percent of the former having had liberal mothers and 31 percent having had liberal fathers.

One of the intriguing questions about religious changes among students, of course, has been whether or not these changes last beyond college. It has already been seen that the number returning to conventional religion after college is no greater than that during college and that a substantial number continue to defect after college. Another approach for assessing the likelihood of students returning to conventional loyalties is to examine the effects of life changes typically occurring in the years immediately after graduation. The present data allow us to assess the effect of marriage (either during

or after college), going to graduate school, taking up full-time employment, and entering the armed forces. Marriage and employment have
usually been suspected of reinforcing commitments to organized religion,
while graduate school has been thought to further erode these commitments. Arguments have been made on both sides of the issue for military
service.

Of these factors, only working and military service are significantly
associated with religious identities at the second time period, taking into
account religious identities at the first time period. More of the Christians
(19 percent) enter the armed forces after college than of either the apostates
(4 percent) or the nonreligious (8 percent). Converts have the highest
proportion of all in military service (22 percent). None of the current
mystics and only 2 percent of the former mystics are in the armed forces.
While it is difficult to know which causes which, it appears, therefore, that
military service tends to be associated with loyalty to conventional religion
more than with defection from it. As far as working is concerned, 69
percent of the Christians have become employed full-time, compared with
61 percent of the converts and 54 percent of the nonreligious but only 29
percent of the apostates. Forty-four percent of the current mystics are
employed, as are 43 percent of the former mystics. Once again, therefore,
becoming involved in commitments to the established social order seems to
be associated with conventional religious loyalties as well.

CONCLUSION

The results we have presented in this chapter will have to be tested among
other groups of college students before much can be said by way of generalization. In making such comparisons, several qualifications should be kept
in mind. First, Berkeley is a highly selective campus; other, more diverse
student populations might show different relations than some of the ones
found here. Second, our sample being limited to males precludes generalization about religious defection among females. Third, our discussion has
been concerned with discovering statistically significant sources of religious
change. Most research, in contrast, has reported only the correlates of religious variables measured at a single time. Fourth, our inquiry has had to
rely on evidence only about religious identity; it would clearly be desirable
to know if other dimensions of religious commitment show the same relations. Finally, we have focused on factors temporally prior to religious
changes that could, therefore, be regarded as *causes* of religious change. This
does not deny, of course, that some of these factors may also be influenced in
turn by differences in religious identity.

These qualifications considered, the sources of religious defection and experimentation uncovered in our analysis of the Berkeley students appear similar in many ways to those found previously in our discussion of the general public. The role of exposure to current sources of cultural innovation, found in Chapter 1 to be an important source of religious experimentation, seems to be operative among college students as well. It is interesting that factors facilitating such exposure seem to be significant sources of religious defection only before entering college. That they are not important later, of course, may be because the Berkeley campus itself provides such a high level of exposure to cultural innovations that individual differences affecting exposure cease to be important.

Countercultural involvement has been very much in evidence as a source of religious defection and experimentation, both among the general public and among the Berkeley students. We have argued that this involvement partly reflects a broader cultural milieu which legitimates experimentation with alternatives to established institutions, whether religious or secular. We have also suggested that the counterculture has functioned as a substitute for religious sources of social solidarity among many young people, at the same time helping to differentiate them from the adult society. The importance of the counterculture as a source of religious defection in these data raises the question, of course, whether religious nonconventionality among students will last as the counterculture of which it has been a part fades, or whether it will also gradually wane as maturation channels students away from the counterculture. In answer to this question, it bears mentioning that some evidence from national polls has suggested that the values of the counterculture may not have faded at all, but rather may have diffused to larger and larger audiences.[17] Nonetheless, our own data has indicated that certain life changes, especially becoming employed, may well cancel out the effects of countercultural participation. For this reason, the possibility must be seriously entertained that the extensive religious defection and experimentation witnessed on campuses during the late 1960s may be only short-lived for those who were a part of it.

Two final conclusions also seem worthy of mention. Evidence of psychological stress among youthful religious experimenters, seen in Chapter 1 to be a significant correlate of religious experimentation in the Bay Area sample, is absent in these data. It should be noted, however, that Berkeley students occupy a highly privileged position in relation to many other young people. The role of stress may be less for them as a source of religious experimentation than for others for this reason. The other observation emerging from the student data has to do with the role of parental religious

17. For instance, see Yankelovich, *The New Morality*.

convictions as a source of religious defection, an important source of early religious defection, as we have seen. While there is considerable evidence that religious defection among young people represents a form of generational conflict, it should be recognized from this evidence that generational continuity in religious defection is also at work. The religious apostasy of students partly reflects the religious apathy of their parents. Conflict and continuity between young people and their elders need not be incompatible. In many cases, nonreligion has been only the logical extension of religious nominalism.

CHAPTER 8

Nominal and True Believers

We have suggested, drawing on a variety of evidence, that religious commitment has declined relative to the prominence it enjoyed prior to the cultural restructuring that took place during the 1960s. The question remains whether religion continues to be a decisive force in the lives of those who have stayed committed to it or whether it has also lost influence among its own members. Has the core of American religion stood firm, even though its ranks have been thinned by apostasy and experimentation, or has it too been weakened by the forces shaping the larger society?

Stated thus, we can probably not supply an answer that will be agreed on universally. Nor should we. What we offer are some comparisons between those few in the Bay Area who adhere to the traditional hallmarks of Christianity, either conservatively or more liberally defined, and those who remain only nominally identified with Christianity, those who have defected altogether, and those who have become attached to new, experimental forms of religion. The purpose of this chapter is to explore the extent to which such differences affect the lives of those who have chosen these alternative modes of religious expression.

To make these comparisons, we must have a means of distinguishing alternative religious orientations. Our data offer various possibilities for making these distinctions. Rather than relying on the responses to any single question, therefore, we shall use a combination of questions about religious belief and practice. *Conservatives* are operationally defined as persons who definitely believe in God or believe their lives are strongly influenced by God, take an active part in church or attach great importance to church activity, and believe in an afterlife with rewards for some and punishments for others. *Liberals* manifest the same characteristics, except that they do not believe literally as the conservatives do in an afterlife with rewards and punishments.[1] The *nominally religious* are persons who are involved in church or value church activities but do not believe in God or feel their lives are not influenced by God, or they believe in God or feel God influences their lives but do not take part in church or value church partici- pation. To be considered nominally religious, they must also not identify themselves as atheists, agnostics, or as having no religious beliefs. The *nonreligious* tend to explicitly reject mainstream religion by identifying themselves as nonreligious, atheists, or agnostics, or by saying that they don't believe in God or that they feel that God has no influence on their lives. *Experimentalists* have to say that they are uncomfortable about the word "God," although they do believe in something "more" or "beyond," and that their religious beliefs are Eastern, mystical, humanist, or some "other" religion (see Table 51).

By these criteria, 15 percent of the sample are classified as conservatives. This proportion seems to be fairly appropriate, judging from responses to other questions. For example, 13 percent of the sample say that God's influence determines their lives almost entirely, 16 percent say that God has been the major influence in shaping their lives, 18 percent believe in a traditional view of life after death, 14 percent attribute suffering in the world to the devil, and 19 percent say they attend church every week. Liberals comprise 23 percent of the sample, meaning that about 38 percent of the sample altogether is classified as religiously committed in either a conservative or liberal manner. This proportion also seems fairly represen- tative of the Bay Area, judging from other questions. For example, 39 percent of the sample are active in churches or religious groups, 37 percent say they pray every day, 39 percent say it is of great importance in their lives to follow God's will, 30 percent say that people not obeying God is a major cause of suffering in the world, 43 percent say they think about the exis- tence of God a lot, and between 40 and 45 percent feel that God exists and actively answers prayer and influences history. Those classified as nominally religious make up 29 percent of the sample, a similar proportion to that expressing nominal commitment to religion on other questions, such as saying that God has a "small" influence on one's life (27 percent), that it is of "some" importance to follow God's will (37 percent), that people can learn "something" about life from religion (35 percent), or that people not

---

1. Belief in life after death varies strongly, of course, from conservative to liberal denomina- tions; for example, 97 percent of the Southern Baptists in the Glock church-member data, in comparison with 36 percent of the Congregationalists, felt it to be completely true that "there is a life beyond death." See Rodney Stark and Charles Y. Glock, *American Piety: The Nature of Religious Commitment* (Berkeley and Los Angeles: University of California Press, 1968).

Table 51. **CHARACTERISTICS USED TO DISTINGUISH RELIGIOUS TYPES** (Total Weighted Sample)

| | Modes of religious expression: | | | | |
	Conservative	Liberal	Nominal	Nonreligious	Experimental
Percent who:					
Take part in church, synagogue, or other religious group	93%	90%	4%	0%	26%
Definitely believe in God	98%	81%	73%	13%	0%
Don't believe, atheist, agnostic	1%	2%	2%	54%	0%
Believe in something "beyond"	0%	4%	9%	18%	100%
Life after death with rewards and punishments	100%	0%	10%	3%	0%
Believe in reincarnation	0%	8%	6%	3%	28%
Protestant, Catholic, Jewish	90%	88%	81%	24%	0%
Atheist, agnostic, no religion	0%	3%	0%	65%	0%
Buddhist, Hindu, mystic	0%	1%	5%	2%	18%
Number	(148)	(228)	(278)	(257)	(33)

obeying God is a "minor" cause of suffering in the world (20 percent). The nonreligious category constitutes 27 percent of the sample and usually about a fourth of the sample gives nonreligious responses to specific questions as well: 27 percent say they never think about the existence of God, 23 percent never pray, 24 percent attach no importance to following God's will, 20 percent classify themselves as nonreligious, atheists, or agnostics, 24 percent have never experienced the holy or sacred and don't care to, and 18 percent say God has had no influence on their lives. Finally, the experimentalists make up about 3 percent of the sample. On other questions having to do with religious experimentation, the proportions run about the same: 5 percent believe in reincarnation, 7 percent practice meditation using special techniques, 5 percent have taken part in Transcendental Meditation, and 3 percent have participated in Zen.

The particular criteria used to define our five modes of religious expression were chosen because they seemed to discriminate between different religious orientations better than any other combinations of responses in the data. Although they do not yield pure religious types, they isolate respondents who, by almost any definition of the terms, fit the categories in which they are placed. Tables 51 and 52 reveal the following religious profiles for each of the five types.

Conservatives. Although many different criteria have been used to judge religious commitment, these respondents come as close to being devoutly religious in a traditionally conservative sense on every dimension of religious commitment as any group we could conceive. Ninety-eight percent of them definitely believe in God, 95 percent believe their life has been strongly influenced by God, 87 percent attach great importance to following God's will in their lives, 79 percent say they think about the existence of God a lot, and all of them believe in a heaven and a hell—all of which is to say that they seem, certainly in comparison with the other religious types, highly oriented toward the supernatural as traditionally defined. Indeed, two out of three (66 percent) affirm that they have had an experience of closeness with the sacred or holy which has had a lasting influence on their lives, and 81 percent claim that they pray every day. These are also people who overwhelmingly associate themselves with the church. Ninety-three percent say they are currently active in some church or religious group, 90 percent say they are Protestant, Catholic, or Jewish, 90 percent say they attach considerable importance in their lives to taking part in church activities, 67 percent say they attend church every week, and 76 percent think they can learn a great deal about life from religion.

Liberals. By comparison, the liberals are by no means as uniformly committed to such traditional tenets of belief and practice, but religion nonetheless plays an important role in their lives. Ninety percent claim to take an active part in religious groups, and 88 percent identify themselves as Protestants, Catholics, or Jews, but only 39 percent attend church every week (28 percent fewer than among the conservatives). Eighty-eight percent believe in some form of life after death, but most of these say they are unsure what it may be like; nearly one in ten says reincarnation comes closest to his beliefs about life after death. Similarly, 81 percent believe definitely in God, but only about half (57 percent) pray daily to God, only a third (34 percent) say they have experienced the holy in a deeply meaningful and lasting way, only four of ten (39 percent) say that people not obeying God is a major cause of suffering in the world, and about that many (37 percent) say that following God's will is not of great importance to their lives. In comparison with the conservatives, therefore, liberals tend to have, on the average, about twenty percent fewer persons who are strongly committed to the traditional practices of their faith. On specifically liberal beliefs, however, they give decidedly greater assent than the conservatives; for example, 40 percent agree that man evolved from lower animals, compared with 19 percent among the conservatives.

The nominally religious. A large majority of the people in this category continue to identify with mainstream religion in some way; for instance, four out of five (81 percent) claim to be Protestants, Catholics, or Jews, and three out of four (73 percent) believe definitely in God. Yet only a minority expresses the kind of commitment to the specifics of their faith that characterizes conservatives and liberals. Only one in three values following God's will (34 percent), believes suffering comes about because people don't obey God (31 percent), or prays every day (32 percent). Even fewer are actively involved in religious activities. None attends church every week, and only 4 percent are involved at all in churches or religious groups. Only 21 percent attach importance to church participation, 51 percent fewer than among the liberals and 69 percent fewer than among the conservatives. The nominally religious have not dissociated themselves entirely from conventional religion, therefore, but for all intents and purposes they have broken any formal commitments they may have had to it.

The nonreligious. In contrast to the nominally religious, the nonreligious have disengaged from religious involvements and for the most part have taken an overtly negative orientation toward such involvements as well. None of them is active in religious groups, none attends church, and only 4 percent attach value to church participation. Ninety percent have never had an experience of contact with the sacred that they consider important, 87 percent express doubt about God's existence, 85 percent attach little or no importance to following God's will, and only 3 percent believe in heaven or hell. Furthermore, they tend to explicitly regard themselves as nonreligious; for example, nearly two-thirds (65 percent) identify themselves as atheists, agnostics, or as having no religious beliefs. These characteristics are quite different, of course, from the conservatives and liberals, and they are also considerably more pronounced than among the nominally religious. For example, 59 percent never pray, compared with only 12 percent of the nominalists; 50 percent think people can learn little or nothing from religion, compared with 16 percent of the nominalists; and 59 percent say that God has had no influence at all on their lives, whereas none of the nominalists chose this response. The nonreligious, as operationally defined here, are scarcely 100 percent detached from religion, but they have severed their ties to a much greater degree than any of the others.

The experimentalists. These respondents, of whom there are only a few, resemble the nonreligious in having cut themselves off from established faiths, yet they remain open to the transcendent, and a sizable proportion expresses interest in some form of nonconventional religion, whether Eastern philosophy, mysticism, or the occult. All of them feel uncomfortable about the word "God," but rather than aligning themselves with atheism or agnosticism, they indicate belief in something "more" or something "beyond." None of them believes in a traditional view of life after death, but all believe in some kind of afterlife, with 28 percent saying that the idea of reincarnation comes closest to their views. None of them identifies with Protestant, Catholic, or Jewish faiths, but neither do they call themselves nonreligious; 18 percent say they are Buddhists, Hindus, or mystics, another 31 percent say they are humanists, and the remainder identify themselves as "other" or as being uncertain how to characterize their beliefs. Their nonconventionality is shown in a variety of ways. For instance, 34 percent say they have had a lasting experience of being close to the sacred (the same percentage as among liberals), and an even larger proportion (47 percent) say they have experienced harmony with the universe (no more than a fourth of any of the other categories say they have had this experience). On belief, considerably more of the experimentalists believe in the influence of the stars on their lives (79 percent) than believe God influences their lives (43 percent) or than value following God's will (15 percent).

There is no way to construct an entirely fool-proof typology using data from the real world, of course, so there are undoubtedly those in our scheme who have been misclassified as conservatives when they are not, as nonreligious when they are not, and so forth. But from every indication we have available, it seems reasonable to suggest that rather dramatic religious

Table 52. **RELIGIOUS BELIEFS AND PRACTICES (Total Weighted Sample)**

		Modes of religious expression:			
	Conservative	Liberal	Nominal	Nonreligious	Experimental
My life has been strongly influenced by God or other supernatural force	95%	79%	60%	9%	43%
Important to follow God's will	87%	63%	34%	5%	15%
People not obeying God is a major cause of world's suffering	66%	39%	31%	8%	10%
Experienced close contact with the holy, had lasting effects	66%	34%	18%	10%	34%
Can learn a lot about life from religion	76%	61%	41%	14%	38%
Man evolved from lower animals	19%	40%	46%	74%	92%
Important to take part in church	90%	72%	21%	4%	18%
Attend church weekly	67%	39%	0%	0%	4%
Pray every day	81%	57%	32%	6%	15%
Number	(148)	(228)	(278)	(257)	(33)

differences exist between the conservatives, the liberals, the nominally religious, the nonreligious, and the experimentalists. Let us, therefore, examine the resultant differences in other areas of these respondents' lives.

MEANING AND PURPOSE IN LIFE

Beginning with matters primarily of importance to the person (as opposed to social issues), we would expect to find differences between respondents of different religious orientations in their responses to questions about meaning and purpose in their lives. Three items were available in our data to test this expectation, one that asked how much people thought about the purpose of life, a second that asked how meaningful they felt their lives to be, and a third that asked whether or not they felt they knew the answer to the purpose of life. Since religion has been one of the main channels through which people have approached questions of meaning and purpose, we guessed that the more religiously oriented would probably be more likely to say they'd thought about such questions than the less religious. This is what the data show, although the differences are small (see Table 53). Conservatives are most likely to say they think about the purpose of life a lot (45 percent), followed by the experimentalists (42 percent). Liberals are less likely to think about this question (32 percent), but are still somewhat more likely to think about it than either the nominally religious (26 percent) or the nonreligious (22 percent).

With regard to the answers to the question about meaning in life, the results are somewhat different. Conservatives are more likely than others to say their life is very meaningful (67 percent). Among the other orientations, however, there are virtually no differences. The percentages who say their life is very meaningful vary only between 55 percent and 58 percent. Conservatives are also considerably more likely than the others to say they have an answer to the purpose of life (63 percent). Here, the differences among the others are somewhat larger, but still vary only between 29 percent (among the liberals) and 21 percent (among the nonreligious).

The pattern that emerges, therefore, is that conservatives are most likely both to ponder the purpose of life and to feel they have found answers, probably because their religious faith supplies these answers. The experimentally religious wonder about the purpose of life about as much as the conservatives, but with less satisfactory results. They remain seekers. As for the others, it seems to make little difference that some are liberally religious while others are nominally religious or nonreligious. Liberals are somewhat more likely to think about purpose in life and to find answers, but the differences are small and represent only about a fourth of the respondents in any of the three categories. All three types say their lives are meaningful in about the same proportions.

PERSONAL MORALITY

Matters of personal morality have also been the subject of much religious teaching. Historically, the church has been the champion of sexual fidelity, virtue, honesty, diligence, and other moral standards. More recently, these issues have often divided conservatives from liberals, the one wishing to uphold both the spirit and the letter of biblical injunctions, the other advocating a new, more relative or situational morality. Such issues have also been points of contention between those who have abandoned religion and those who have not and, certainly, between the more experimental and the more conventional religions.

As we might well expect, therefore, the differences associated with different religious orientations on questions of morality are quite powerful (see Table 54). One of the questions we asked respondents was whether they approved or disapproved of "an unmarried couple living together." Only 20 percent of those we have classified as conservatively religious say they approve. Twice as many of the liberals (41 percent) approve. Even more of the nominally religious approve (55 percent). More still of the nonreligious say they approve (78 percent). And among the experimentalists, seven out of eight (87 percent) approve. Another question bearing on sexual conduct asked about "more freedom for homosexuals." This idea gains support from only 15 percent of the conservatives, but from almost half of the liberals (43 percent). On this question, the nominally religious are actually somewhat less likely to give assent (38 percent) than the liberals. The nonreligious, however, are much more approving than any of the conventionally religious: 65 percent of them say they favor more freedom for homosexuals. Again, the experimentalists almost universally (88 percent) give their approval.

We also asked a more general question about "living up to strict moral standards" to see how much importance is attached to this value by people having different religious orientations. Here, of course, we would expect the pattern of support to be reversed. Sixty-three percent of the conservatives say this is of great importance in their lives, as compared with 45 percent of the liberals. Substantially fewer of the nominally religious (29 percent) and fewer still of the nonreligious (24 percent) say the same. Among the experimentalists, only about a fifth (12 percent) as many as among the conservatives attach importance to this value.

Table 53. **MEANING AND PURPOSE IN LIFE (Total Weighted Sample)**

		Modes of religious expression:			
	Conservative	Liberal	Nominal	Nonreligious	Experimental
Think a lot about the purpose of life	45%	32%	26%	22%	42%
My life is very meaningful	67%	55%	56%	55%	58%
Have an answer to the purpose of life	63%	29%	27%	21%	28%
Number	(148)	(228)	(278)	(257)	(33)

Table 54. **PERSONAL MORALITY (Total Weighted Sample)**

		Modes of religious expression:			
	Conservative	Liberal	Nominal	Nonreligious	Experimental
Approve of cohabitation	20%	41%	55%	78%	87%
Favor more freedom for homosexuals	15%	43%	38%	65%	88%
Important to live up to strict moral standards	63%	45%	29%	24%	12%
Might say I was sick to get an extra day off work	36%	27%	37%	51%	59%
Might consider buying a stolen radio or TV	4%	9%	12%	25%	30%
Number	(148)	(228)	(278)	(257)	(33)

Finally, we asked two situational questions having to do with basic honesty. The first asked respondents whether they felt they might, or definitely wouldn't, "say you were sick when you really weren't in order to get an extra day off." The second asked for the same responses regarding "buy[ing] a radio or TV from someone who had stolen it and was selling it cheap." The responses to the first appear somewhat surprising. More of the conservatives (36 percent) than of the liberals (27 percent) say they might lie to get an extra day off. Whether this is because the conservatives are more mindful that "the flesh is weak," or whether it may stem from the fact that more of the conservatives may be working or from some other factor, we cannot say. The other responses are more in keeping with what we would expect, however. The nominally religious are more likely than the liberals to say they might do this (37 percent say they feel they might). Even more of the nonreligious give an affirmative response (51 percent). And the largest proportion is again among the experimentally religious (59 percent). On the second question (buying a stolen radio or TV), the conservatives fall in line again (only 4 percent say they might), followed by the liberals (9 percent), then the nominally religious (12 percent), then by the nonreligious of whom the proportion saying they might is more than twice as large (25 percent) as for the conventionally religious, and finally, the experimentally religious (30 percent).

If behavior follows conviction, these results indicate that religion does make a considerable difference in the ways in which people conduct their lives morally and sexually. Traditional morality still finds support from traditional faith, whereas the nonreligious and especially the religious experimenters seem to have largely abandoned these traditions. Let us see whether religious orientations have the same influence on personal values.

PERSONAL VALUES

What we have in mind here are values such as "job security," having a beautiful home, a new car, and other nice things," "a high-paying job," "children," "lots of friends"—those values that are often associated with the American way of life itself. In asking these questions, we weren't sure what to expect as far as religious differences are concerned. Churches, especially the more conservative ones, have often preached against the pursuit of material success and worldly pleasures. At the same time, they have been known to inadvertently encourage their parishioners along the road to material happiness and often have been the focus of criticism for doing so. Having children seems less ambiguous, at least as a value historically associated with the churches, but again little is known about its

current relation with religious teachings. In general, conformity to dominant values in one area has tended to be associated with conformity in other
areas as well. But in the present context, it isn't clear whether the religious
conservatives, the liberals, the nominally religious, or the nonreligious
should be considered as the most conformative orientation. Only the religious experimenters seem clearly likely to reject such conventional values,
and even they have sometimes been characterized as wanting "something
more" out of life, while not wishing to give up their attachment to the more
mundane niceties of modern life.

The data show that the various religious types mostly score about the
same on these personal values. Conservatives are slightly less likely than
liberals to stress a high-paying job and lots of friends and are slightly more
likely to value having children, but these differences are small and on the
other values there are no differences at all between the two (see Table 55). As
between the liberals and the nominally religious, virtually the same percentages attach importance to all of the values listed. This is also pretty
much the case for the nonreligious, except that fewer of them than of the
liberals or nominally religious value having children. Thus, none of the
major religious orientations seems to make much difference as far as commitment to these kinds of personal values is concerned. The experimentally
religious, however, tend to be set apart in their rejection of these values.
Only about half as many of the experimentalists as of the other orientations
value job security, high pay, or lots of friends, only about a third as many
value a nice home, car, and other such possessions, and they resemble the
nonreligious in valuing children less than the religious.

COUNTERCULTURAL ACTIVITIES

We have already seen that countercultural activities tend to be associated
with religious defection and experimentation. Are they also associated with
being nominally religious, as compared with being religiously committed?
Are they more common among liberals than among conservatives? One of
the questions we asked respondents was whether they would like to try
living in a commune (or perhaps had lived in a commune) or whether they
either disapproved of communes or, though approving, felt communes
were not for them. Another question asked respondents to say whether they
liked to smoke dope (marijuana) a lot or whether they didn't like dope that
much or had never tried it. We also asked whether or not they had ever
experienced being "high" from drugs. And to get at a more political
dimension of the counterculture, we asked respondents if they had ever been
in a demonstration.

Table 55. **PERSONAL VALUES (Total Weighted Sample)**

			Modes of religious expression:		
	Conservative	Liberal	Nominal	Nonreligious	Experimental
Attach importance to:					
Job security	46%	46%	46%	41%	25%
A beautiful home, new car, and other nice things	14%	14%	16%	16%	5%
A high-paying job	13%	21%	21%	21%	12%
Having children	52%	46%	52%	35%	35%
Having lots of friends	31%	37%	34%	33%	16%
Number	(148)	(228)	(278)	(257)	(33)

Table 56. **COUNTERCULTURAL ACTIVITIES (Total Weighted Sample)**

			Modes of religious expression:		
	Conservative	Liberal	Nominal	Nonreligious	Experimental
Would like to live in a commune	7%	9%	10%	19%	41%
Like to smoke dope	2%	4%	11%	21%	49%
Been "high" on drugs	12%	14%	22%	43%	71%
Took part in demonstrations	8%	10%	13%	28%	38%
Number	(148)	(228)	(278)	(257)	(33)

The experimentally religious, as we should expect, are more likely than any of the other religious types to have participated in the counterculture in these ways: 41 percent of them say they would like to try communal living, compared with only 13 percent of the total sample; 49 percent say they like to smoke dope a lot, compared with only 5 percent of the total sample; 71 percent have been "high" on drugs, compared with only 27 percent of the total sample; and 38 percent have participated in demonstrations, compared with 17 percent of the total sample. The nonreligious also score above average on these activities, although not as high as the experimentally religious (see Table 56). Nineteen percent say they would like to live in a commune, 21 percent like to smoke dope a lot, 43 percent have been high on drugs, and 28 percent have been part of demonstrations. These activities may well be the *cause* of nonreligiosity and religious experimentation, as we have argued previously. Having become nonreligious or a religious experimenter, however, it seems likely that one's propensities to participate in or to support countercultural activities would be reinforced.

The nominally religious are considerably less likely to have taken part in countercultural activities than the nonreligious—9 percentage points less likely to be interested in communes, 10 percentage points less likely to like drugs, 21 percentage points less likely to have experienced a high, and 15 percentage points less likely to have participated in demonstrations. They are only slightly more likely to have taken part in these activities than the religiously committed liberals, however. The largest difference is on having been high (8 percentage points) and the smallest is on attitudes toward communes (1 percentage point). The fact that virtually all of the liberals take part in church, while virtually none of the nominally religious do, seems to make little difference, therefore, in how the two orient themselves to the counterculture.

What is also surprising is that conservatives differ little from liberals on these activities. To be sure, conservatives are less likely to have taken part in the counterculture than liberals, but on each of the items the two are separated by only a two percentage point spread. This is despite the fact, it should be recalled, that conservatives are almost twice as likely as liberals to attend church every week and to have had deep and lasting religious experiences. Furthermore, conservatives are over 20 percentage points more likely to value following God's will, to attribute suffering to not obeying God, and to pray every day, and all of them believe in a traditional view of life after death, in comparison with none of the liberals.

In sum, whether one is conservative, liberal, or nominally attached to mainstream religion seems to make little difference in these data as far as one's attitudes toward the counterculture are concerned, at least in comparison with being nonreligious or religiously experimental. The major differences on countercultural involvement in this sample seem to be between those still identified with conventional religion and those not identified with it, rather than between the more committed and the less committed within conventional religion.

POLITICAL CONSCIOUSNESS

It has been widely suggested that political attitudes vary depending on one's religious views, conservatives in religion being conservatives in politics and liberals in one being liberals in the other. Of the numerous studies examining the relations between religion and politics, however, just about as many have found no relations between the two as have found relations, and some have even found relations in the "wrong" direction. Most of these studies have dealt with specific policies or with specific political issues. Part of the reason for religion not being associated more strongly with political attitudes may be that such issues are simply not salient or that, more generally, the religious may not have a keen sense of political consciousness. As one indication, studies comparing the relations between religious and political attitudes among political leaders with those among the general public, or those among the highly educated with those among the less educated, or those among college students with those among adults, have generally found stronger relations in the former, presumably because they were more politically conscious than the latter.

For these reasons, we asked some questions to find out how politically conscious respondents were before asking them questions about more specific policy issues. Part of political consciousness, of course, is simply how informed a person is, on which we have no data. But perhaps a more important aspect of political consciousness is how people *explain* events happening in their society. In other words, some people probably understand social problems as problems stemming from the social and political structure of the society itself, while others would probably attribute these problems to individuals, to fate, to the supernatural, or to some other cause. Karl Marx's pointed criticisms of religion, of course, were precisely that religious believers tended to attribute social problems to the divine and therefore failed to see them as problems of the society itself, problems about which something could be done.

To find out something about political consciousness, we asked respondents how much they agreed or disagreed with a variety of explanations frequently given to account for the existence and persistence of poverty in

American society. We had found through preliminary interviews that people were usually willing to countenance several explanations to greater or lesser degrees rather than having their minds made up firmly enough to choose only one explanation. To discover how many respondents do, in fact, explain problems such as poverty by reference to the supernatural, one of the explanations presented was "God gave people different abilities so that the work of the world will get done." As expected, this explanation finds greatest support from the more religious, varying strongly among our five religious types. While only 27 percent of the religious experimenters and only 35 percent of the nonreligious agree with this statement, 81 percent of the conservatives agree, 72 percent of the liberals agree, and 59 percent of the nominally religious agree (see Table 57).

We also asked two questions to test the frequency of individualistic explanations: "Poor people are born without the talents to get ahead," and "The poor simply aren't willing to work hard." The extent to which religion has been associated with individualistic values and morals in American history led us to suspect that we might find the same patterns for these explanations as we did for the supernatural explanation. The data suggest somewhat different patterns, however. Almost the same proportions agree with the statement about poor people not having talents, whether their religious orientation is conservative, liberal, nominal, or nonreligious; only the experimentally religious are considerably less likely than the others to agree with this explanation. As for the poor not working hard, conservatives, liberals, and the nominally religious all agree in about the same proportions. The nonreligious are somewhat less likely to agree, although the differences are small. The experimentalists again are the least likely of all to agree. We cannot be entirely sure of the proper interpretation of these results, but what they suggest is that individualistic explanations do not erode as people become liberal, nominally religious, or nonreligious, in the same way that supernatural explanations do. The view that poor people don't work hard seems to be somewhat more common among the religious than among the nonreligious; again, this seems to be where the difference lies rather than between the different ways of being conventionally religious.

We also asked respondents to give their opinions of two statements involving social or political explanations of poverty. One explained that "the poor are poor because the American way of life doesn't give all people an equal chance." The other suggested a more overt political cause: "The poor are poor because the wealthy and powerful keep them poor." Both statements elicited almost identical responses. On each, about half the

Table 57. EXPLANATIONS OF POVERTY (Total Weighted Sample)

			Modes of religious expression:		
	Conservative	Liberal	Nominal	Nonreligious	Experimental
Agree that a major reason for poverty is:					
God gave people different abilities so that the work of the world will get done	81%	72%	59%	35%	27%
Poor people are born without the talents to get ahead	18%	16%	20%	21%	7%
The poor simply aren't willing to work hard	26%	30%	29%	22%	12%
The American way of life doesn't give all people an equal chance	51%	51%	52%	70%	78%
The wealthy and powerful keep them poor	54%	51%	55%	71%	79%
Number	(148)	(228)	(278)	(257)	(33)

conservatives, liberals, and nominally religious agreed, compared with about 70 percent of the nonreligious and almost 80 percent of the religious experimenters.

Political consciousness, therefore, does appear to be less pronounced among the conventionally religious than among the nonreligious or among the nonconventionally religious. Whether one is conservative or liberal, however, seems to make little difference as far as political explanations for poverty are concerned. Nor does it appear to make much difference whether one is actively involved in organized religion or only nominally identified with it.

ATTITUDES TOWARD SOCIAL POLICIES

If social problems are less likely to be conceived in political terms by the religious and if the different ways of being religious seem to bear little relation to this likelihood, than it seems doubly unlikely that conservatives, liberals, and the nominally religious will differ significantly from one another on specific social policies. This is, indeed, the conclusion best supported by the data.

One of the questions asked was whether respondents supported a guaranteed annual wage program for the poor or whether they felt the poor should look out for themselves except for private charity and government-supported jobs. Conservatives, liberals, and the nominally religious score virtually the same on this question: 30 percent, 33 percent, and 28 percent respectively support a guaranteed wage program. The nonreligious are substantially more likely to give their support (41 percent), and the highest rate of support is among the experimenters (53 percent). Another question asked about approval of "new tax laws making it impossible for anyone to become extremely wealthy." On this question, the religious also score somewhat lower than the nonreligious, although the conservatives give almost as much support as the nonreligious. The religious experimenters again score considerably higher than the others (see Table 58).

A similar pattern is evident on questions concerning liberal or radical changes in the American governmental structure. The conventionally religious are least likely to support major changes in the government, to say that an avowed revolutionary should be treated like anyone else, and to identify their own political position as liberal or radical. They are followed on these questions by the nonreligious and finally by the religious experimenters, who are overwhelmingly supportive of political change. Conservatives do tend to score somewhat lower in their support of political

Table 58. POLITICAL ATTITUDES (Total Weighted Sample)

| | | Modes of religious expression: | | |
	Conservative	Liberal	Nominal	Nonreligious	Experimental
Support a guaranteed annual wage program for the poor	30%	33%	28%	41%	53%
Favor new tax laws making it impossible for anyone to become extremely wealthy	39%	31%	36%	44%	65%
Our form of government needs a major overhaul	42%	42%	45%	53%	76%
An avowed revolutionary should be treated like anyone else	40%	46%	47%	61%	81%
Liberal or radical	17%	26%	26%	49%	87%
Vote for affirmative action candidate	12%	22%	14%	25%	56%
Important to help women get equal rights	36%	50%	40%	55%	74%
Number	(148)	(228)	(278)	(257)	(33)

change than liberals, at least on two of the items, but liberals and the nominally religious score virtually the same.

We also asked two questions having to do with equality for minority groups. One was a story-type question which read:

Imagine two candidates, Smith and Jones, are running against each other for a seat in the state government. In the state there are a lot of black people, but only a few of them have been hired for state jobs.

JONES says the state should make special efforts to hire blacks until they get their rightful share of jobs.

SMITH says the state should pay no attention to color and hire people who are best fitted for the job whether they are black or white.

You may not be completely happy with either Jones's or Smith's point of view, but they are the only choice you have in the voting booth. How would you vote? Jones or Smith?

The other question asked how much value respondents placed on "helping women to get equal rights." As with other questions about social policy, the conventionally religious are less inclined to support the affirmative action candidate and women's rights, followed by the nonreligious, who in turn are less supportive of these policies than the experimentally religious. On these questions an important difference appears among the conventionally religious types, however. Liberals are more likely to support these policies than conservatives. They are also more likely to support them than the nominally religious. Here is one instance, then, where religious orientations seem to carry over into the political sphere, with commitment to religious liberalism reinforcing liberal attitudes toward minority rights.

What we have seen, in sum, is that religious conventionality tends to be associated with greater unwillingness to countenance social reform than either nonreligiosity or religious experimentation. On most of these issues, however, the differences between conservatives, liberals, and the nominally religious tend to be minimal in comparison with those who have abandoned conventional religion entirely.

CONCLUSION

The purpose of this chapter has been to see whether the core of true believers remaining in the religious mainstream, however their numbers may have been reduced, still differ significantly from the nominally religious and from the nonreligious on important matters of value, policy, and life style, or whether the core of mainstream religion may have grown weaker both in size and in the influence it exerts over its members. We have also sought to determine if there are differences within the religious core itself between those whose theology tends toward the liberal and those whose theology tends more toward the conservative. What we have found may come as no surprise to readers familiar with past studies similar to this one. But the results must surely be disheartening to those committed to the proposition that religious faith should make some difference in the lives of those who believe.

Despite the fact that religious conservatives in our sample tend to espouse traditional beliefs and practices to a much greater extent than liberals, the two differ only on matters of meaning and personal morality. Conservatives tend to think about the meaning of life, feel their lives are meaningful, and believe they have found the answer to the purpose of life more often than liberals. They also tend to adhere more commonly to traditional moral standards, but more specifically, it seems, only to standards of sexual conduct, since the two questions we asked about honesty produced mixed results. On less personal matters, we have witnessed a slight tendency for liberals to be more supportive of equal rights for minorities than conservatives, but on most policy issues theology seems to have little influence. Virtually the same proportions among conservatives and liberals support major governmental change, economic reforms, and countercultural activities. They differ in their propensity to attribute social problems such as poverty to God's design, but they show no differences in their use of social or political explanations for such problems. Nor do they differ in the extent to which they value material possessions in their lives.

If conservatives and liberals resemble one another in most respects, the same can also be said about the nominally religious in comparison with both liberals and conservatives. Despite the fact that virtually all the liberals, for example, take part in church activities, in comparison with virtually none of the nominally religious, the two differ minimally on most of the items we examined. There are scarcely any differences regarding meaning and purpose or personal values. On morality issues the nominally religious are less likely to support strict moral standards and are more likely to countenance cohabitation and dishonesty at work, but are no more likely than the liberals to express tolerance toward homosexuals or to say they'd buy stolen goods. The only difference between the two on countercultural activities is that more of the nominally religious have experimented with drugs. Both are equally likely to agree with political explanations of poverty, although the nominally religious are less likely to also attribute poverty to God's plan. The liberals are somewhat more likely to favor equality for minority groups, but on matters of economic and governmental reform there are no important differences.

Within the religious mainstream, therefore, strong differences in theological dispositions and in levels of commitment seem to be associated with only minimal differences in the kinds of values, life styles, and political attitudes we have been able to examine. Outrightly rejecting conventional religion, however, seems to have greater consequences, although not on everything. Items about meaning and purpose and about values show no major differences between the nonreligious and any of the conventionally religious categories. On all the morality items, counterculture items, political consciousness items, and social policy items, however, the nonreligious are consistently from 10 to 20 percentage points more likely to take a liberal orientation than the nominally religious or the liberals, and, of course, they are even more likely to be liberal than the conservatives.

Only the experimentalists consistently differ from the other religious orientations on practically all the items examined. They think about questions of meaning more than any of the other groups except the conservatives, although they do not feel they have found answers. They are consistently more liberal on morality items than any of the others, including the nonreligious. They are the only group to reject conventional values having to do with job and family. And they score higher than any of the others on countercultural activities, political consciousness, and support for liberal social policies.

To summarize, the religious mainstream can be said to exert an influence over the lives of those identified with it, in the sense that they tend generally to be more conventional and more conservative than those having outrightly dissociated themselves from it. Whether this is a direct influence, though, seems somewhat doubtful, given the minimal differences within the religious mainstream itself between persons varying in commitment and style of belief. For them, at least in the present sample, the major influence of religious commitment itself continues to be on matters of personal morality. On more public or political issues, their church attachments seem not to have informed their opinions to any significant degree. Why this may be so, as well as the relations between these findings and the larger picture of religious change that we can now piece together, is the subject of the concluding chapter.

III. CONCLUSIONS

III. CONCLUSIONS

Chapter 9

The Coming Of
Religious Populism?

In this concluding chapter, I want to try to draw together a number of themes implicit in the foregoing chapters and cast them into a somewhat larger framework that will perhaps illuminate more fully some of the social processes seemingly involved in the recent religious experimentation. This attempt will remain speculative in the final analysis, of course, since many of the processes with which we must concern ourselves are still unfolding.

The recent experimentation in American religion has taken many forms. There have been movements rooted in Asian religious traditions. There have been Jesus People and similar movements from within the Christian tradition. There have been experiments with the occult. There have been quasi-religious experiments clothed in the garb of psychological and political movements. There has been experimentation with atheism, agnosticism, and nonreligion. And there have been experiments within the churches themselves in worship, theology, and service. Each of these kinds of experimentation itself encompasses a multitude of more specific groups and innovations. We have learned something of the social sources or consequences of several of these kinds of experimentation from the Bay Area data. We have, of course, failed to learn anything about many of them. What we did learn, we have attempted to summarize as we went along. But in attempting to draw some general conclusions, the fact of *experimentation* itself is a phenomenon requiring some comment, lest the forest be missed for the trees.

The recent religious experimentation in American society, as a general social phenomenon, has probably been nourished to some extent by several long-range tendencies seemingly characteristic of modern societies. Among others, these have probably included the rising role of popular education and the mass media, high standards of living, and cultural pluralism. Over the long haul, each of these developments has probably contributed to the creation of a reservoir of persons exposed to the latest cultural innovations and having the time and interest to experiment with them. In the Bay Area we have seen the direct or indirect effects of these factors at a number of points in our investigation. Although we have not been able to examine it directly, the opportunity for a diverse offering of religious institutions to co-exist and for individuals to choose among them (including the option to choose again and again without damage to feelings of moral consistency) has probably also been enhanced by the autonomy and complexity of a large-scale urban society. The ability to stage-manage diverse, and sometimes conflicting, commitments has been commented upon as a common feature of life in these settings.[1] These conditions seem to go only part way in accounting for the present religious experimentation, however, for there have been times of great religious unrest in societies where these conditions were largely absent, and there have been times of relatively little religious experimentation under essentially the same social conditions.

Judging from some of the larger findings of the Berkeley religious consciousness project, the recent experimental character of American religion also seems potentially attributable in some measure to what might be termed a gradual "re-enchantment" of the natural and social world.[2] This process, if it has indeed taken place, has taken place slowly and imperceptibly, making its existence difficult to establish with any degree of certainty. Over a period of some time, however, there seems to have been some indication of this process being manifested in at least three ways.

The first way might be thought of as a long-range reinfusion of divine immanence into the realm of human events. Conceptions of mankind ruled over by a transcendent, omnipotent, inscrutable deity whose inerrant will

1. Erving Goffman's convincing observations of the dramaturgical character of everyday life suggest the importance of presentational rituals both for the sustenance of the self and for the preservation of social order. Indeed, Goffman has argued that these rituals have become a major repository of sacredness in secular societies. See especially, Erving Goffman, "The Nature of Deference and Demeanor," *American Anthropologist* 58 (June 1956): 473–502; and Erving Goffman, *The Presentation of Self in Everyday Life* (Garden City, N.Y.: Doubleday, 1959). It takes only a small leap of inference from Goffman's observations to suggest that morality and integrity may cease to be defined as qualities somehow internal to the individual but as an individual's ability to stage-manage himself in such a way as to act consistently in similar situations and to avoid situations demanding conflicting role performances.

2. Following Weber, the usual assumption, of course, has been that modernity has been accompanied by a gradual *disenchantment* of the world. As more has been learned about the nature of myth and ritual, however, it has become more difficult to sustain this simple evolutionary perspective. Rather than the sacred simply receding in the modern world, it has become infused into different objects, such as the individual, public opinion, the state, and nature, all of which tend to be attributed the *mana* once reserved for the gods and treated accordingly with the respect of taboo.

must be sought and obeyed seem to have gradually receded in the face of conceptions placing man and God in partnership, a partnership in which God increasingly seems to have become the silent partner. The effect of this tendency, to the extent that it has taken place, has probably been to attribute an increasing sense of efficacy both to the individual and to the world of nature.

The second tendency has been what some have regarded as a gradual unfettering of the individual from the laws of nature and their incumbent obligations bestowed upon him by the Enlightenment, itself a product of the first development. This "new individualism," as it has been articulated by many of the contemporary religious movements themselves, tends to give the individual the perceived capability, formerly reserved for the gods, of not only discovering reality and truth (his role in Enlightenment individualism), but of creating them symbolically and experientially.[3]

Third, a gradual re-enchantment of social events also seems to have taken place, unleashing them from supernatural intervention on the one hand and from natural causation, such as genetic, racial, geographic, and morphological factors, on the other. Social factors, one might say, have tended to become animated forces themselves, capable of constraining even the individual, although subject in turn to human manipulation. If these tendencies toward re-enchantment, especially of the individual, have occurred, they have probably contributed to the legitimacy of experimentation, including religious experimentation, by granting the individual both a capacity and an obligation to make of himself what he will.[4]

The other condition that has probably contributed measurably to the recent experimentation in American religion, judging from our investigation in Chapter 6, is the changing relation of American youth to the dominant social order. On the surface, this change seems to have been one of tacit acceptance being replaced by overt criticism of the society's conventional norms, coupled with relatively widespread adoption of life styles and attitudes running counter to these norms. The initially political tenor of these developments during the 1960s seems to have been survived by experimentation with nontraditional modes of religious expression, sexual conduct, and spare-time activities. Underlying the formation and persistence of this counterculture, however, and perhaps ironically, has been a gradual *incorporation* of youth into the main institutional structure of the

3. Goffman writes, "Many gods have been done away with, but the individual himself stubbornly remains as a deity of considerable importance" ("The Nature of Deference and Demeanor," p. 502).
4. Some evidence on these possibilities has been presented in my book, *The Consciousness Reformation* (Berkeley and Los Angeles: University of California Press, 1976).

society—the enfranchisement of eighteen-year-olds being a symbolic indication, but the increasingly recognized role of higher education as an apprenticeship period for entry into professional and technical occupations, the economic role of young people as an important consumer market, and the reliance of the military on young people who tend to perceive themselves as having the same rights as other citizens, being perhaps more to the point. The social inclusion of youth appears to be a widespread phenomenon, at least in modern countries. It has been precisely this inclusion, giving young people a sense of being able to make legitimate claims upon the social order of which they have become a part (judging from what has been found in studies of other types of collective protest), that seems to have at least partly underlain their propensity to engage in critical and nonconventional activity.[5]

At the same time, the countercultural commitments associated with the young seem to have facilitated the establishment of "youth" as an identifiable *social category*, no longer merely a limited age category or even a psychological stage, as Kenneth Keniston has described it, but a distinct aspect of the social organization of modern societies, included as part of these societies and yet not simply absorbed anonymously into them. The distinctive modes of dress, living arrangements, language, and religious orientations of people identifying with this subculture have tended to provide visible symbolic boundaries separating youth as a social category from the remainder of the society. These boundaries tend to maintain an autonomous social "space" in which tasks necessitated by the society can be accomplished, the most important of which may be the recruitment of personnel to occupy the adult roles of the society and the articulation of personal interests in these role demands. These tasks by no means seem easy to accomplish in complex, industrialized societies having both a highly differentiated division of labor and a constantly changing technological base. The youth subculture seems to provide an atmosphere of relative freedom, in comparison with that of the adult society, to experiment with alternative courses of behavior, to explore, and to change, thereby enhancing the likelihood of these tasks being accomplished. While young people have tended to be incorporated into the larger social order, the youth subculture,

5. The importance of incorporation into the social order as a precondition of modern forms of collective violence has been argued persuasively by Charles Tilly, "Collective Violence in European Perspective," in Hugh Davis Graham and Ted Robert Gurr (eds.), *Violence in America: Historical and Comparative Perspectives* (New York: Bantam Books, 1969), pp. 4–45. Evidence on the relations between student protest and the political incorporation of youth for a number of societies has been presented in John M. Meyer and Richard Rubinson, "Structural Determinants of Student Political Activity: A Comparative Interpretation," *Sociology of Education* 45 (1972): 23–46.

therefore, has probably helped to protect them from becoming prematurely locked into commitments to the society's major social institutions.

Summarizing briefly, the recent religious experimentation appears to have been facilitated by, among other social and cultural conditions, relatively high levels of education and economic prosperity, cultural pluralism, belief systems giving the individual a sense of responsibility for discovering his own conceptions of ultimacy, and a changing relation of young people to the larger society. These factors have probably functioned as preconditions making religious experimentation possible, while other factors, perhaps more unique to the person, have influenced the choice of specific experiments.

The effects of the new religious experimentation on the religious mainstream have not yet been investigated sufficiently to suggest what their major significance may be. Clearly, the new religions have been perceived as a hostile force in some quarters, resulting in efforts to close ranks against them and to check their progress. In other quarters, they have been welcomed as a source of revitalization to the churches. From either standpoint, it seems evident that some of the values associated with the new religions have been diffused into the religious mainstream. The widespread interest in psychic and ecstatic experiences witnessed in the Bay Area, or the fact that even among the most religiously conservative of our respondents 20 percent approved of cohabitation, 12 percent had had a drug experience, 12 percent had participated in encounter or sensitivity groups, and 34 percent expressed some belief in astrology, can be cited as examples. Perhaps more importantly, although the data are less clear on this point, the new religions seem to have initiated a renewed interest in the experiential dimension of religion, stressing personal experience in place of doctrinal or ecclesiastical authority.

Another possible effect of the new religious experimentation, one that has not received much consideration and therefore seems deserving of some comment, derives from the *symbolic* role that deviant groups have sometimes been known to play. Deviant behavior, by definition, lies beyond the pale of conventionally accepted standards of conduct. As such, it dramatizes what the limits of conventional behavior are, or, as it has sometimes been put, deviance ritually defines the boundaries of acceptable behavior.[6] In this sense, the fact that many of the new religious movements have derived from sources outside the Judeo-Christian tradition (or from beyond western civilization) seems to have potentially broadened the definition of what may

6. See Kai T. Erikson, *Wayward Puritans: A Study in the Sociology of Deviance* (New York: Wiley, 1966).

now be regarded as "conventional" religion. Put differently, the extreme nonconventionality of some of the new experiments may have "made room" for greater diversity within conventional religion. One can get a sense of this possibility from comparing the 1960s and early 1970s with the 1950s, in which the boundaries of conventional religion seemed to be ritually defined, not by the presence of new religions, but by the threat of "atheistic Communism." In that period, the distinctions between normality and deviance in American religion seemed to be drawn essentially between believers and nonbelievers, church-goers and nonchurch-goers, those loyal to the Judeo-Christian faith and those opposed or indifferent. (Hence, President Eisenhower's well-worn remark, "Our government makes no sense unless it is founded in a deeply religious faith—and I don't care what it is.") By comparison, the religious experimentation of the 1960s and early 1970s seems to have set the limits of religious respectability farther out, such that even atheism, agnosticism, and humanism have come to lie more within the normal range.

Another way of looking at the boundary-defining functions of deviant behavior is to say that the presence of distinct external boundaries, as between believers and nonbelievers or between traditional faith and the new religions, may focus attention away from distinctions that might otherwise be made within the religious mainstream, such as distinctions between Protestants and Catholics or between Christians and Jews. External threats, especially if they are more symbolic than "real," often seem to produce a reaffirmation of certain common-denominator values, while topics of disagreement and potential disunity tend to be downplayed. This consequence may manifest itself either as overt tolerance of differences or merely as an unwillingness to focus attention on them.

There seems to be some evidence that the boundaries giving American religion its distinctive characteristics have been changing in this manner. If polls are believed, prejudices between Protestants and Catholics and between Christians and Jews have gradually subsided, in comparison with levels of several decades ago, as has intolerance of atheists. The ecumenical movement, though less successful than many had hoped, has stressed dialogue among the major Judeo-Christian faiths, seemingly with a reduction of out-group antagonisms. This is not to say that differences and divisions among church members have ceased, but certainly there is an impressionistic sense that overt attacks and open criticisms against members of other faiths have become less frequent. There also seems to be some evidence of a renewed interest in those common-denominator values which, although only partly accurate, have been characterized as the American civil religion, values derived in large measure from the religious mainstream and advanced, often implicitly, in the interest of consensus around national purposes and identities. Both the civil religion and the increased tolerance manifested among the major faiths toward one another suggest that violations of boundaries within the religious mainstream may have become less important as mechanisms by which the nature of American religion is dramatized.

In contrast, violations of boundaries on the fringes of mainstream religion seem to arouse considerable attention. For instance, parents normally apathetic toward religious activities have brought lawsuits against representatives of new religious movements for allegedly kidnapping and brainwashing their sons and daughters. Churchmen who would no longer countenance attacks on papacy or Judaism have, on occasion, openly ridiculed the promises of Eastern gurus. Religious ethnic groups have occasionally expressed fears that the new religions may erode the traditional loyalties of their youth. Even the most liberal of the religious mainstream have sometimes found themselves critical of the apparent authoritarianism evident in some of the new religions. The presence of such deviance-defining activities suggests that the new religions may have inadvertently helped to clarify the outer limits of the religious mainstream. From this perspective, therefore, the structure of American religion may have become somewhat "geodesic" in character, maintained, as it were, less by internal divisions than by an external shell which defines the limits of the structure but gives ample freedom of movement within.

To the extent that these are accurate descriptions of the religious mainstream, they can likely be attributed to the new religious experimentation only to a degree, however, for they also probably stem from some basic structural vulnerabilities within mainstream religion itself. One of these vulnerabilities which has been commonly noted seems to derive from the voluntarism and denominational diversity of American religion, long one of its distinguishing elements. To this historic diversity has been added the additional diversity of new experimentation in worship, in theology, in church structure, and in outreach and social service programs, owing partly to the same social unrest evoking the new religions. A characteristic feature of diversity among organizations within a single institutional sphere appears to be a degree of competition among these organizations to attract and retain participants. Competition of this sort tends to reduce the autonomy of organizations to pursue their own interests and ideals, making them subject to the demands of potential participants for whom they must compete. A common mode of adaption under such circumstances, whether in religion, in the economy, or in other spheres, appears to be a standardization of organizational products along the lines of common consumer interests to maximize their appeal, coupled with a reduction of product differentiation to relatively superficial "packaging" characteristics.[7]

The impact of increased diversity within American religion probably also tends to be compounded by the re-enchantment of the individual of which we spoke earlier. The individual seems to have, in a sense, been given the right to choose among competing conceptions of the ultimate, meaning that different individuals may legitimately choose differently. To the extent that individuals exercise this option, it tends to place religious organizations in an ambiguous situation. Their role tends to become one of offering attractive alternatives to the individual, but they tend to lack the authority they once had to command permanent loyalty.[8]

The term that seems to capture most appropriately the characteristics we have been describing is "religious populism." The distinguishing features of populism include: (1) a primary belief in the "intrinsic and immediate validity of the popular will," (2) fluid standards subject to fads and crazes, (3) diversity in ideas and organization (sometimes noted as the Janus character of populism), (4) resentment of elites and elite intellectuals, and (5) organizations that treat people as members of a mass audience or market.[9]

The nascent contours of populism in American religion can be seen along each of these lines, both in the religious mainstream and in the new religions. Validity of the popular will tends to be a corollary of the sovereignty of the individual in matters spiritual. Toqueville recognized this tendency in American religion some years ago: "If we examine it very closely, it will be perceived that religion itself holds sway there much less as a doctrine of revelation than as a commonly received opinion."[10] Of course, there seems to be an inherent tension between conformity to the majority opinion and the assertion that each person should choose that faith which his conscience dictates. This was not what Tocqueville had in mind, however. For there is

7. These characteristics of American religion have been discussed in detail by Peter L. Berger, "A Market Model for the Analysis of Ecumenicity," *Social Research* 30 (Spring 1963): 77–94.

8. I am indebted to Phillip E. Hammond for his patience and insight in discussing many of these ideas with me, some of which were summarized in a joint paper entitled "Religion —The Next Fifty Years" read at the annual meetings of the Pacific Sociological Association, March 1976, in San Diego, California.

9. These characteristics of populism have been discussed by William Kornhauser, *The Politics of Mass Society* (New York: Free Press, 1959), pp. 103–105; Richard Hofstadter, *Anti-Intellectualism in American Life* (New York: Vintage Books, 1963), pp. 151–169; and Angus Stewart, "The Social Roots," in Ghita Ionescu and Ernest Gellner (eds.), *Populism: Its Meaning and National Characteristics* (New York: Macmillan, 1969), pp. 180–196. The direct quotation is from Kornhauser, p. 104.

10. *Democracy in America,* vol. II (New York: Vintage Books, 1945), p. 12. Tocqueville adds, "It may be foreseen that faith in public opinion will become for them a species of religion, and the majority its ministering prophet" (p. 12).

tension only if the popular will is conceived of as monolithic. Where the popular will consists of fluid and diverse standards, as in populism, the individual chooses from a smorgasbord of available faiths according to his conscience, but the smorgasbord itself is the reflection of popular will. The offerings tend to be dictated by popular demand more than by divine revelation, tradition, or religious hierarchy. The diversity and fluidity of ideas and organization characteristic of populism also seem to have been evident in American religion. Not only has there tended to be an increasing array of creeds and structures to choose from, but the popularity of different theological positions or of different religious movements has sometimes shifted from year to year (as the trajectories of god-is-dead and black theology well illustrate), and there appears to have been an increasing fluidity of organizational structure itself, whether through formal mergers and schisms within denominations or through less formal modes of cross-denominational and interfaith cooperation at the local levels. The populist attitude of skepticism toward elites and elite authority seems to have also been in evidence. Most clearly in the new religions but in the churches as well, the authority of direct experience with God, with self, or with nature seems to have become fashionable, while trust in scriptural doctrines, church creeds, and ecclesiastical declarations has come to seem remotely passé. And we have already considered the extent to which religious organizations have come to treat their clientele as undifferentiated mass markets.

The idea of religious populism, it should be noted, stands in contrast with that which has been known as religious pluralism. Pluralism implies a relatively stable balance of power among a limited number of competing groups. Populism is characterized more by fluid levels of popularity among a greater array of ideas and organizations. Pluralism consists of distinctive traditions set off from one another by clearly defined boundaries that are consciously maintained through explicitly organized efforts. In religious pluralism there are common assumptions shared by all the major parties represented, to be sure, and these assumptions provide a basis for mutual forbearance and cooperation. But these common assumptions derive from the distinctive traditions themselves. Populism, in contrast, does not divide easily into clearly defined traditions. Its major boundaries are more at the edge, defining loosely what may be considered a legitimate expression of the popular will and what may not. This is not to say that populism contains less variety than pluralism, for its very fluidity and, in a sense, shapelessness provide room for considerable variety. Divisions of importance fall less clearly along established organizational lines, however, and they often tend to be masked by purely surface characteristics associated with organizations in their attempts to differentiate themselves from one another. In the absence of well defined internal boundaries, moreover, there comes to be greater emphasis placed directly upon those common beliefs and core practices that can unify and integrate the largest majority. A further difference of some importance is that pluralism affords a relatively high degree of institutional autonomy for its elites, whose foremost responsibilities include preserving the distinctiveness of their respective organizations such that the goals of those organizations can be pursued effectively. Populism, typically associated with grass-roots demands to a greater extent, provides less autonomy for its elites, requiring them to respond in relevant ways to the populace at whose will they serve.

Populism, so conceived, seems scarcely new to American religion; indeed, some might wish to argue that it, rather than pluralism, has predominated. Pluralism, by the same token, seems hardly to have vanished from the American context or been replaced by religious populism. Yet the possibility that there are populist tendencies in American religion seems to merit special attention for at least two reasons. The first is simply that pluralism has become a widely-used catch-word for characterizing American religion, to the extent that whatever populist features American faith may have have tended to be neglected. In this regard, it is probably instructive to note that considerably more attention has been paid to populist and mass tendencies in the study of American politics than in the study of American religion. The second reason for paying special attention to the idea of populism in the present context is that the features of populism, however much a part of the American past, seem to have been reinforced and dramatized by the new religions. Within the new religions themselves there seems to have been great diversity and fluidity, great emphasis upon the needs and experiences of the individual, and considerable skepticism toward established religious elites and their authority, together with expressions of concern that their own elites be responsive and approachable. New religious movements seem to have brought these values into sharp relief, allowing them to be adopted in sectors of the religious mainstream where they had perhaps been but latent predispositions prior to the appearance of the new religions. As deviants on the fringes of American religion, the new religions may also on occasion have caused internal realignments of interest in the major faiths, or on other occasions caused new divisions to be added to existing ones. Not infrequently, it seems, they have probably also been a stimulus for new experiments and efforts to recapture the loyalties of those, especially among the young, whose commitment had been lost.

Whether there will continue to be tendencies in the direction of greater religious populism will probably depend on a number of factors in the larger society. Durkheim's observation that religious beliefs are formed and reformed in periods of collective effervescence squares well with the historical record of sudden shifts in prevailing religious trends, and both suggest the precariousness of predictions rooted in extensions of the past. It is too early yet, for example, to tell what effects may have resulted from the nation's celebration of its bicentennial, a civil religious ceremony of the highest importance from a Durkheimian view. But the spectacle of young people, still clothed in the countercultural appearances of the 1960s, singing "God bless America" with teary-eyed emotion, contrasted sharply with the great outpourings of collective protest so characteristic of their predecessors of only a half decade before. From the vantage point of the 1950s, few would probably have predicted the emergence of new religious experimentation of the proportions it had taken by the early 1970s. By the same token, the religious patterns of the early 1970s may turn in directions least expected. We have learned, to take another example, that the religious developments of recent years seem to have been heavily conditioned by the changing relations of young people to the larger society. These changes appear to have come about in part from the sheer expansion in numbers of young people during the 1960s and from the attendant social strains accompanying this expansion. Demographers point out, however, that the population of the future will likely be characterized by proportionately fewer young people and proportionately greater numbers of middle-aged and elderly people. To the extent that the religious interests of different age groups are likely to differ, for which there is considerable evidence, important changes in the religious sphere may develop in response to these new demographic patterns. These changes may lead to an even greater variety of religious offerings or to a consolidation of religious orientations around new collective themes.

We have also seen evidence of the importance of high educational levels and prosperous economic conditions, the former seeming to contribute a mood of tolerance vital to the coexistence of a panoply of diverse religious and quasi-religious modes of expression, the latter providing opportunities for experimentation especially with those forms of religion offering that "something more" which prosperity alone does not buy. But neither continuously rising levels of education nor uninterrupted economic prosperity seem assured. A significant contraction of either could possibly lead to a significant reduction of religious diversity and a return to the more conventional beliefs of the past, on the one hand, or to a new variety of religious movements appealing less to those wanting "something more" than to those needing "something else."

What may influence religious trends even more than domestic social conditions, however, is the nation's relation to the rest of the world. Surprisingly little attention has been given to the effects of these broader conditions in the study of religion, yet their importance would seem to be of the first magnitude. A decisive ingredient in the unrest producing the new religious movements of the early 1970s was undoubtedly America's involvement in Vietnam, just as the nation's reluctant acknowledgment of a strong new ideological counterforce in the world during the 1950s was probably an important factor in the religious revival it experienced in that time. The common-denominator values of the American civil religion, it seems, may be particularly susceptible to such international influences, being marked by the nation's efforts to differentiate itself from other nations of the world and to redefine its mission to the world. The formative ingredients entered into the American civil religion at both its founding and its time of greatest cleavage, for example, were probably shaped as much by the nation's awareness of its image in the world as by any desire for internal harmony or integration. If the twentieth century has witnessed a crisis in America's civil religion, as some have argued, is it perhaps not in part because of world events which have inhibited the evolution of a mature national identity consolidated around its own unifying themes? The energies of the nineteenth century seem to have been spent largely on economic expansion and industrialization, for it was a time when growth seemed more urgent than national identity. But the indigenous cultural renaissance so typical elsewhere in the aftermath of such periods seems to have happened here to less of an extent than might have been expected, for no sooner had a degree of economic autonomy been achieved than the United States was plunged into the affairs of other nations, twice going to war in Europe and twice taking up arms in Asia. The interdependence of the United States and the world seems to have taken root too deeply for any significant extirpation from international affairs to occur in the foreseeable future (even if autarky were desirable). And yet, if America has realized its inability to police the world, as some have suggested, and finds itself turned inward to some extent, of which there has been some indication, perhaps its own Edwardian period of cultural consolidation, including a revitalization of its civil religion, could still come about.

In the end, the character of American religion, whether predominately populist or some other form, rests heavily with the churches and with church leaders themselves. We have suggested that church leaders have been placed in a vulnerable position by the social and cultural trends of recent years. This vulnerability seems to expose them to direct pressures from the populace to whom they must appeal, and seems to weaken the institutional underpinnings of their authority. They have sometimes been expected to speak out not only on purely theological questions but on a wider range of moral, ethical, and political issues about which they may have felt ill-qualified to speak. The other side of the matter, however, is that populism seems to contain an implicit corrective to these pressures, especially in its skepticism toward established leaders and established authority. Skepticism of this sort tends to afford a degree of autonomy from popular demands. In the face of religious diversity and experimentation, this autonomy, in turn, may be part of what is needed for creative theological reflection and efforts to renew religious organizations.

APPENDIX

Supplementary Tables

Table A-1. **HOROSCOPES, DEPRIVATION, AND COUNTERCULTURAL INVOLVEMENT**

		Percent who are quite interested in their horoscopes:			
			Deprivation Index		
Index of Countercultural Involvement		Low 0	1	2	High 3
Low	0	4%	12%	8%	*
		(161)	(92)	(26)	(4)
	1	9%	13%	11%	17%
		(147)	(108)	(37)	(6)
	2	9%	19%	26%	*
		(102)	(70)	(35)	(5)
High	3	12%	11%	6%	*
		(50)	(54)	(32)	(4)

Table A-2. **ASTROLOGY BY DEPRIVATION BY COUNTERCULTURAL INVOLVEMENT, GOODMAN ANALYSIS OF SIGNIFICANCE**

Model	Parameters Included	LRX²	df	p
H_1	(AB)(BC)	46.23	12	.000
H_2	(AC)(BC)	15.97	12	.193
H_3	(AB)(AC)(BC)	3.65	9	.95
Comparison of models:				
H_1-H_3		42.58	3	.001
H_2-H_3		12.32	3	.01

A = interest in horoscopes; B = counterculture; C = marginality

H_1	(AB)(BC)	51.60	12	.000
H_2	(AC)(BC)	29.15	12	.004
H_3	(AB)(AC)(BC)	8.03	9	.60
Comparison of models:				
H_1-H_3		43.57	3	.001
H_2-H_3		21.12	3	.001

A = belief in astrology; B = counterculture; C = marginality

Table A-3. **MYSTICISM ITEMS**

Item	Mean	Standard Deviation	Factor I*	Factor-Score Coefficient
Experienced harmony with the universe	2.342	1.094	.613	.267
Been deeply moved by the beauty of nature	3.287	.855	.558	.219
Value getting to know your inner self	2.086	1.000	.553	.224
Attracted to yoga, Zen, or TM	2.534	.703	.501	.184
Value learning to be aware of your body	2.203	.995	.472	.165
Can learn a lot from walks in the woods	1.997	.971	.469	.162
Do meditation using special techniques	2.233	.564	.462	.156

*Iterations required = 5; eigen value = 1.901; variance explained = 100 percent; algorithm is from SPSS, Type PA2

Table A-4. POLITICAL ITEMS

Item	X̄	SD	Varimax rotated factor matrix*			Factor score coefficients		
			I	II	III	I	II	III
Political position	4.575	1.733	.663	.023	.142	.412	−.068	−.018
Demonstrated	1.785	.411	.507	.025	.383	.236	−.063	.179
Tolerant of radicals	3.592	.799	.466	.077	.107	.195	−.010	−.011
Support poverty programs	2.356	.527	.442	.099	.028	.190	.006	−.051
Government needs change	2.548	.783	.409	.128	.003	.174	.023	−.059
Work for social change	2.146	.926	.207	.710	.077	.056	.492	−.033
Attended political meetings	1.477	.500	.146	.074	.689	−.056	−.018	.557
Help solve social problems	1.955	.874	.070	.698	.096	−.061	.451	.018
Written to political official	1.569	.496	.040	.064	.446	−.050	.004	.242
Eigen values			1.877	.813	.559			
% of variance			57.8	25.0	17.2			

*Factor I = "Liberalism"; Factor II = "Social Concern"; Factor III = "Political Action"

Table A-5. MORAL RELATIVISM ITEMS

Item	$\overline{X}$	SD	Varimax rotated factor matrix*		Factor score coefficients	
			I	II	I	II
Approve of an unmarried couple living together	1.455	.644	.725	.093	.437	−.081
Favor legalizing marijuana	1.586	.667	.622	.113	.283	−.010
Favor more freedom for homosexuals	1.561	.600	.605	.301	.256	.262
Approve of communal living	2.012	.623	.408	.139	.125	.054
Would play hooky from work	1.647	.670	.115	.332	−.016	.275
Would buy stolen goods	1.961	.570	.036	.235	−.030	.191
Eigen values			1.598	.159		
% of variance			91.0	9.0		

*Factor I = Moral Relativism

Table A-6. **LOG LINEAR ANALYSIS OF POLITICAL ACTION, MYSTICISM, ROLE DIFFERENTIATION**

Model	Parameters Included	X^2	df	p
H_1	(BC)(AC)	46.76	2	.000
H_2	(BC)(AB)	17.68	2	.000
H_3	(BC)(AB)(AC)	6.06	1	.014
Comparison of models:				
H_1-H_3		40.70	1	.001
H_2-H_3		11.62	1	.001
Odds ratios for saturated model:				
(AB),	$c = 1$,	odds ratio = 1.72		
(AB),	$c = 2$,	odds ratio = 3.29		

A = political activism, 1 = high, 2 = low; B = mysticism, 1 = high, 2 = low; C = role differentiation, 1 = high, 2 = low

Table A-7. **SIGNIFICANCE OF TEST ITEMS FOR RELIGIOUS CHANGES BEFORE COLLEGE**

Item	Difference in models (df = 3)* Chi-square	p
Importance of religion to mother	42.2	.001
Importance of religion to father	51.2	.001
Parents' annual income	3.4	.25
Mother's education	4.9	.15
Father's education	3.7	.25
Father's occupation	10.7	.05
Mother encouraged independence	2.8	.25
Father encouraged independence	3.2	.25
Mother encouraged self-expression	1.5	.50
Father encouraged self-expression	0.1	.99
Mother gave things for love	2.2	.50
Father gave things for love	1.4	.50
Mother gave love and affection	13.2	.01
Father gave love and affection	14.6	.01
Mother politically liberal	3.6	.25
Father politically liberal	2.9	.25
High school GPA	1.1	.75
Math SAT score	6.1	.10**
Verbal SAT score	17.9	.001

*Chi-square value of model (12)(23)(13) minus chi-square value of model (12)(23), where 1 = religion as freshman, 2 = religion raised in, and 3 = test item indicated

**Marginally significant

Table A-8. **SIGNIFICANCE OF TEST ITEMS FOR RELIGIOUS CHANGES DURING COLLEGE**

Item	Difference in models (df = 3)* Chi-square	p
High school GPA	0.6	.80
Math SAT score	3.1	.30
Verbal SAT score	4.1	.20
Considers himself an intellectual	4.9	.15
Plans on going to graduate school	7.5	.10**
Bothered by unhappiness	0.6	.90
Bothered by hopelessness	1.2	.75
Nervous, tense	3.5	.25
Worries a lot	1.9	.50
Lonely a lot	5.1	.10**
Been in a demonstration	7.1	.10**
Done community organizing	8.1	.05
Favored living together before marriage	15.7	.01
Approved of premarital sex	9.1	.05
Marijuana important to life style	9.2	.05
Like to live in commune	18.0	.01
Father's religiosity	14.0	.05
Mother's religiosity	6.6	.10**
Parents' annual income	5.3	.15
Father's education	2.9	.30
Mother's education	5.7	.15
Father's occupation	7.2	.10**
Mother gave love and affection	1.9	.50
Father gave love and affection	6.6	.10**
Mother politically liberal	5.8	.15
Father politically liberal	3.4	.30

*Chi-square value of model (12)(23)(13) minus chi-square value of model (12)(23), where 1 = religion at time-2, 2 = religion at time-1, and 3 = test item indicated

**Marginally significant

Table A-9. **SIGNIFICANCE OF TEST ITEMS FOR RELIGIOUS CHANGES AFTER COLLEGE**

Item	*Difference in models (df = 3)** *Chi-square*	*p*
Identified with new life styles	14.3	.01
Used drugs	12.2	.01
Been living with a girlfriend	8.4	.05
Favored living together before marriage	13.8	.01
Very critical of conventional morals	8.1	.05
Approved of nonviolent confrontation	7.2	.10**
Parents' annual income	7.1	.10**
Mother's education	2.3	.75
Father's education	3.3	.25
Father's occupation	3.2	.25
College GPA	1.4	.70
Problems feeling lonely	1.6	.75
Problems finding friends	4.2	.15
Problems with girls	1.0	.75
Problems with money	2.9	.25
Problems with grades	3.1	.25
Mother politically liberal	12.2	.05
Father politically liberal	16.7	.01
Married during college	2.9	.25
Married by time-2	6.1	.15
Been in graduate school	4.1	.25
Employed 30 hours per week at time-2	14.7	.01
Entered armed services	13.5	.01

*Chi-square value of model (12)(23)(13) minus chi-square value of (12)(23), where 1 = religion at time-2, 2 = religion at time-1, and 3 = test item indicated (senior cohort)

**Marginally significant

INDEX

Design: U.C. Press staff
Composition: University of California Press
Lithography: Edwards Brothers, Inc.
Binding: Edwards Brothers, Inc.

Text: VIP Garamond
Display: VIP Optima semi-bold
Paper: EB book Natural, basis 50